SHADES OF
TRUTH

Praise for the Book

In our sharply divided political discourse, *Shades of Truth* is graphic in its compilation of facts and bold in its exposure of the perceived designs of an adversary. It sheds much light on the strategy of denigration, premised on a carefully packaged dream sequence that has sought to submerge our democratic polity's quest for transparency, accountability and inclusiveness in an alternate paradigm of exclusion and homogenization. The book also candidly acknowledges the shortfalls of an earlier period that may have contributed to the current happenings.

—**M. Hamid Ansari, Former Vice President**

Shades of Truth is a comprehensive analysis of the functioning of the Modi government in the last four years. It highlights the failure of this government to fulfil important promises made to the people on the eve of the Lok Sabha elections in 2014. This book is a powerful indictment of the Modi government's performance. There has to be a meaningful national debate on issues raised by Kapil Sibal.

—**Dr Manmohan Singh, Former Prime Minister**

Facts that add up to a dire warning: Unless this poisonous vine is scorched in 2019, it will choke the country. Essential documentation. Essential reading.

—**Arun Shourie, Former Union Minister**

SHADES OF TRUTH

~A JOURNEY DERAILED~

KAPIL SIBAL

Published by
Rupa Publications India Pvt. Ltd 2018
7/16, Ansari Road, Daryaganj
New Delhi 110002

Sales centres:
Allahabad Bengaluru Chennai
Hyderabad Jaipur Kathmandu
Kolkata Mumbai

Copyright © Kapil Sibal 2018

The views and opinions expressed in this book are the author's own and the facts
are as reported by him which have been verified to the extent possible,
and the publishers are not in any way liable for the same.

All rights reserved.

No part of this publication may be reproduced, transmitted,
or stored in a retrieval system, in any form or by any means, electronic,
mechanical, photocopying, recording or otherwise,
without the prior permission of the publisher.

ISBN: 978-93-5304-601-9

First impression 2018

10 9 8 7 6 5 4 3 2 1

Printed by Thomson Press India Ltd., Faridabad

This book is sold subject to the condition that it shall not,
by way of trade or otherwise, be lent, resold, hired out, or otherwise circulated,
without the publisher's prior consent, in any form of binding or cover
other than that in which it is published.

*I dedicate this book to my grandchildren—Jai, Gayatri,
Gauri, Anina, Mira and Diya.
I hope they will passionately protect
the democratic values of my country.*

THERE HANGS A TALE

Shades of Truth
There hangs a tale
Of promises made
And dreams for sale

Will breach the heights
We failed to climb
The showman's act
A pantomime

Data is oft
Moulded to form
No jobs, the young
Now feel forlorn

Safe havens are
For those who kill
The victims just
Don't fit the bill

A widow's wail
Is all in vain
The girl child dead
Now feels no pain

Don't kill brothers
To save a cow
Their blood will stain
The land we plough

In silence all
Our masters watch
Gloat, take pride
In victories notched

Caged parrots are
The new Trishuls
The long arms of
The czars who rule

Diktats at will
Had frozen lives
Millions struggling
Just to survive

Deals off the shelf
Have caused a stir
Transparency
Is now a blur

Our steady pace
Of growth has stalled
What we had built
Defaced and mauled

Speak out aloud
Time will not wait
Let not the hounds
Decide our fate

In troubled times
Together stand
Do not think twice
Extend your Hand

CONTENTS

Introduction   *xi*

Part One: Modi Sarkar Decoded
1. Deconstructing the Modi Magic   3
2. Democracy in Danger   59
3. Beyond Courtrooms   72
4. Aadhaar and the Right to Privacy   92
5. Foreign Policy: Hits and Misses   100

Part Two: The UPA Years: Myths and Reality
6. In the House of the People   137
7. Transforming India's Knowledge Landscape   160
8. Decline of the UPA Government: When Perceptions Outplayed Facts   188
9. 2G: A 'Scam' of Monumental Proportions   195
10. Arab Spring Comes to India   215
11. Coal Scam: A Spark That Caused a Fire   226

Epilogue   235
Acknowledgements   238
Index   241

INTRODUCTION

In the run-up to the 2014 Lok Sabha elections, Narendra Modi caught the imagination of most Indians. Ordinary citizens living simple lives were carried away by the promise of change. The desire for a better tomorrow was at the heart of every individual. Modi not only promised the moon but gave a clarion call for fundamental change in systems of governance—change that was to transform India. This was nothing but realpolitik at play.

Modi is no Messiah and all those of us in politics, who are well versed with the functioning of the government, knew that this Messiah would fail. Four years down the road, the conversation for change and the promises made with persuasive articulation are no longer repeated. Each day, a new acronym is mouthed for effect. Modi is no longer heard to say, 'You gave Congress 60 years, give me 60 months and I will transform India.' Now he wants an extension. He now asks people to wait for 2022 when India turns seventy-five.

It is said that a consummate politician manipulates people's emotions and mindsets and institutions, often for electoral benefit. To me, this is unprincipled politics. The art of manipulation sometimes succeeds. In the long run, however, such leaders get exposed. The story of manipulative politics and its possible outcome needs to be told.

My worst fears about having Prime Minister Modi at the helm of affairs, given that he ruled Gujarat with an iron hand, have come true. Democracy can only flourish when you respect opinions, which might not be in sync with your own thought processes. It can only flourish when you have your ear to the ground and are prepared to listen to the rumblings that are destined to reach you. This is particularly true in a complex country suffused with colours of diversity. No monolithic structure can hope to be democratic. It is important for all those who are fortunate to be clothed with the mantle of power to understand what democracy is before they can be democratic.

It is easy to distinguish democracy from other less representative forms of government, but it is difficult to define. Let me make an attempt. Planet Earth is a gift to all those who have stepped on it in the past, and will do so in the future. It is only fair that its bounty should be shared, and that too, as equitably as possible. That is a democratic way of looking at dealing with assets that belong to mankind.

Aggrandisement by the powerful may be an expression of might but is essentially undemocratic. Another attribute of Planet Earth is that it is both diverse and accommodating. There is no element of uniformity in its landscape. Even the colour green has thousands of unique shades. It is the multitude of colours, their diversity and sheer beauty that makes our home an exciting place to live in.

This diversity has its imprint on the human race. Individuals living here and the ones yet to be born are all unlike each other. Our social contract is to ensure that this uniqueness is preserved in an orderly manner. Each voice is important and each opinion must be counted and respected. All this exists within the boundaries of our decision to live together in the form of a nation-state regulated by law that recognizes the complexities of living together. The global order should also be subject to the same essential attributes of diversity and comity.

Any imposition on this thought is anti-democratic. This is equally true of attempts to impose cultural uniformity. Religious beliefs are diverse and must be respected, subject to minimum standards of human conduct which is always contextual. Representative government, backed by a majority mandate, is democratic; but imposition by the majority of its beliefs, its cultural moorings and its perception of values on the minority is repressive and undemocratic.

Our Prime Minister has failed to understand the true essence of democracy. In Chapter 1 of this book, 'Deconstructing the Modi Magic', I have focussed on the consistent assault by this government on institutions that are constitutionally obligated to be watchdogs of the Executive or Legislative excesses which seek to weaken democratic structures. The chapter also gives an insight into how those belonging to a particular political mindset have jeopardized lives and caused schisms in society. They instil fear in the minds of the marginalized and the minorities. The silence of the Prime Minister in the last four years, while such unsavoury incidents are in full play, is disturbing. I have dwelt upon the promises made by Prime Minister Modi in the run-up to the Lok Sabha elections and how the development agenda has been put in cold storage while the agenda of the Hindutva brigade gets traction. Divisive politics has gathered pace as the next Lok Sabha elections are around the corner.

In the last four years, key institutions of our democracy have been undermined. The supremacy of the law is under attack and processes of law are being used to serve political outcomes. Representatives of the people have become the voice of agendas, seeking to propagate a majoritarian sentiment. Civility in public discourse has touched a new low. These are some of the issues that I have dealt with in Chapter 2, 'Democracy in Danger'.

This book would not have been complete without dealing with the Judiciary. The importance of independence of the Judiciary is fundamental to the survival of democracy. I have analysed recent events which have thrown up serious questions about the functioning of the judicial system. These issues need to be addressed rather than being brushed under the carpet. My thoughts on this subject are elaborated in Chapter 3, 'Beyond Courtrooms'.

Some recent pronouncements by the Supreme Court have far-reaching consequences. Declaring privacy to be a fundamental right is a historic verdict. How it plays out in its implementation is yet to be seen. We are awaiting the judgement of the apex court on the Aadhaar issue. The possible misuse of Aadhaar data by the government will subvert democracy. This issue is discussed in Chapter 4, 'Aadhaar and the Right to Privacy'.

To my mind, it was also important to analyse this government's foreign policy. Peace in our neighbourhood is necessary for the nation to secure its development imperatives. Our neighbourhood is far less secure than it was in 2014 and our relations with neighbours have deteriorated in the last four years. China is flexing its muscles and our inconsistent policies have led us nowhere. The foreign office has been sidelined. The enthusiastic backslapping and informality at a personal level, when dealing with prime ministers and presidents of other countries, is hardly conducive to serious diplomacy. Foreign tours of the Prime Minister are mega events, managed by collaborators, which tend to project the Prime Minister's persona. It is quiet diplomacy that is necessary to establish bilateral relationships on a surer footing. The new dynamics of the Trump presidency has added yet another dimension to our relationship with global powers. How India will respond to the trade wars that are likely to erupt requires both prescience and wisdom. We need to cushion ourselves from the impact of these developments. I have discussed these issues in Chapter 5, 'Foreign Policy: Hits and Misses'.

The United Progressive Alliance's (UPA's) vision of the significance of science & technology (S&T) and the importance of transformational reform in the education sector were issues addressed by our government. Attempts to transform education to make it relevant to the contemporary world were consistently opposed by the BJP when it was in Opposition. Four years have passed. No significant decisions have been taken to address issues to boost output in S&T and find innovative ways to improve quality and provide for autonomy in higher education. Instead, academic freedom is sought to be throttled and the environment in universities vitiated. These issues find resonance in Chapter 6, 'In the House of the People' and Chapter 7, 'Transforming India's Knowledge Landscape'.

The rise and fall of governments is a normal phenomenon. The UPA's decline was a result of it being a coalescence of forces in opposition. We also failed to effectively articulate our responses to criticism of our policies. We believe that opposition of both State and non-State players gathered momentum, with the public seeking answers and pushing for change. The charge that the UPA government was afflicted by policy paralysis was widely publicized. The government was seen to be weak and the clamour for change received public support. Though the change in the corridors of power came about, the promises made by the harbingers of change are still a distant dream. Chapter 8, 'Decline of the UPA Government: When Perceptions Outplayed Facts', deals with it.

It is necessary to draw attention to events prior to 2014, which led to the decline of the UPA. After the report of the Comptroller and Auditor General of India (CAG), with the Opposition and the media baying for blood, the Judiciary cancelled both telecom licences as well as all coal allocations. This was the beginning of the end of UPA-II. The impact of these events on the economy, with the rise in NPAs, are issues that needed to be addressed. I have done that in Chapter 9, '2G: A "Scam" of Monumental Proportions', and Chapter 11, 'Coal Scam: A Spark That Caused a Fire'. In the course of analysing events prior to 2014, I have also discussed in Chapter 10, 'Arab Spring Comes to India', the circumstances leading to the Anna movement and the opportunists who, on the shoulders of Anna, launched themselves politically and became a relevant force in Indian politics.

The functioning of this government in the last four years requires to be assessed. I have done that by analysing this government's policies. I fear that the government has intentionally embarked upon a dangerous journey to change the character of the Indian State. This government has slowly, but surely, undermined the values that any democratic polity should fiercely protect.

I consider it my duty to dwell upon some of the policies of the UPA and how they addressed issues impacting the quality of governance. No one should be so arrogant as to state that all policy prescriptions were both rational and justified. No government can claim that. There could be enough reasons to criticize the policies of the UPA. Such criticisms may well be justified. The purpose of adverting to some of the UPA's policy decisions is not to provide justifications but to explain the intent behind them. It must be remembered that the UPA was running a coalition government. We had several coalition partners who had their own points of view in respect of both policies and decision-making. Any regional party which had to satisfy its electorate was an active participant as an alliance partner. The Union government needed to handle the alliance partners with sensitivity. That in itself is a difficult task. That Prime Minister Manmohan Singh handled them with great maturity and was able to take forward the essential agenda of the UPA, is commendable. It does not mean that there were no fault lines that emerged; they did. The essential task of any government is to lift people out of poverty, to ensure that our democratic structure is strengthened, that the diversity of India is protected, that the problems of the marginalized and minorities are addressed. It is their responsibility to create the conditions for ease of doing business without oppressive bureaucratic regulations; to set in place building blocks for the future, persuading the global community to acknowledge India's potential; and above all to conduct our foreign policy, ensuring friendly relations with our neighbours and treating each nation as a potential friend. We tried to do all this and part of our efforts in doing so is reflected in the chapters in this book that deal with the UPA years.

All this needed to be told. This book is an attempt to do that.

Part One

MODI SARKAR DECODED

Chapter 1

DECONSTRUCTING THE MODI MAGIC

It is no mean feat to govern and manage a population of about 1.3 billion people. The challenges facing India, in a complex interconnected world, are humongous. Millions are steeped in poverty, deprived of basic necessities of life. For the poor, quality education and affordable healthcare are distant dreams. They lack the essentials to live with dignity. Discrimination based on religion, caste and creed, despite constitutional guarantees, is a way of life. Despite migration to urban centres, about 60 per cent of our population lives in villages, agriculture being their mainstay. The size and nature of holdings of a vast majority of those surviving on agriculture are not enough to provide surplus resources for their vertical movement in society. Most agricultural holdings are less than one hectare, which is barely enough to meet their daily needs, let alone take them out of poverty. More than 732 million people in India are without access to toilet facilities.[1] Of the 40 per cent population living in urban centres, a large percentage lives amidst pestilence. Lack of drainage facilities and a hostile environment make daily life a challenge. All households do not have access to clean drinking water. Governments have attempted in the past to reduce poverty but achieved limited success.

---

[1]https://www.wateraid.org/uk/publications/out-of-order-the-state-of-the-worlds-toilets-2017

Challenges at Different Levels

The fact that only 3.17 crore people pay taxes, as was disclosed by the Finance Minister in his 2017 Budget speech, suggests the gap between the vast majority of people at the margins and those who live in luxury. Over the years, this gap has increased. This open and visible inequality finds resonance in various protests throughout the country. Unrest within the farmer community is reflective of the government's inability to ensure optimum prices for their produce. Cushioning provided by way of Minimum Support Price (MSP) does not match the exponential increase in input costs. The growing demand for reservation in government jobs reveals the inability of the system to provide sustainable employment. Our youth are unemployed because the private sector has not expanded at a steady pace to provide them with adequate livelihood opportunities. Technology solutions have, in fact, resulted in loss of jobs, which in turn increases levels of unemployment or underemployment. The small and medium enterprises (SMEs) sector within the business community finds it difficult to cope in a competitive global environment. Borrowing at high rates of interest makes it tough to run business enterprises competitively. Their inability to adopt technology because of inadequate resources is another impediment. Sectors of the economy that absorb a large workforce, mainly textile, leather and the informal sector, are languishing because of their inability to use technology in a globally competitive environment. Transformation of these sectors requires huge investments. Added to these are archaic rules and regulations which impede ease of doing business. Further, corruption at all levels is endemic.

The different civilizational levels at which India resides is yet another challenge. A multireligious, multiracial and multilingual civilization is an asset; yet it has its own problems. The issues arising therefrom have remained unresolved. The ethos of our Constitution is far removed from the reality of societal interactions on the ground. That is the India we live in and that is the India we need to transform.

The common man wants change. With the communications revolution, the poor and the marginalized are exposed to the world as never before. They are aspirational and hungry for the opportunities available to others, far removed from their shanties in which survival is a daily challenge. They wait for the day when their children will have access to quality education. In the absence of universal health coverage, they lack resources to afford private healthcare. Access to education and healthcare are central to the lives of individuals. Without either, deprivation will haunt their future.

As a nation, our priority should be to lift millions out of poverty and provide them opportunities to fulfil their aspirations. But governments with limited resources find it difficult to meet their legitimate expectations. Administrations face several impediments as they attempt to implement policies. The complexity of India—its sheer size, coupled with diversity—makes it tough for standard policy prescriptions to be uniformly applied. The distribution of resources, in the context of the size and diversity of India, has its own fault lines. It is easy to criticize but solutions are hard to find.

Modi and the Promise of Change

The clarion call given by Narendra Modi for change was welcomed by millions who had hoped for a better tomorrow.

Modi mesmerized crowds and came to power. He was and is a dealer in hope. He sold many dreams and continues to do so. His electoral victories are evidence of his ability to enthuse people.

In the run-up to the 2014 Lok Sabha elections, Modi exploited every opportunity to establish an emotional bond with those he addressed. His eloquence made people believe in him. People saw in him the prospect of change that they yearned for; not a change in the processes of government but that which would empower them to deal with their everyday troubles. He had the advantage of a new entrant in national politics. He carried no baggage; therefore, he could promise the world to whoever he spoke to.

He asked the farmers why they were forced to commit suicide and blamed the policies of the UPA for it. During one of his 'Chai pe Charcha' programmes on 20 March 2014, he termed farmer suicides a 'national agony' and said, 'The NDA shall stand behind all farmers hit by natural calamities… I shall not be able to sleep peacefully till I do something for you.'[2] Addressing a rally in Akola, Maharashtra, on 30 March 2014, he insisted that the UPA had turned Lal Bahadur Shastri's slogan of *'Jai Jawan Jai Kisan'* into *'Mar Jawan Mar Kisan'*.[3] He wondered why farmers did not receive remunerative prices for their produce. He lamented that while input costs had gone up, procurement prices did not provide the returns farmers deserved. Furthermore, he promised that if he came to power, the farmer would be compensated not just for the cost of his produce but also 50 per cent of the cost as additional remuneration. He realized that making such a promise would earn him the sympathy of farmers.

He gave the youth something to cheer about. For the millions unemployed, he promised to provide jobs. On 21 November 2013, at an election rally in Agra, he said, 'If BJP comes to power, it will provide one crore jobs which the UPA government promised but could not fulfil.'[4] The BJP's manifesto reinforced Modi's words: 'The country has been dragged through 10 years of jobless growth by the Congress-led UPA government. Under the broader economic revival, BJP will accord high priority to job creation and opportunities for entrepreneurship.'[5]

To the young women in urban centres, he promised an environment of security. What happened to Nirbhaya was a national shame; it was an uncivilized act and the genuine public outcry reflected societal angst. Modi promised change. Millions were swayed by his rhetoric and nobody questioned why women could not be protected during the post-Godhra riots in Gujarat.

To the business community, he promised an environment where investment would be easy without unfriendly regulations, replicating the ease of doing business that he provided in Gujarat. The community rallied behind him. As corporate houses owned both the print and electronic media, Modi was omnipresent, exhorting people to believe in his promise

---

[2]http://www.firstpost.com/india/farmers-suicides-are-a-national-agony-says-modi-1443757.html
[3]http://economictimes.indiatimes.com/news/politics-and-nation/narendra-modi-woos-farmers-says-mar-jawan-mar-kisan-is-upa-slogan/printarticle/32974322.cms
[4]http://www.dnaindia.com/india/report-one-crore-jobs-if-bjp-comes-to-power-narendra-modi-1922835
[5]http://www.bjp.org/images/pdf_2014/full_manifesto_english_07.04.2014.pdf

for change and eloquently convincing them to buy into his dream.

He had allied with industry when he was Gujarat's chief minister. Participants at 'Vibrant Gujarat'[6] extolled Modi for his business-friendly utterances. The state represented a model of development that brought prosperity. No one questioned the nature of that prosperity and whether or not it had reached the marginalized, backward communities and Adivasis in Gujarat. Modi highlighted how every village in Gujarat had access to electricity all 365 days.[7] Even if someone questioned that statement, the facts were never investigated.

The billions of dollars of investment promised at 'Vibrant Gujarat' summits was just a chimera. Between 2003–04 and 2016–17, investment projects, completed as a percentage of new investments announced, was only 25 per cent.[8] Yet 'Vibrant Gujarat' was perceived to be a miracle. The media became a willing partner in this enterprise. It celebrated the virtues of a modern, aggressive leader like Modi as if Gujarat had been transformed. Modi was perceived to be a chief minister who was ahead of all others, even though the facts did not back that claim.

Most importantly, he promised that billions of dollars stashed abroad as black money would be brought back to India and that once that happened, every citizen of this country would get ₹15–20 lakh.[9] Launching his 'Chai pe Charcha' campaign in Ahmedabad on 12 February 2014, Modi said, 'We will bring back each and every penny deposited abroad by Indian citizens. I am committed to this because this money belongs to the poor people of India…'[10] His propaganda machine was on overdrive.

He had hired and persuaded professionals from elite institutions in the US to come and help him deliver his message. His social media

---

[6]Biennial investors' summit organized by the Gujarat government since 2003.
[7]http://economictimes.indiatimes.com/news/politics-and-nation/modi-to-mulayam-making-gujarat-means-providing-24/7-electricity/articleshow/29253390.cms?intenttarget=no
[8]http://www.livemint.com/Politics/DUArdx5enj9jeu6O2OUVYP/Vibrant-Gujarat-Marketing-gimmick-or-investment-driver.html
[9]https://www.youtube.com/watch?v=EbdFJ2vg3ic
[10]http://timesofindia.indiatimes.com/india/I-will-bring-back-black-money-and-distribute-it-to-honest-taxpayers-Modi/articleshow/30295281.cms

campaign had an army of supporters committed to his dream.[11] The UPA was castigated for being ineffectual and suffering from policy paralysis. That perception gained ground. He assured the people that policy paralysis would be replaced by the activism evident in Gujarat. Modi promised the emergence of India as an economic superpower.

The Wait for 'Achhe Din'

Four years down the road, that dream has been shattered. The events that have unfolded during this period prove that Modi never meant what he promised.

The much-debated issue of appointment of a Lokpal which would have ensured transparency in government, has still not seen the light of day. In 2011, the Lokpal Bill became a topic of conversation in almost every home in this country, especially amongst the middle class. This legislation was to empower ordinary citizens to complain against corrupt public servants and prosecute them. The BJP, then in Opposition, pushed for it. However, since Modi came to power, the issue has been put in cold storage. No Lokpal has been appointed (The Lokpal and Lokayuktas Act 2013 was passed by the Congress-led UPA government and notified on 1 January 2014). While hearing a petition filed by an NGO on the delay in appointment of the Lokpal on 23 November 2016, the then Chief Justice of India, Justice T.S. Thakur, pulled up the Modi government and said, 'We can't allow a situation where a law or an institution like Lokpal becomes redundant.'[12] Modi realized that an institution like Lokpal would jeopardize the functioning of his own government. He charged the UPA government with corruption but now seeks to protect his own from any form of investigation on charges of corruption.

The Lokpal was a sword to strike at the UPA, castigated for its lack of resolve to combat corruption. However, multiple legislations have not

---

[11]http://www.business-standard.com/article/politics/modi-s-cyber-army-foot-soldiers-preparing-for-long-march-ahead-114052200218_1.html
[12]http://indiatoday.intoday.in/story/lokpal-appointment-supreme-court-pulls-up-centre/1/817642.html

helped eradicate this menace. The Prevention of Corruption Act (PCA) of 1988, which deals with public servants and provides procedures to bring them to book, has had no real impact on the prevailing endemic levels of corruption. In fact, there is a general perception, also shared by Members of Parliament (MPs), that if such sweeping powers as provided in the Lokpal and Lokayuktas Act, 2013, vest in investigating agencies, it might lead to a regime where those who are themselves perceived to be corrupt will be given the absolute authority to deal with corruption. The scandals that have recently emerged—and many more which may never see the light of day—have shown the investigating agencies to be guided by biased agendas and selective in dealing with corruption. Some of them holding the reins of power are, in fact, perceived to be protecting the corrupt. I suspect that before the end of the term of this government, if Modi perceives that he may lose power in 2019, he will be inclined to pass an amended Lokpal Bill.

As for black money, in the run-up to his campaign for prime ministership, the vulgar extravaganza displayed on television channels suggested that the BJP was flush with funds. Media planners placed the tab on Modi's media campaign at ₹5,000 crore.[13] Any party with such enormous resources cannot possibly be serious about its commitment to eradicate black money. But most modern day politicians pay scant respect to principles. Double standards are the norm. In the February–March 2017 Assembly elections, soon after demonetization, enormous flow of funds was visible wherever the BJP campaigned. The legitimate earnings of ordinary folk were frozen during demonetization while the Uttar Pradesh election witnessed rampant use of cash.

After he became the prime minister, Modi not only failed but also completely forgot that he had promised to bring back black money stashed abroad. Nearly five months after assuming office, the government told the Supreme Court on 17 October 2014 that it could not reveal the names of Indians having accounts in foreign banks due to the Double Taxation Avoidance Agreement (DTAA), a position that was earlier taken by the

---

[13]http://www.hindustantimes.com/india/bjp-s-advertisement-plan-may-cost-a-whopping-rs-5-000-cr/story-y8x34eYh26xwoAxeRuaCoO.html

UPA. Finance Minister Arun Jaitley defended the government's stand by saying, 'Is the present NDA government led by Modi in any way reluctant to make some names public? Certainly not. But they can be made public only in accordance with the due process of law.'[14]

This government now says that any such accounts opened after 2017 will be made public, pursuant to an agreement between India and foreign powers under the Common Reporting Standard (CRS) on the Automatic Exchange of Information (AEOI) portal. But why can't the names of account holders prior to 2017 be revealed—a demand made on the floor of the Lok Sabha by the then BJP in Opposition? Sushma Swaraj, erstwhile Leader of the Opposition, in her spirited interventions, accused the UPA of protecting the corrupt despite the Finance Minister's statement that the names could not be revealed. When the Congress reminded the BJP of the promise Modi had made, there was no response. Modi realized that his promise was only a 'jumla' meant to convince the public that the UPA was corrupt and protecting the corrupt.

Modi has failed miserably in his developmental agenda, which has bedevilled the Indian economy in the last four years with rising unemployment, lack of growth, a stagnant agricultural sector, inflation in essential commodities (especially food items), failure to protect the farmers and inability to give an impetus to manufacturing.

Addressing the Deeper Malaise

India's exports had been robust during the tenure of the UPA; but falling exports are a drag on the growth story of the NDA. The average growth rate of exports during the 10 years of UPA rule (2004–14) stood at 18.1 per cent, while during the first three years of NDA rule (2014–17), the average growth rate was negative. Perhaps the reason was that export earnings were largely based on oil imports converted into petrochemicals and other plastic-based commodities. With the fall in the price of crude oil during 2015–16, the consequent price of crude-based products fell

---

[14]http://timesofindia.indiatimes.com/india/Now-Modi-govt-too-refuses-to-name-foreign-bank-account-holders/articleshow/44863834.cms

substantially. But the differential between the price of imported crude and the sale of petrol and diesel at the gas stations went into the kitty of the treasury with increased excise.[15] The consumer did not benefit and exports suffered. We, of course, cannot lose sight of the fact that global slowdown also reduced global demand for consumer products. China's rate of growth had come down from 10 per cent to a mere 6.5 per cent. The third element in declining exports was the appreciation of the rupee against the dollar.[16]

Some experts attribute declining exports to a malaise deeper than the reasons set out above. The reality is that Indian merchandise exports are very narrow-based—we export low-value commodities such as cotton yarn or apparel rather than technical textiles. The poor logistics infrastructure along with a weak trade facilitation regime is also the cause of our poor performance. Our cost of logistics as a percentage of Gross Domestic Product (GDP) is anywhere between 13 and 14 per cent compared with 7 to 8 per cent in developed countries. Besides, India has failed to negotiate improved market access for the country's exports. We face prohibitive tariff and non-tariff barriers in both developing and emerging markets. In Europe and other developed markets, Indian exports face non-tariff barriers. While we are somewhat generous in providing unilaterally, duty-free market access to Bangladesh and other countries, we do not get the same treatment from other nations. Japan is an example where, through the Comprehensive Economic Partnership Agreement (CEPA), India's pharmaceutical products have benefited from tariff reductions.

Another reason for our poor export performance is the high import duties we impose on raw materials and intermediates while keeping the duties on finished products low, which discourage production and export of value-added items. For instance, apparel can be imported duty-free but its raw material attracts a 10 per cent duty.[17]

---

[15] http://www.livemint.com/Money/9FCR8AHiK2FuW5D6p9G9kI/With-crude-oil-prices-rising-will-govt-roll-back-excise-dut.html
[16] http://www.thehindubusinessline.com/opinion/columns/why-indias-exports-are-falling/article9370929.ece
[17] http://thediplomat.com/2015/11/whats-behind-indias-big-export-decline/

The NDA, in the last four years, has not focussed on the consistent decline of our exports. Of course, the saving grace is that exports of services have shown only a moderate decline. The NDA should have entered into trade pacts and persuaded nations to lower their tariffs, easing the flow of exports from India. Reducing cost of finance and logistics would have enabled exporters to be competitive in the global market.

If one compares the prices of essential food items on 1 January 2014 with those prevailing on 1 January 2017, the percentage of upward variation is between 3.37 per cent and 75 per cent. Pulses, tea, milk, sugar, mustard oil, vanaspati, salt, wheat, rice and atta all cost dearer today. And this is when the price of crude oil came down from $108 a barrel to $53 a barrel during the same period. Despite this global downward trend in crude oil prices, diesel was sold at ₹53.78 per litre in January 2014, as against ₹57.82 per litre three years later. Similarly, an LPG cylinder, which was subsidized, was sold at ₹414 on 1 January 2014 against ₹434.71 three years later.[18] So, while the government got an enormous cushion because of the reduction in crude prices, the benefit was not passed on to the consumer.

Since the beginning of 2018, international crude oil prices have firmed up. As of June 2018, the price of the Indian crude basket was hovering around the $75 a barrel mark, still below the $100 a barrel average of the first five months of 2014. However, petrol and diesel prices have gone up exponentially and, as on 25 June 2018, they are being sold at ₹75.69 and ₹67.48, respectively, in Delhi.

In the run-up to the Lok Sabha elections in 2014, Modi attacked the Congress for the high rate of inflation during the UPA years. He assured that if the governments of Morarji Desai and Atal Bihari Vajpayee could arrest price rise, his government could do it too.[19] However, after assuming power, when the inflation rate touched a five-month high in June 2014, the government changed tack. BJP spokesperson Siddharth Nath Singh maintained, 'There is no immediate prescription like instant Maggi

---

[18]http://www.livemint.com/Money/FTH16NAd2e2LrlCqpyVXeM/Jet-fuel-price-hiked-by-86-subsidised-LPG-by-Rs2-per-cyli.html
[19]http://www.narendramodi.in/gu/its-time-to-defeat-inflation-its-time-to-defeat-congress-6053

noodles by which inflation can be brought down.'[20] This double standard is also reflected in Modi's statements on this issue as Gujarat Chief Minister. He insisted that controlling inflation was the sole responsibility of the Centre and that its failure could not be passed on to state governments.[21] However, after becoming the prime minister, he did an about-turn and said that it was the joint responsibility of the Centre and the states to curb inflation.[22]

We were earlier told by the Leader of the Opposition in the Lok Sabha, Sushma Swaraj, that GDP numbers did not fill stomachs and assuage pangs of hunger. That is probably true, but at least the economy was growing at all times by more than 7 per cent with an average of 8.5 per cent during UPA-I and 7.5 per cent during UPA-II.

Modi failed to realize that for growth, one needs to overcome barriers to investment and provide massive incentives to the manufacturing sector—something which provided the foundation for catapulting the Chinese economy. But in India, the manufacturing sector isn't gaining much ground.[23] The announcement of the BJP just ahead of the Uttar Pradesh elections (2017) that all abattoirs in the state would be shut down[24] is hardly a way to deal with the leather industry, which employs a massive workforce.[25] Knitwear and hosiery is another sector which needs to be incentivized. The automobile sector was, of course, doing well. Now thanks to Modi, it has slumped after demonetization.[26]

Those who throng Modi's events abroad perceive him as riding a

---

[20] http://gt.ibnlive.in.com.akadns.net/news/no-immediate-remedy-like-instant-noodles-to-control-inflation-bjp-leader/479745-37-64.html

[21] http://www.outlookindia.com/newswire/story/modi-criticises-sonia-pm-on-price-rise-issue/674150

[22] http://www.timesnow.tv/india/video/pmspeakstoarnab-read-full-text-here/44827

[23] http://www.ncaer.org/news_details.php?nID=187

[24] http://timesofindia.indiatimes.com/city/kanpur/all-slaughterhouses-in-uttar-pradesh-will-be-shut-from-march-12-amit-shah/articleshow/57092121.cms

[25] http://webcache.googleusercontent.com/search?q=cache:http://www.iilfleatherfair.com/leatherfair/chennaileather//about_leather_industry.php&gws_rd=cr&ei=LSKsWN_DK4j7vgSHu52QDA

[26] http://www.businesstoday.in/sectors/auto/automobile-sales-hit-60-month-low-in-december/story/244899.html

galloping stallion and dazzling the world with acronyms. But resulting expectations are seldom realized. Consider this: In September 2015, 2.3 million people applied for 368 vacant posts for government peons in UP, many of them postgraduates and even PhDs.[27] Similarly, in August 2016, over 0.5 million people, including graduates and postgraduates, applied for 3,275 contractual posts of sweepers in Kanpur Municipal Corporation.[28] Modi talked of creating 10 million jobs per annum.[29] The irony is that even the upcoming Statue of Unity of Sardar Patel in Gujarat has been outsourced to a Chinese foundry.[30] Modi's public statements and commitments made in the run-up to the 2014 Lok Sabha elections of providing employment were a hollow promise with no intent to carry it through, since there was no well-thought-out strategy to provide the promised jobs. Most of these laudable, oft-repeated campaign jumlas were purely political, meant for electoral consumption and gain, without any clue to the course of action required to transform promises into reality and consequently, ameliorating the aam aadmi's economic condition.

Unless you decipher what the growth story of India is likely to be—which sectors of the economy are likely to provide jobs, the key sectors that will attract private sector investment and those that require public investment depending on the leverage provided by higher GDP numbers—there can be no steady course for employment generation and absorption. Once these sectors are identified, policymakers will have to create the infrastructure for those skills to be developed amongst the youth. That, in turn, requires massive changes in imparting education. What is required is change of curriculum in schools, transformation in the design and delivery of diploma courses in technical education, and a tectonic shift in dealing with those seeking graduate and postgraduate

---

[27] http://www.thehindu.com/news/national/other-states/23-lakh-apply-for-368-peon-posts-in-uttar-pradesh/article7660341.ece
[28] http://indianexpress.com/article/education/over-5-lakh-post-graduates-graduates-apply-for-sweepers-posts-in-up/
[29] https://www.firstpost.com/india/modi-promises-one-crore-jobs-if-bjp-comes-to-power-1243037.html
[30] http://timesofindia.indiatimes.com/city/ahmedabad/Iron-man-statue-is-outsourcing-magnet/articleshow/55136676.cms

degrees. We need to put in place a plan for skill development both in schools and universities. Massive investment in the education sector for quality teachers is a national imperative. In the last four years, our government's education policy has been regressive without an eye on the future.

Inspector Raj, which was sought to be demolished with the BJP coming to power, is alive and kicking. The Income Declaration Scheme (IDS) saw taxmen going to businesses and extracting involuntary disclosures. Of course, the Finance Minister took credit for that. Behind every post-demonetization deposit is the lurking fear of the taxman. With demonetization as the first step in targeting people with black money, Modi had publicly stated his intention to target 'benami' transactions next.[31] The prevalent fear that Modi may orchestrate yet another 'surgical strike' is partly the reason for depressed demand and adverse growth.

The mounting bank NPAs (Non-Performing Assets)—now more than 10 per cent of gross advances—need to be tackled to ensure that public sector banks have clean balance sheets. The small allocation of ₹10,000 crore in the 2016–17 Budget was hardly enough to even begin to deal with this contentious problem.[32] In his 2018 Budget speech, Jaitley spoke about the ₹80,000 crore bank recapitalization bonds, but this in itself will not prevent further deterioration in the quality of assets of these public-sector banks. Prosecution of heads of banks for extending loans will further adversely impact the ability of banks to extend credit. In an environment where investors are hesitant to invest, along with an uncertain economic roadmap, any hope to increase GDP will be just a chimera. The Finance Minister, in his Budget proposals for 2018–19, has not drawn a roadmap for economic growth either.

---

[31]http://www.business-standard.com/article/economy-policy/will-take-action-against-benami-property-says-pm-modi-116111300253_1.html
[32]http://economictimes.indiatimes.com/industry/banking/finance/banking/budget-2017-with-a-meagre-rs-10k-crore-allocation-psu-banks-are-in-for-a-tough-time/articleshow/57027736.cms

Deepening Agrarian Distress

Modi's assertion that he would transform the agriculture sector to put an end to farmer suicides is yet another promise that he has miserably failed to fulfil. Farmer suicides in the Marathwada region of Maharashtra and in other states such as Karnataka, Telangana, Madhya Pradesh, Chhattisgarh and Andhra Pradesh, have shamed us and continue to do so.[33] According to the National Crime Records Bureau (NCRB) Report, 'Accidental deaths and suicides in India, 2015', 12,602 farmers and agricultural labourers committed suicide in 2015. This was 2 per cent higher than 12,360 such suicides recorded in 2014. Out of these, 8,007 were farmers, while 4,595 were agricultural labourers. In 2014, the corresponding numbers were 5,650 farmers and 6,710 agricultural labourers. The data makes it apparent that suicides by farmers rose by 42 per cent between 2014 and 2015.[34] For reasons not yet known, no data on farmer suicides has been released by NCRB for the past two years—2016 and 2017.[35]

The reasons for farmer suicides are multifarious, though when in Opposition, Modi blamed UPA policies for the same. Now his government states that farmer suicides have nothing to do with government policies. Union Minister for Agriculture and Farmers' Welfare Radha Mohan Singh, in a written reply to a question in Parliament on 24 July 2015, included reasons like love affairs and impotency.[36] Similarly, on 29 April 2015, Haryana Agriculture Minister O.P. Dhankar called farmers committing suicide 'cowards'.[37]

Modi promised seeds at low cost and a procurement price of produce that would enable farmers to receive 50 per cent more than the cost.

---

[33]http://indianexpress.com/article/india/india-news-india/farmer-suicide-case-in-india-crop-failure-drought-dry-zones-indian-monsoon-2984125/
[34]https://www.newslaundry.com/shorts/42-rise-in-farmer-suicides-in-2014-15-says-ncrb-data
[35]http://www.newindianexpress.com/nation/2018/mar/16/no-data-available-on-the-number-of-farmer-suicide-cases-after-2016-government-1788243.html
[36]http://www.hindustantimes.com/india/agriculture-minister-lists-love-affairs-as-reason-for-farmer-suicides/story-2g8jCPaeS0ZyydtkBViMSL.html
[37]http://indianexpress.com/article/india/india-others/farmers-who-commit-suicide-are-cowards-haryana-agriculture-minister/

Both promises remain unfulfilled. If we compare the MSP per quintal to production costs, MSP for paddy was ₹950 per quintal in 2009–10 against a production cost of ₹670 per quintal, which translated to a 42 per cent profit for farmers. In 2015–16, MSP for paddy was ₹1,410 per quintal against an estimated production cost of ₹1,324 per quintal, resulting in only 6.5 per cent profit to the farmer. In 2016–17, MSP for paddy was ₹1,470 per quintal which barely covered the cost of production.[38]

The procurement prices of wheat, paddy and other agricultural produce in recent years have been much less than the prices received by farmers during the UPA government. Between 2014 and 2016, the Modi government hiked MSP of paddy by only 3.9 per cent (average) per year, while during 2011–13, the UPA had increased it by 9.5 per cent (average) per year. Similarly, for wheat, the figure stood at 4.1 per cent (average) per year under the Modi government as against 7 per cent (average) per year during the UPA.[39]

The recent announcement by the Modi government to hike the MSP of 14 kharif crops for the 2018–19 season[40] is not going to benefit the farmers much. The MSP hike announced for paddy is lower than the year-on-year hike in 2007–08, 2009–10 and 2012–13. Similarly, hike in MSP for cotton (long staple), which is 26 per cent this year, is way lower than 48 per cent in 2008–09. The same is true for sunflower seeds hiked by 31 per cent this year against a hike of 47 per cent in 2008–09.[41] The hike is way less than what the Swaminathan Commission had recommended, which was 50 per cent over comprehensive costs. It also remains to be seen how this increase in MSP is administered. The farmer is going to benefit only if a proper procurement mechanism is set up and effectively implemented. In some states like West Bengal, Assam, Uttar Pradesh and Bihar, in the case of paddy, market price has fallen below the MSP for

---

[38] http://cacp.dacnet.nic.in/ViewReports.aspx?Input=2&PageId=39&KeyId=598
[39] http://www.livemint.com/Politics/xHI61mhVtZlmIR5p9zmh6M/A-pay-cut-for-farmers.html
[40] https://economictimes.indiatimes.com/news/economy/agriculture/modi-government-approves-hike-in-msp-for-kharif-crops/articleshow/64852476.cms
[41] https://thewire.in/agriculture/msp-hike-agriculture-farmers-narendra-modi-government

a number of years in the absence of proper procurement. It is apparent that this announcement is nothing more than vote-bank politics as kharif crops are harvested between October and November—the period when Assembly elections will be held in the three agrarian states of Chhattisgarh, Madhya Pradesh and Rajasthan.

Groundwater is depleting across the country and soils are turning acidic. 'More crop per drop' (a Centrally Sponsored Scheme aimed at enhancing water use efficiency by promoting technological interventions like drip and sprinkler irrigation technologies, and encouraging farmers to use water saving and conservation technologies) is a claim which will take several years to realize. The growth in agriculture during the present dispensation has been far from satisfactory. The growth rate in agriculture for 2017–18 is estimated at 2.1 per cent. Though the growth rate in agriculture for 2016–17 clocked 4.9 per cent, the growth rate in the preceding period of the Modi government was a dismal 0.7 per cent in 2015–16 and -0.2 per cent in 2014–15. Modi has failed to deliver on the policy prescriptions that he promised.

As a nation progresses, we must draw inspiration from the past and provide solutions to people for the problems they face in the present. It is in this context that Mahatma Gandhi talked of reforming agriculture and improving productivity. He talked about village industries and the importance of self-sufficiency for sustainability. It is the Mahatma who espoused the cause of labour-intensive industries to reduce levels of unemployment—a concept of growth and social justice that is relevant even today. The solutions that the Mahatma espoused may not be relevant today since solutions to problems of today must be contextual. While we must, through our economic policies, give an impetus to growth, we cannot possibly forget those at the bottom of the pyramid who live in abject poverty.

Modi does not seem to have grasped this concept. While agriculture is the mainstay for large sections of the rural population, the fragmentation of land has affected millions of marginal farmers who live off their labour but have no surplus to fuel the economy. At the same time, there are very few opportunities for rural youth since manufacturing activity has not resulted in the growth of jobs. Therefore, we have outflow from the rural sector into the cities, as well as states where there is demand for labour; but this labour is unskilled. These migrating farmers have no choice but to work on a daily wage to supplement the meagre resources of their families.

Make in India: A Shooting Star Destined to Fade

Modi's penchant for making grand announcements helps to project himself not just as an energetic prime minister but also as someone with a grand vision who does things differently. The Make in India programme is one such example, which essentially is a restatement of UPA-I's National Manufacturing Policy (NMP) of 2011.[42] Under this policy, Dr Manmohan Singh wished to raise the share of manufacturing in the GDP from 16 per cent to 25 per cent.

But the genesis of this programme can be traced to the 1960s and early '70s, when an import substitution programme was put in place to develop enterprises in India, as technology was hard to come by. The aim was to manufacture goods in India. So, instead of Make in India, we had embraced the concept of Made in India. That programme was unsuccessful. The automobile sector was then dominated by the Walchand Group and the Birlas, who manufactured Fiat and Ambassador cars in the absence of competition, which short-changed the consumer. The consumer paid exorbitant prices for highly inefficient cars. All that changed with the opening up of the economy in 1991 by Dr Manmohan Singh, the then finance minister under the Congress government led by P.V. Narasimha Rao. With liberalization, we embraced an economic culture in which the Indian economy was open to competition and the free market was given enough space to produce goods and services. But over the years, owing to government policies, an entrepreneur in India does not have the kind of space and freedom to chart a course without State interference. In fact, entrepreneurs are handicapped by the high cost of credit and a regime

---

[42]https://chunauti.org/2016/02/15/ab-ki-baar-cut-and-paste-sarkar-the-case-of-make-in-india/

of bureaucratic approvals which consume time and lead to corruption and above all, an economic regime which is susceptible to patronage.

While embarking upon this alleged new enterprise and following it up with a slick campaign, Modi did not realize that Make in India can never be successful unless the regime is free of bureaucratic shackles. The exclusive licensing of technology cannot be the basis for bringing about a paradigm shift in the manufacturing sector.

Further, Make in India does not address our economy's backbone—the SMEs which account for 45 per cent of our industrial production and contribute 40 per cent to our exports while providing employment to over 80 million people.[43] This sector has really no role to play in this programme. Globally, small firms and businesses form the mainstay of employment in manufacturing and services sectors. In South Korea, 80 per cent of the jobs are provided by small firms; in Japan, they provide 66 per cent of employment and have long been the workhorses of construction and manufacturing through a tightly knit system of subcontracting.[44] Make in India does not give a fillip to manufacturing; all it does is to allow multinationals to tie up with either the Defence Research and Development Organization (DRDO) or some of the public sector enterprises for manufacturing in India. Make in India is another jumla, a shooting star that will eventually fade away.

If India is to become an economic powerhouse, the quality of manufacturing and services must improve. We must have an ecosystem that supports growth and, unless we value the significance of technology and harness it, this initiative will become directionless. In 1991, India's services sector contributed 49 per cent to our GDP. In 2015–16, this sector contributed 66 per cent.[45] It is, therefore, clear that our economy is driven by the services sector and is not product oriented. Unless we incentivize the producer and help him make goods, our manufacturing sector will continue to lag.

---

[43]http://www.smechamberofindia.com/about_msmes.aspx
[44]https://scroll.in/article/717955/what-is-missing-from-modis-make-in-india-plan-its-not-thinking-small-enough
[45]http://pib.nic.in/newsite/PrintRelease.aspx?relid=136868

What is needed is an environment where quality goods can be produced at lower costs and be competitive in the global market. Free movement of goods throughout India, the rationale behind the GST, will help lower costs of production. But, for that to happen, we must ensure that India has an enabling ecosystem in place. We need ease of doing business for Indian entrepreneurs, rather than responding only to the ease of doing business for foreign entities in general and multinationals in particular. All this can happen if we have quality human resource with the skill sets necessary to create products. Low energy costs and reduced rates of indirect taxes are essential for growth. There should be easy availability of resources at low cost, with sufficient profit margins for producers. The absence of steady and uninterrupted electric supply results in loss of production while the use of diesel in power generating sets increases costs. We need to incentivize exports to make us competitive in the global market. Our competitiveness also depends on a cost-friendly ecosystem. Has Modi grasped all this? If he has, what steps has he taken other than announcing Make in India, which ultimately allows foreign entities, especially in the electronics sector, to make their products in India?

We also need a robust mechanism that fosters growth of intellectual property. In the health sector, India needs to discover new molecules to address the impact of diseases that afflict this part of the world. Even though our service industry is robust, the IT sector still does not produce intellectual property to enrich companies that eventually hope to play a global role. The telecom sector is an ideal example where we have attracted huge investments but have not created products and unique services which, in turn, can enrich companies like Airtel, Idea and Reliance. Our telecom sector does not cater to the manufacturing of telecom products but uses telecom products of foreign manufacturers to provide services. Most of Airtel's products for providing services are imported. If the Indian economy is to achieve double-digit growth, it is the Make in India programme that must be given a fillip through a process of liberalization which caters to the creation of intellectual property. The Modi regime has taken no steps in this direction. All that it has done is to pat itself on the back through revenue earnings in the auction of spectrum. Modi may fill the treasury through public auction of spectrum, a national asset, but that won't help India lead the way or achieve double-digit growth. We need thoughtful and innovative policy prescriptions.

Taking the Shine Off Start-ups

Startup India was initiated with an eye to create employment and generate jobs. A sum of ₹10,000 crore was set aside during the Budget of 2015–16, but in his Budget speech for 2016–17, the Finance Minister did not mention if any part of that fund was utilized. In fact, an allocation of ₹600 crore made earlier was reduced to ₹100 crore in 2016–17. The Finance Minister had also set up an India Aspiration Fund, as part of the Startup India initiative, to catalyse tens of thousands of crores of equity-linked investments in start-ups and Micro, Small and Medium Enterprises (MSMEs). All this has come to naught.[46]

A survey conducted by InnoVen Capital in its India Start-up Outlook Report 2017 highlights the perspective of founders and chief executive officers of Indian start-ups, with respect to fundraising and investor sentiment, challenges confronting start-ups and policy and government initiatives. The survey captured responses of over 170 start-up leaders across bootstrap as well as funded ventures. The report suggested that approximately 65 per cent believe the Indian start-up is in a technological bubble, and 80 per cent of them felt that the bubble was close to bursting soon. Commenting on the fundraising environment in 2016, 63 per cent of the respondents who had attempted to raise funds said they had an unfavourable funding experience with almost half of these returning unsuccessful.[47] After demonetization, fundraising is even more problematic. One of the biggest problems in Startup India is the difficulty in listing. The preferred option is either to list in India or offshore so

---

[46]http://timesofindia.indiatimes.com/trend-tracking/govt-makes-no-allocation-for-startup-fund-for-next-fiscal/articleshow/57169870.cms
[47]http://www.innovencapital.com/sites/default/files/InnoVen%20Capital%20Startup%20outlook%20report%202017.pdf (last accessed on 08.10.2017)

that they can invest back in more start-ups. In the absence of cheaper finance and investment in digital infrastructure, the start-up scene will continue to be sombre. Even after GST, it will take some time for the benefits of tax rates to help the ecosystem both in the manufacturing and services sector.

Clearly, Startup India does not have the economic wherewithal to make it a success. The programme is misconceived because it seeks to give an impetus to start-ups through public investment and contributions. Such programmes should not be State-incentivized. The economy should give enough opportunities to the private sector for start-ups.

High rate of churning of jobs is an endemic problem that start-up ecosystems face across the world. In India, the problem worsened after the ill-conceived decision of demonetization. Instead of ease of doing business, entities have ceased to do business. On 17 March 2017, Forbes reported that demonetization and scarce capital availability led to a 10 to 50 per cent drop in employee hiring in the start-up ecosystem that year.[48] This sudden decline in recruitments has taken the shine off start-ups. According to Sunil Goel, managing director of Global Hunt in *The Economic Times*, 'It used to take about eight weeks to complete the decision-making process (regarding hiring), but now that cycle has gone up to almost 16 weeks. Momentum has slowed down.' Other than hiring, the rate at which pink slips are being given to employees has also increased. According to a research platform, Xeler8, start-ups fired 9,200 employees in 2016, compared to 500 the previous year. This trend continued in 2017–18 as several mid-sized companies issued layoff notices to hundreds of employees in a bid to trim costs and conserve cash. India's third largest online marketplace, Snapdeal, decided to layoff at least 1,000 employees. Fashion retailer Yepme also laid off an unspecified number of people from its warehousing and quality control teams. Vivek Gaur of Yepme maintained that even though they were planning to break even in 2017, owing to demonetization, sales were down, resulting in the company's decision to move its focus outside India. Clearly, the bloodbath in the

---

[48]https://www.forbes.com/sites/krnkashyap/2017/03/17/the-demonetization-effect-indian-startups-cutting-jobs-amid-uncertainty/#5056b2687089

country's start-up ecosystem continues unabated. Demonetization, more than the tough funding environment, has increased job cuts and lowered levels of hiring.

The Government, a Continuum

To some extent, Modi has been successful in appropriating schemes started by the UPA and projecting them as his own. The Swachh Bharat Abhiyan, for instance, is the Nirmal Bharat Abhiyan of the Congress-led UPA. The Pradhan Mantri Kaushal Vikas Yojana (PMKVY) is the UPA's skill development mission. The UPA had created the National Skill Development Fund (NSDF), National Skill Development Council (NSDC) in 2009, and National Skill Development Agency (NSDA) in 2014. The financial inclusion programme of the UPA is the BJP's Pradhan Mantri Jan-Dhan Yojana (PMJDY)—a basic savings bank accounts programme. In 2005, the RBI directed banks to open 'no-frills' accounts, also known as 'zero balance' accounts.[49] In 2013, banks were directed to extend the financial inclusion plan to 2016.[50] The Digital India initiative was a UPA scheme, called the National e-Governance Plan (NeGP). The Pradhan Mantri Awas Yojana-Gramin (PMAY-G) is a change of name from the Indira Awas Yojana, which was launched by Rajiv Gandhi in 1985 to provide housing for the rural poor. The Modi government has merely increased the amount sanctioned for this housing scheme. Now people entitled to the benefits will get ₹1.2 lakh against the earlier sanctioned amount of ₹70,000 under the UPA government. In addition, the beneficiaries will now be able to take a loan of ₹70,000 and get ₹12,000 to construct a toilet.

Pratyaksh Hastantarit Labh, popularly known as PAHAL, allows consumers of LPG cylinders to claim their subsidies directly in their bank accounts. This is nothing but the UPA's work-in-progress Direct Benefit Transfer (DBT) scheme. The objective of the scheme was to seed

---

[49]https://www.rbi.org.in/Scripts/NotificationUser.aspx?Id=2669&Mode=0
[50]http://www.thehindubusinessline.com/money-and-banking/banks-told-to-submit-financial-inclusion-plan-for-next-three-years/article4634041.ece

150 million LPG connections with bank accounts. Modi renamed it and launched it in 54 districts in mid-November 2014.[51]

In 2008–09, the UPA government launched a national project to test farm soils and encourage the use of appropriate fertilizers on the basis of such tests to boost soil health and productivity. More than 50 million Soil Health Cards were issued to farmers across the states and Union territories by March 2012. The Modi government claims that this is its original programme.[52]

The Deendayal Upadhyaya Gram Jyoti Yojana (DDUGJY) was launched by this government as a key initiative for rural electrification. In reality, it is a new name for the Rajiv Gandhi Grameen Vidyutikaran Yojana (RGGVY). As many as 1,012,287 villages, previously without electricity, were connected to the grid from 2002 to 2012. Under the 12th Plan (2012–17), the target was electrification of 12,468 unelectrified villages, intensive electrification of 0.2 million electrified villages and free electricity to 13.3 million Below Poverty Line (BPL) households, including those belonging to the Scheduled Castes (SC) and Scheduled Tribes (ST), at a cost of ₹23,709 crore. This government informed Parliament that the RGGVY was subsumed under the DDUGJY.

The Pradhan Mantri Krishi Sinchayee Yojana (PMKSY) is a revamped version of the UPA's Accelerated Irrigation Benefit Programme (AIBP) launched during the 11th Plan (2007–11). It finances chosen unfinished irrigation projects. The Paramparagat Krishi Vikas Yojana (PKVY), wherein every farmer is to get ₹20,000 per acre every three years, clubs the UPA's organic farming schemes/programmes.

The Jawaharlal Nehru National Urban Renewal Mission (JNNURM) launched by the UPA in 2005, is now the Atal Mission for Rejuvenation and Urban Transformation (AMRUT), launched in April 2015 by the Modi government.[53] This improved version widens its objectives both in

---

[51] http://www.deccanchronicle.com/141019/business-latest/article/direct-benefit-transfer-lpg-sop-back
[52] http://factchecker.in/agriculture-ministry-old-schemes-renamed-other-misleading-claims/
[53] http://timesofindia.indiatimes.com/india/JNNURM-2-0-to-be-named-after-Vajpayee/articleshow/46102222.cms

size and scale. The JNNURM targeted 63 cities, while AMRUT will cover 500 cities with a population of over 1 lakh. The JNNURM was largely Centre-driven, while AMRUT decentralizes the mission, giving powers to the states to monitor and implement the projects.

Modi claims that he has transformed India and that we live in a new, energized Bharat. What is clear is that government is a continuum and Modi's claim of transformation is nothing more than a play of words. This is yet another of Modi's stratagems to hide the facts and, through his unmatched rhetoric, boast that he seeks a better India for our citizens.

Manipulation of Data

While the BJP is a deft manipulator of public opinion, its ability to manipulate data is a matter of graver concern. Since it came to power, the Central Statistics Office (CSO) decided to change the base year from March 2005 to March 2012 while calculating GDP. GDP is calculated on a fixed base year to ensure that inflation does not affect the data. The GDP in the year 2010 would be: gross consumption + investment + government spending + (export–import) at 2004–05 prices. Now that the base year is 2012, it has increased the value of the GDP because inflation in 2004–05 was very low compared to the figure in 2011–12. In the new calculations, corporate activities and data on household spending and the informal sector have also been included.

However, the major shift in GDP calculations was to evaluate economic activity at market cost rather than factor cost (the GDP at factor cost means valuation at the production stage and not at the consumption stage). Here taxes are added and prices are increased. These major changes by the CSO have adjusted the GDP figures significantly. The problem is that the rate of economic growth does not change. So if the new GDP data suddenly puts India's growth at 7.6 or 7.1 or 6.75 per cent, this figure does not represent any increased economic activity on the ground—one of the reasons for former Reserve Bank of India (RBI) Governor

Raghuram Rajan to question the growth numbers.[54] If we apply the new methodology to the growth rate in 2013–14 under the UPA, the GDP would have grown at the rate of 6.9 per cent, whereas on the basis of the old series, it was 4.7 per cent.[55] The manipulation of numbers and change in methodology do not improve people's lives but provide enough grist to spin doctors led by Modi to claim the transformational change in their political outreach. It is sad that in a democratic country the government has chosen to manipulate figures to give the impression of prosperity. People are, by and large, unaware of the basis of calculating GDP. However, in the long run, those feeling the pinch of abject poverty may not be taken in.

Demonetization—Yet Another Jumla

Modi's decision (perhaps not that of the Modi government) to demonetize 86 per cent of the currency on 8 November 2016, was yet another false step in convincing people that his government genuinely wished to eradicate the black economy. He had failed to bring back home the black money stashed abroad. One way of changing the nature of the discourse on unaccounted-for wealth stashed abroad was to deal with the black economy at home.

While the objective of reducing black money in a growing economy is laudable, the means to achieve it without much thought was not only questionable but also resulted in unprecedented dislocation of the economy. This 'surgical strike' on black money caused a massive loss of jobs—the closing down of businesses, especially in the informal sector; destruction of the livelihoods of daily wagers and migrant labour, etc. Apart from a negative impact on self-help groups and cooperative banks,

---

[54] http://indianexpress.com/article/india/india-news-india/raghuram-rajan-sceptical-about-gdp-calculation/

[55] http://www.thehindu.com/business/Economy/base-year-change-pushes-201314-gdp-growth-to-69/article6839570.ece

demonetization left the farmer in a state of utter despair.[56,57,58] It halted India's growth story.

Modi must have known that 86 per cent of our cash economy, represented by legal tender in the form of ₹500 and ₹1,000 currency notes, cannot represent unaccounted-for wealth. Cash alone does not represent black money, but unaccounted-for transactions do. Moreover, cash merely represented 6 per cent (3.7 per cent to 7.4 per cent, according to the UPA's May 2012 White Paper on Black Money tabled in Parliament[59]) of unaccounted-for wealth in India, the balance being invested in real estate, gold and perhaps exchanged in foreign currency.[60] Those transactions were not the target, for that might have impacted Modi's own party and businesses closely associated with the corridors of power.

Any economist could have told him that in paralysing the economy, India's GDP would be severely affected with a negative impact on economic growth. The Economic Survey of 2017 lowered GDP growth forecast to 6.5 per cent for 2016–17 and projected a growth rate between 6.5 per cent and 7.5 per cent for 2017–18.[61] Similarly, the RBI and various rating agencies, investment banking firms and financial research companies revised the GDP growth rate downwards from earlier estimates. The lingering impact of demonetization was clearly visible in the growth rate in the first quarter of 2017–18, which slowed to a three-year low of 5.7 per cent in April–June

---

[56] http://indianexpress.com/article/india/demonetization-35-per-cent-job-losses-50-per-cent-revenue-dip-says-study-by-largest-organisation-of-manufacturers-4465524/?utm_source=VKD&utm_medium=website&utm_campaign=e-letter&utm_content=VKD

[57] http://www.livemint.com/Industry/BRp44zlczj0jeTFyf8vKeP/Demonetization-has-negative-impact-on-jobs-SMEs-says-Assoc.html?utm_source=VKD&utm_medium=website&utm_campaign=e-letter&utm_content=VKD

[58] http://www.hindustantimes.com/india-news/demonetization-will-hit-farmers-informal-workers-long-term-outlook-positive/story-ghWMZfVuXnsvkiPWCF4iKM.html

[59] http://www.prsindia.org/uploads/media/White%20Paper%20Black%20Money/WhitePaper_BackMoney2012.pdf

[60] https://scroll.in/article/822390/only-16-of-every-250-fake-notes-were-detected-in-india-in-2015-16

[61] http://indianexpress.com/article/business/economy/note-ban-shaves-off-gdp-growth-rate-by-up-to-0-5-pc-in-ficsal-year-2017-4500529/

(Q1 period) of 2017–18 from 7.9 per cent in the Q1 period of 2016–17.[62] The Economic Survey 2018 has projected GDP to grow by 6.75 per cent in 2017–18, while the RBI has lowered it to 6.6 per cent. According to provisional estimates by Central Statistical Organisation (CSO), growth rate of GDP for 2017–18 is 6.7 per cent.[63]

The immediate effect of demonetization was the negative impact on the informal sector. A study by the All India Manufacturers' Organisation (AIMO), which represents over 3 lakh MSMEs and large-scale industries engaged in manufacturing and export activities, found that in the first 34 days after demonetization, they suffered 35 per cent job losses and a 50 per cent dip in revenue. It also projected a 60 per cent drop in employment and loss in revenue of 55 per cent before March 2017.[64] According to CMIE's July 2017 report, demonetization resulted in the loss of roughly 1.5 million jobs in the first four months after 8 November 2016.[65] Migrant labourers working on daily wages lost their jobs;[66] it impacted the leather, textile, hosiery, glassware, automobiles,[67] diamonds[68] and other industries;[69] tea and coffee plantation workers;[70] and those holding Indian currency. Sales in the retail sector diminished radically.[71] With inventories still unsold,

---

[62] http://www.thehindubusinessline.com/economy/first-quarter-gdp-grew-57-per-cent-cso/article9838210.ece
[63] http://pib.nic.in/newsite/PrintRelease.aspx?relid=179666
[64] http://indianexpress.com/article/india/demonetization-35-per-cent-job-losses-50-per-cent-revenue-dip-says-study-by-largest-organisation-of-manufacturers-4465524/
[65] https://www.cmie.com/kommon/bin/sr.php?kall=warticle&dt=2017-07-11%2011:07:31&msec=463
[66] http://www.hindustantimes.com/india-news/the-flight-of-the-migrants-jobless-labourers-return-home-after-demonetization/story-1H5HeMuLpTe7ZZTbG8hEnL.html
[67] http://economictimes.indiatimes.com/industry/auto/news/industry/demonetization-cash-crunch-brings-auto-industry-to-a-screeching-halt/articleshow/55883126.cms
[68] http://www.catchnews.com/yahoo/india-news/diamond-industry-loses-its-sparkle-thanks-to-modi-s-demonetization-1482850147.html
[69] http://indianexpress.com/article/business/economy/demonetization-brings-labour-industry-to-standstill-4392814/
[70] http://www.livemint.com/Politics/YQQKZovaUAXBrNUP3rEFTO/Demonetization-hits-plantation-workers-in-south-India-hard.html
[71] http://www.zeebiz.com/india/news-post-demonetization-organised-retail-sector-likely-to-post-low-single-digit-growth-in-q3-fy17-india-ratings-10755

demand slackened and our fast-paced economy, the foundations of which were laid by the UPA, slowed down.

Legitimate money in the hands of ordinary folk was deemed to be black, and the pain it caused was witnessed by the long queues of frustrated citizens desperately wanting to withdraw legitimate money from their bank accounts only to be informed of the non-availability of cash. There is evidence to the effect that before 8 November, the BJP had bought properties in Bihar[72] and deposited money in banks in West Bengal, suggesting that perhaps the party sought to protect its own cash and legitimize it in other forms before the demonetization announcement.[73]

Just before the Assembly elections to five states in 2017, Modi suddenly changed tack and started talking about the plight of the poor, not realizing that in Gujarat, over the years, the poor Adivasis were last in his priority. His empathy for the poor was not the result of any change of heart—he sought to provide the rationale for demonetization. He suggested that the rich were being targeted.[74] Behind that action was the belief that the poor would smile in silence. That was a miscalculation. Modi, perhaps, did not realize that the rich, by manipulating the banking system, would not suffer; whereas millions at the bottom of the pyramid would feel the pain of demonetization. The trading community felt cheated and isolated as several medium and small enterprises lost business and closed.

The full impact of demonetization is yet to be seen. The decision was not based on sound thinking but was yet another jumla before the elections in five states, in the hope that Modi would be perceived to be against the corrupt. But people have understood that the BJP is flush with cash. Modi thought that demonetization was a masterstroke as it would paralyse his political opponents who would be unable to match the BJP in money power.

---

[72]http://www.catchnews.com/india-news/bjp-paid-crores-in-cash-to-buy-land-before-note-ban-amit-shah-authorised-deals-1480425007.html
[73]http://www.newindianexpress.com/nation/2016/nov/11/west-bengal-bjp-knew-about-demonetization-deposited-rs-1-crore-hours-before-announcement-cpm-1537470.html
[75]https://www.thehindu.com/news/national/Demonetization-has-equalised-the-rich-and-the-poor-claims-Modi/article16447877.ece
[74]http://www.newindianexpress.com/nation/2016/nov/11/west-bengal-bjp-knew-about-demonetization-deposited-rs-1-crore-hours-before-announcement-cpm-1537470.html

That demonetization was a sham was demonstrated by the RBI's annual report for 2016–17, which said that 99 per cent of the demonetized banknotes returned to the banking system—of the estimated ₹15.44 lakh crore that was rendered invalid, ₹15.28 lakh crore came back.[75]

Thus, the decision taken on 8 November by the Modi government to delegitimize the use of ₹500 and ₹1,000 currency notes has turned out to be counter-productive. There has been a mismatch between NaMo's objectives and DeMo's outcome. Down the road, cash is back in a significant way. As per RBI data, currency with the public in 2018 has reached a record high of over 18.5 lakh crore, more than double the 7.8 lakh crore post-demonetization.[76] The total currency in circulation has also increased exponentially to 19.3 lakh crore from a low of about 8.9 lakh crore post-demonetization.[77] It is, therefore, clear that after 19 months of demonetization, the dream of India becoming a cashless economy has faded away. Even though the volume of digital payments has touched 1.9 billion in April 2017 as compared to 1.4 billion in April 2016, showing a growth of 37 per cent,[78] the claim that digital payments will substitute the cash economy was yet another jumla, because the favoured mode of payments across Asia is cash. In fact, despite the push for a cashless economy, over 50 per cent of the people in India prefer using cash.[79] Clearly, the decision of 8 November was an ill-thought decision merely to shock and awe instead of being a genuine effort for transformational change. That indeed is the tragedy of most decisions taken by this government since these are motivated solely by the aim of gaining public support, without understanding the consequences they entail.

---

[75]http://www.business-standard.com/article/economy-policy/rbi-annual-report-99-of-demonetised-currency-back-into-the-system-117083000891_1.html
[76]https://www.thehindubusinessline.com/economy/currency-with-public-hits-record-high-post-demonetization/article24127708.ece
[77]https://www.thehindubusinessline.com/economy/currency-with-public-hits-record-high-post-demonetization/article24127708.ece
[78]http://niti.gov.in/writereaddata/files/Digital%20Payments%20-%20Progress%20Report-April%202017.pdf
[79]https://www.financialexpress.com/economy/cashless-economy-dream-not-yet-cash-is-still-the-king-says-cto-of-this-digital-payments-major/1180011/

Modi Doublespeak

In the last four years, the crime graph has been on the ascendance. According to a report of the NCRB, there was an increase of 2.9 per cent in instances of crime against women in 2016 as compared to 2015, including an increase of 12.4 per cent in rape cases over the same period. Delhi recorded the highest overall rate of crime against women in 2016.[80]

Modi has not been able to—perhaps he never intended to—put in place an institutional framework for reducing crimes against women. With the police's inability to protect Nirbhaya, the UPA became the target of public wrath. The candlelight marches and manhandling of protesters fuelled disenchantment. The UPA was perceived to have failed on this front, and yet, in the last four years, despite increasing instances of such heinous crimes, candlelight marches are absent and public angst missing. Recent incidents like the January 2018 rape and the brutal murder of a Dalit girl in Jind, Haryana, and the gang-rape and murder of an 11-year-old girl in Panipat have not evoked such reactions. Either these instances have not been highlighted enough, which alone can persuade the government to reduce the frequency of such crimes, or there is a new agenda— diversion of public attention every day. The quality of administration in Yogi Adityanath's Uttar Pradesh can be gauged by the fact that one of its own MLAs, Kuldeep Sengar, has been booked for raping a minor girl, and his brother Atul Singh for mercilessly killing the 55-year-old father of the victim. The Uttar Pradesh government left no stone unturned in its attempt to shield the accused. The Kathua rape represents the demonic mindset of those who committed the crime, and the setting up of the Hindu Ekta Manch to defend the accused is indefensible.[81] That humanity can stoop to such a low to make a young innocent girl a pawn shows that we have not learned any lesson after the Nirbhaya incident. The fact remains that Modi's promise of providing a secure environment for our women has not even been attempted.

---

[80] https://www.dailyo.in/variety/ncrb-data-2016-crimes-against-women-human-trafficking-cyber-crime/story/1/20867.html
[81] https://www.frontline.in/cover-story/ekta-manch-that-aims-to-divide/article10107269.ece

In the run-up to the Lok Sabha elections, Modi promised that he would deliver a scam-free India to the people. Even now Modi backs this eloquently; he repeatedly reminds India of how UPA was scam-tainted. However, Modi turns a blind eye to the endemic corruption symbolized by the Vyapam scam and the serious allegations made against chief ministers of states where the BJP is in power. Rajasthan Chief Minister Vasundhara Raje was alleged to have provided patronage to Lalit Modi; Madhya Pradesh Chief Minister Shivraj Singh Chouhan's name figured in the Vyapam as well as Dental and Medical Admission Test scams and Chhattisgarh Chief Minister Raman Singh was alleged to be part of the PDS scam. Similarly, scams involving the Gujarat State Petroleum Corporation Ltd (GSPC),[82] Adani's over-invoicing (of coal and electricity generation equipment[83]), Vijay Mallya, and most recently, Union Minister Giriraj Singh (allegedly in a land grabbing case in Danapur, Patna[84]), have been kept under the lid.

The Birla-Sahara bribery papers would have created a national furore in any other dispensation. Surprisingly, the Supreme Court buried the controversy. It held that such entries have no evidential value. However, an investigation could have unearthed the truth behind such entries. But we have seen no genuine attempts at investigating the matter. The Rafale fighter jet deal continues to remain shrouded in mystery. Modi did not take into confidence the then Defence Minister Manohar Parrikar, when on a visit to Paris in April 2015, he announced the purchase of 36 Rafale aircraft off-the-shelf. On the eve of Modi's visit to France, at a customary press conference, the then Foreign Secretary S. Jaishankar told the media that Hindustan Aeronautics Limited (HAL) was Dassault Aviation's partner, thereby suggesting that the public sector undertaking HAL was ready to seal the deal. Modi broke convention by announcing the deal on foreign soil and surprised everyone by snatching the deal away

---

[82] https://www.financialexpress.com/economy/cag-raps-gspc-for-mismanagement-rs-19576-crore-investment-in-kg-block/232001/
[83] http://www.caravanmagazine.in/vantage/dri-investigation-50000-crore-over-invoicing-scam-judicial-logjam
[84] http://www.thehindu.com/news/national/union-minister-giriraj-singh-booked-in-land-grabbing-case/article22687397.ece

from HAL. In March 2015, Dassault and HAL had publicly announced that the deal was 90 per cent done. By April 2015, on his visit to France, the deal was undone. The stepmotherly treatment of a PSU surprised even those in government. Modi preferred a private company to a PSU for reasons that he knows best.

The Finance Minister says that the price of the fighter jet cannot be put in the public domain since it has never been done in the past, for it impacts the secrecy and non-disclosure clause. This is contrary to the practice in the past. The Congress Defence Minister placed before Parliament the price of acquisitions for the Defence Services.[85] And of course, the biggest scam in Independent India—demonetization—continues to unfold. Modi has been successful in ensuring that every scandal is brushed under the carpet and the Ministry of Information and Broadcasting is used to ensure that the voluminous evidence, though available, does not become a part of any public discourse. The print media is equally targeted.

The Nirav Modi scam, to the tune of ₹14,000 crore, is perhaps the biggest banking scam since Independence. Nirav Modi was allowed to leverage letters of undertaking given by Punjab National Bank to secure payments from foreign banks. What needs to be investigated is the disposal of the money that was earned by Nirav Modi and the manner in which he was allowed to flee the country in January 2018.

The escapes of Vijay Mallya and Nirav Modi suggest complicity of official machinery. Crony capitalism has been institutionalized under the Modi government. Transparency International and other organizations have suggested that, in this part of the world, India is the most corrupt nation.

Corruption cannot be brushed under the carpet through political manipulation. Serious attempts to deal with corruption require transparent processes of investigation to make systems of governance accountable. Perhaps, the most corrupt agencies are those which exercise statutory powers, allowing officials to collaborate with the prospective accused, for a price. Political funding required to fight elections and its overarching

---

[85]https://economictimes.indiatimes.com/news/politics-and-nation/congress-shows-antony-replies-questions-rafale-price-secrecy/articleshow/62858422.cms

influence are the root causes of corruption. Unless we reform our institutional processes, reduce levels of poverty and make people and institutions accountable, corruption will eat into the interstices of the body politic.

Machiavellian Par Excellence

There are three elements of Modi's political strategy that make him a Machiavellian par excellence. First is to constantly sell a dream to the people of India, launch schemes and make public statements catering to people's aspirations. Swachh Bharat, for example, is aspirational. Every Indian wants her or his backyard to be clean. The poor who live in pestilence want a clean environment in which their children can play, instead of drains full of muck or putrid ponds. All of us want garbage to be removed as quickly as possible, protecting us from the stench that emanates when the authorities have not done their job. Modi holding a broom is symbolic of that aspiration of a Swachh India. Make in India, too, is emotive, evoking feelings of nationalism, while Startup India is a symbolic break from the past, as if Modi has switched on the ignition for India to move forward. Yet, over the years, only hope has been generated, and very little is seen on the ground.

Varanasi remains one of the most polluted cities in India[86] and its banks have a limited cosmetic ambience.[87] The Ganga is as dirty as ever. The National Green Tribunal (NGT), on 6 February 2017, rapped government agencies, 'Everyone says they are doing a lot to clean Ganga, but not a single drop of the river has been cleaned.'[88] Yet Modi, through his aspirational announcements, seeks to gain political momentum and be perceived as a doer.

The second element of Modi's governance is his attempt to be perceived

---

[86]http://www.counterview.net/2016/12/modis-varanasi-most-toxic-city-of-india.html
[87]http://www.business-standard.com/article/current-affairs/clean-india-a-distant-dream-in-pm-modi-s-varanasi-116121800219_1.html
[88]http://www.hindustantimes.com/india-news/public-money-wasted-not-a-drop-of-ganga-cleaned-ngt/story-W0sHleMHqdLuNmYXdxnsZI.html

as a statesman by talking of programmes like Beti Bachao, addressing the masses through Mann Ki Baat and generally pandering to the middle class. Perhaps the most non-transparent prime minister India has ever had, Modi never stops talking of transparency in governance. His government is also perhaps the most non-accountable, yet Modi never hesitates to talk of accountability.

The third element is Modi's ability to allow the RSS to push forward its agenda and, at the same time, distance himself from it. In fact, in the last four years, the Prime Minister has not spoken on the issues that have confronted the nation. In July 2016, when Kashmir turned into a volatile battleground between the security forces and local residents after the killing of Hizbul Mujahideen militant Burhan Wani, our Prime Minister chose not to participate, even as both Houses of Parliament debated the issue. The raging controversy over Dalit scholar Rohith Vemula's suicide and the events at JNU left the nation surprised. When other ministers exchanged charges and countercharges, the Prime Minister remained silent. In June 2015, when the issue of Lalit Modi having escaped investigation with government help raged, the proceedings in Parliament seeking an explanation from the government and a statement from the Prime Minister were blocked. Our garrulous Prime Minister, who doesn't hesitate to speak his mind, again chose not to address the issue even in his monthly radio address, Mann Ki Baat.

The spread of religious intolerance has surged since Modi came to power in 2014, in sharp contrast to the UPA's 10 years. Communal campaigns like love jihad, ghar wapsi, beef bans, dress codes and moral policing have generated an atmosphere of hatred against minorities. The PM allows his ministers to make statements that would shame any right-thinking person, hoping that a polarized nation will unite the majority community to benefit the BJP politically.

Indeed, the impression one gets is that such controversies were allowed to stay the course because it benefits the BJP. That is why, instead of dousing the fire, the Prime Minister, on all such occasions, chooses to let the fire rage. His silence, in fact, encourages all those elements within the party, and close to it, to allow the fuelled divisive discourse to flourish.

Videos on social media platforms motivated by right-wing elements spread venom and go viral, making communities insecure and fearful. All this is engineered to consolidate the Hindu vote bank.

Perpetuating the Majoritarian Sentiment

Modi understands better than most others how to exploit the majoritarian mindset. It all started with L.K. Advani's Rath Yatra. The demolition of the Babri Masjid paid huge political dividends.

Prosecutions launched in the aftermath of the Mumbai bomb blasts in March 1993 (allegedly masterminded by Dawood Ibrahim in response to the January 1993 Mumbai riots), in which 257 people were killed and 713 injured, tell a story of their own. A total of 123 accused were prosecuted and 100 convicted through the designated Terrorist and Disruptive Activities Act (TADA) special court set up at Arthur Road; 11 were given capital punishment and 31 life sentences.[89] Those who were sentenced deserved to be punished.

The Mumbai riots of December 1992 and January 1993, that followed the Babri Masjid demolition in which 900 were killed and 2,036 injured, have a different story to tell. Of the dead, 575 were Muslims, 275 Hindus and 50 from other communities. However, just three convictions took place. On 10 July 2008, a Mumbai court sentenced former Shiv Sena MP Madhukar Sarpotdar and two other party activists to a year-long rigorous imprisonment in connection with the riots.[90] Sarpotdar was immediately granted bail[91] and on 20 February 2010, he passed away without serving a day's sentence.[92] Those named in the Srikrishna Report were never dealt with. Inspector Nikhil Kapse, found guilty of killing six innocent

---

[89]http://www.thehindu.com/news/national/full-list-of-accused-and-punishment-in-the-mumbai-blast-case/article7481121.ece
[90]http://in.reuters.com/article/idINIndia-34444720080709
[91]http://timesofindia.indiatimes.com/city/mumbai/Sena-leader-Sarpotdar-gets-bail-in-Mumbai-riot-case/articleshow/3281328.cms
[92]http://www.dnaindia.com/mumbai/report-sena-leader-madhukar-sarpotdar-dies-1350425

Muslims, was promoted.[93] Shiv Sena members found with unlicensed guns were not charged. The commission indicted the Mumbai police force as communal and charged 31 policemen as well. Srikrishna recommended 1,350 cases to be reopened, but the special task force reopened only five. Those too ended in acquittals.

Even more troublesome are the statements made by important rightwing leaders in 1998. The then Chief Minister of Maharashtra Manohar Joshi said on 22 April 1998, 'Everything that our party undertakes is done after due thought and, therefore, I have no regrets for my party's role during the riots...' The Srikrishna Report was perceived as 'biased against the majority community', according to Shiv Sena leader Subash Desai. Uddhav Thackeray insisted, '...we did not start the riots; we only retaliated to protect our people. We are not ashamed of defending our people. In fact, we will retaliate even harder if anybody tries to create trouble again.'[94]

It is this majoritarian sentiment that Modi grasped and used to his advantage in the aftermath of the Godhra train incident in 2002. In this regard, it would be significant to set out comparisons between the manner in which two sets of accused in the Godhra and post-Godhra incidents were dealt with.

In the case of the Godhra train burning incident, of the 94 accused who were prosecuted, 31 were convicted, 11 were awarded the death penalty, 20 were given life imprisonment and the rest were acquitted, thereby highlighting the quality of the investigation. It can be argued that those acquitted were given the benefit of the doubt, but the element of discrimination lies in the fact that throughout the course of the trial, none of the accused were released on bail. Maulvi Umerji and Mohammad Hussain Kalota, two individuals who were most crucial from the prosecution's point of view, were charged as the masterminds. Interestingly, Umerji, the most respected cleric in Godhra and Kalota, was the chief political opponent of the BJP in a town which was communally sensitive. He was the president of the Godhra Municipal Council at the time of his

---

[93]http://www.bhindibazaar.asia/haj-house-imam-still-suspended-despite-acquittal/
[94]http://www.sabrang.com/cc/comold/may98/report.htm

arrest. The theory that a conspiracy was hatched by political and religious leaders of a particular community in Godhra was a smokescreen. Umerji never got bail even after the charges of terrorism were removed in 2009. While he languished in jail, six of his children were married off. He died of a brain haemorrhage in January 2013.[95]

Contrast this with the treatment meted out to the post-Godhra riots accused—a large number of them belonged to the majority community, whether at Naroda Patiya or Gulbarg Society where Ehsan Jafri and others were killed and set on fire, or at places where women and children were massacred with impunity as acts of retribution.[96] The significant elements of the prosecution and trial in these cases suggest that not all the accused were brought to book and many were released on bail during the course of the trial. In fact, many fresh FIRs with names of the alleged accused were not allowed to be lodged on the pretext that FIRs during the incidents had already been lodged and were being investigated. Allegations that the members of commissions set up by the then Gujarat government were handpicked and were meant to exculpate those directly or indirectly involved in the post-Godhra events may have an element of truth in them.[97] During a 2007 investigative sting operation carried out by *Tehelka* magazine on the Gujarat riots, Arvind Pandya, the counsel appointed by the Gujarat government to defend itself before the Shah-Nanavati Commission, claimed that Justice K.G. Shah 'is our man' and Justice Nanavati was there 'for money'. He was referring to the Commission of Inquiry appointed by the Gujarat government in May 2002 to probe the Godhra incident and the riots.[98]

Another curious feature was the invocation of Prevention of Terrorism Act (POTA) in the Godhra train carnage on 28 February 2002 for the offences allegedly committed only a day earlier—27 February 2002. The attempt to apply POTA failed, but it reflected the mindset

---

[95]http://archive.indianexpress.com/news/godhra-attack-accused-later-acquitted-he--never-got-over-his-jail-term-/1060277/0
[96]http://www.truthofgujarat.com/the-death-dance-at-naroda-patiya/
[97]http://www.tehelka.com/2012/09/the-sting-in-the-story/
[98]https://www.youtube.com/watch?v=XCbV5nB8w50

of the administration led by the then Chief Minister Modi.[99] Instead of condemning all those who were responsible for this act of terror, he accused the Muslims of Godhra of possessing 'criminal tendencies'. In an interview with Zee TV on 1 March 2002, he said, 'This is a chain of action and reaction. We want both the action and the reaction to stop.'[100]

Post-Godhra, 1,044 people were killed, 2,500 injured and 223 were reported missing; more than 4,500 houses were destroyed and 18,500 damaged. Loss of property for Muslims was pegged at approximately ₹600 crore, and that of Hindus at approximately ₹40 crore (as per the then DGP Intelligence of Gujarat Police, R.B. Sreekumar's affidavit before the Justice Nanavati Commission of Inquiry). By August 2002, 1,32,532 people had been displaced or forced to leave their homes and were living in 121 relief camps.[101] Till August 2002, 225 women and 65 children were reportedly killed.[102] But for Supreme Court interventions, many of the post-Godhra incidents would not have been investigated—Best Bakery killings, Naroda Patiya massacre, killings in Sardarpura, Gulbarg, Naroda Gam and Dipda Darwaza, the Pirawali Bhagol massacres, the Malav Bhagol incident, and the Sabarkantha killings. All of these incidents will be remembered for the cruelty with which people of the minority community were targeted. The bias of the enforcement agencies[103] reflects a majoritarian culture, which allows for unequal treatment, which in turn sows the seeds of discontent.

There were several instances in Gujarat in which young Muslims were caught, investigated and, in some cases, allegedly killed in fake encounters. This set the stage for Modi becoming a leader who was ready to deal with

---

[99]http://twocircles.net/2009feb14/pota_not_applicable_godhra_train_burning_case_gujarat_hc.html

[100]http://cjponline.org/gujaratTrials/statecomp/pdf%20files/pdfs/Excerpts%20from%20Editors%20Guild%20Report%202002.pdf

[101]Report of the Parliamentary Committee on the Empowerment of Women; Gujarat Home Department had also recorded the same

[102]http://www.gujarat-riots.com/liveslost.htm. Also see:Report of the Parliamentary Committee on the Empowerment of Women; Gujarat Home Department had also recorded the same

[103]http://timesofindia.indiatimes.com/india/NHRC-upset-over-bias-in-Gujarat-FIRs/articleshow/12583920.cms

acts of terror. Several plots to assassinate him were allegedly unearthed. In August 2002, it was reported that three Lashkar-e-Taiba (LeT) terrorists, who were arrested from Delhi and Moradabad, had hatched a plan to kill Modi.[104] In June 2004, Ishrat Jahan and her three accomplices were shot dead as Gujarat police claimed that they had plans to assassinate Modi.[105] This zero-tolerance policy of Modi vis-à-vis alleged terrorists endeared him even more to the majority community.

The ghettoization of the Muslim community and its consequent impact on the Muslim psyche speaks volumes of the mindset of those in power.[106] It would not be fair to come to any firm conclusion, but the needle of suspicion points to wilful acts being engineered to ignite passions that led to violence across the state and then turning the other way while innocent men, women and children were being massacred.[107]

While the UPA was in power, it so happened that in several cases of terrorist activity, members of the majority community had been arraigned as accused. The Malegaon blast of 8 September 2006, the Samjhauta Express blast on 19 February 2007, the Mecca Masjid blast on 18 May 2007, the Ajmer Sharif blast on 11 October 2007 and the Malegaon blast of 2008—all point to right-wing organizations targeting the Muslim community.

In the 2006 Malegaon blast case, nine young Muslims were arraigned as accused at first, seven of whom were granted bail after five years. These nine people (seven of them from Malegaon) were arrested by the Maharashtra Anti-Terrorism Squad (ATS) two months after the blast. The Maharashtra ATS filed the charge sheet in the special Maharashtra Control of Organised Crime Act (MCOCA) court, and after the Central Bureau of Investigation (CBI) took over the investigation in July 2007, filed a charge sheet against the same accused in February 2010. In 2011,

---

[104]http://zeenews.india.com/home/three-let-terrorists-held-plan-to-kill-modi-togadia-cracked_56201.html?pfrom=article-next-story

[105]http://indianexpress.com/article/explained/changing-versions-contesting-claims-how-ishrat-encounter-refuses-to-die/

[106]https://thewire.in/2606/what-juhapura-tells-us-about-muslims-in-modis-india/

[107]http://www.catchnews.com/india-news/meet-the-23-cops-who-embody-gujarat-s-carrot-and-stick-policy-1440404009.html

the case was handed over to the National Investigation Agency (NIA) whereupon these nine accused retracted their confessions alleging that those confessions had been secured under duress. On 5 November 2011, seven of them walked out of jail, while two others continued to be in jail for their alleged role in the 2006 Mumbai train blast case.[108] On 22 May 2013, the NIA filed its charge sheet in the case against four fresh accused, all allegedly RSS members.[109]

A similar trend was seen in the prosecution of other cases. The LeT was first charged for the Samjhauta Express blast to derail the Indo–Pak peace process. It was later discovered that the incident involved the participation of home-grown right-wing factions.[110] In the Mecca Masjid blast, the initial blame was put on Shahid Bilal from Hyderabad and the Harkat-ul-Jihad-al Islami (HuJI).[111] The Hyderabad police claimed that 21 members of the Muslim community carried out the blast in a bid to create communal tension. They were charged with conspiring to wage a war against the State and for transporting explosive substances. In 2008, 17 accused were acquitted for lack of evidence[112] and four others were acquitted in 2014 after seven years of trial.[113]

In the Ajmer Sharif blast in which three died and 15 were injured, most of the accused were allegedly right-wing members of the majority community. The interesting part is that 26 key witnesses in this case turned hostile after June 2014, fearing for their lives, though their statements had earlier been recorded before the magistrate under Section 164 of the Criminal Procedure Code. These witnesses were allegedly active RSS workers or owed allegiance to the Sangh in some capacity or the other.

---

[108] http://indianexpress.com/article/news-archive/latest-news/2006-malegaon-blasts-7-accused-released-from-prison-on-bail/

[109] http://www.thehindu.com/news/national/nia-files-charge-sheet-in-malegaon-blast-case/article4739573.ece

[110] http://www.caravanmagazine.in/reportage/believer

[111] http://www.hindustantimes.com/india/don-t-call-him-bilal-he-is-shahid/story-imC1tMKDctpCq1PSgaXadO.html

[112] http://www.dailypioneer.com/nation/7-yrs-later-4-mecca-masjid-blast-accused-let-off.html

[113] http://timesofindia.indiatimes.com/city/hyderabad/Court-acquits-four-accused-in-Mecca-Masjid-blast-case/articleshow/38573683.cms

The NIA court on 8 March 2017 found Devendra Gupta, Sunil Joshi and Bhavesh Patel guilty of planning the blast and acquitted others, including Swami Aseemanand. Joshi had been murdered soon after the blast. On 22 March, the court sentenced Patel and Gupta to life imprisonment.[114] The same is true of the Samjhauta blast case where 42 witnesses had turned hostile till April 2018.[115]

In another bomb blast in Malegaon in 2008, the then Maharashtra ATS Chief (late) Hemant Karkare found right-wing extremists to be responsible. In this case, the key accused were Sadhvi Pragya Singh Thakur, a former Akhil Bharatiya Vidyarthi Parishad (ABVP) activist, Lt Colonel Prasad Shrikant Purohit and retired Major Ramesh Upadhyay. An outfit called Abhinav Bharat had allegedly played a key role along with a self-proclaimed Hindu seer, Sudhakara Dwivedi. Those involved were regarded as an organized syndicate wishing to adopt a saffron flag with a golden border as the national flag.[116] On 27 December 2017, the special NIA court dropped charges under MCOCA against all the accused.[117]

In 2008, the then President of the BJP, Rajnath Singh, suggested that Sadhvi Pragya, one of the accused, was not a terrorist,[118] while the Shiv Sena charged that she and others were being framed and that the entire Hindu community should support them.[119] In fact, on 18 November 2008, Advani alleged that, when the Maharashtra ATS could not catch the accused in the blast, it got hold of Sadhvi Pragya.[120] On 25 April 2017, she was granted bail by the Bombay High Court.

In the last four years, investigating agencies have been used to protect criminals and give succour to those charged with serious crimes.

---

[114] http://www.financialexpress.com/india-news/ajmer-dargah-blast-case-life-sentences-for-devendra-gupta-and-bhavesh-patel/597739/
[115] https://www.hindustantimes.com/india-news/hostile-witnesses-hurt-prosecution-in-mecca-masjid-blast-case/story-PDCmLR1M4OXTJvixfEYNlK.html
[116] http://www.frontline.in/static/html/fl2603/stories/20090213260313200.htm
[117] https://www.outlookindia.com/website/story/malegaon-blast-special-nia-court-drops-mcoca-charges-against-accused-sadhvi-prag/306062
[118] http://www.tribuneindia.com/2008/20081104/nation.htm#25
[119] http://www.rediff.com/news/2008/nov/01malegaon.htm
[120] http://www.hindustantimes.com/india/advani-speaks-up-for-sadhvi-seeks-probe/story-eqbM5RH7Cx8oZtauHZEgNO.html

Attempts have been made to appoint those who have been close to the ruling establishment in key investigating agencies, including the CBI, Enforcement Directorate (ED) and Intelligence Bureau (IB). Both the Samjhauta Express blast case and the encounter which led to the murder of Sohrabuddin Sheikh have witnessed a spate of U-turns by the CBI as well as the NIA, which seem to have reviewed the evidence in these cases. In fact, the manner in which the Sohrabuddin trial was conducted, leading to bail being granted to the prime accused, is a black mark on the Indian jurisprudence. To the common man, it seems that attempts were being made to pressurize the public prosecutor in one case, and in other cases, to ensure that those who have given evidence to the police are declared hostile during the trial, making sure that there is not enough evidence to convict the accused. The attempt to reverse the outcomes of prosecutions through biased investigators and prosecutors, and maybe through government diktat, is dangerous.

Rohini Salian, the NIA's special public prosecutor in the 2008 Malegaon blast case, has claimed that she was asked to 'go soft' on the case after the Modi government took over.[121,122] In the Ajmer blast case, public prosecutor Ashwini Sharma also went on record saying that the NIA could have done a great deal more to build the case against prime accused Swami Aseemanand and the seven other accused.[123] Even more disturbing is the fact that the police officers accused of serious crimes and undergoing trial were reinducted to the government positions and, in some cases, granted promotions.[124] We have had instances of judges being transferred overnight if they chose to reject certain applications moved by the accused. We have also seen instances of those within the prosecuting agencies being rewarded for having supported the cause of the establishment.

---

[121] http://indianexpress.com/article/india/india-others/since-this-new-govt-came-i-have-been-told-to-go-soft-on-accused-hindu-extremists-special-public-prosecutor/
[122] http://indianexpress.com/article/india/india-others/the-meaning-very-clearly-was-dont-get-us-favourable-orders/
[123] https://scroll.in/article/747397/not-just-rohini-salian-public-prosecutor-in-ajmer-blast-case-is-also-unhappy-with-nia
[124] http://www.catchnews.com/india-news/meet-the-23-cops-who-embody-gujarat-s-carrot-and-stick-policy-1440404009.html

Such actions are entirely inconsistent with the manner in which administrations have dealt with the accused in the past. The brazenness with which this government has rehabilitated those out on bail who were yet accused of very serious crimes, is evidence of its I-don't-care attitude.[125] This also sends a signal to those who support the present dispensation that they have nothing to fear; and that they will be institutionally protected. Those who are opposed to the present dispensation are both persecuted and prosecuted.[126] The message is clear—'if you criticize and tarnish our image, we will use the prosecuting agencies to target you'. This two-pronged strategy of buying loyalty and silencing dissent is the hallmark of the present dispensation.

It is noteworthy that while the law was taking its course in the context of members of the majority community accused of being involved in terrorist activity, important leaders of the BJP were publicly making statements suggesting that the accused had been framed. Had any such statement been made by a member belonging to the community of those accused in the Godhra train burning incident, it would have been regarded as anti-national, and those making such statements would not only have been targeted, but would have been charged with being pro-Pakistan. It is an act of nationalism to suggest the innocence of the accused when members of the majority community are involved. However, it is an act of betrayal if anyone dares speak about the possible innocence of some of those members of the minority community allegedly involved in acts of terror. It is the nature of this discourse that reflects the majoritarian mindset quality when dealing with acts of terror. All acts of terror must not only be condemned, but those involved must be brought to book, regardless of the community they belong to.

Over the years, Modi has been able to ride the wave of this majoritarian mindset and reap enormous political capital in the process. It was in the

---

[125] http://indianexpress.com/article/explained/ishrat-jahan-accused-where-are-they-now-2760476/
[126] http://www.catchnews.com/india-news/meet-the-23-cops-who-embody-gujarat-s-carrot-and-stick-policy-1440404009.html

aftermath of the Godhra incident that Modi realized the simmering anger of the people and chose to exploit it to his political advantage. That is why in the run-up to the 2014 election, Modi never hesitated to vilify the UPA. He alleged that the government was pro-Muslim, anti-Hindu, that it dealt with Pakistan with kid gloves and followed the policy of Muslim appeasement.

After becoming the prime minister, Modi has adopted a more statesman-like posture without losing any opportunity to exploit the same majoritarian sentiment.

Polarization of 'Us' and 'Them'

An enduring theme which runs through this majoritarian mindset is the polarization of 'us' and 'them'. It is the 'us' who talk about love jihad and target young people expressing their emotions without thinking about the religious community they belong to. The concept of ghar wapsi, which is a way of celebrating homecoming, suggests that somehow the association with the other religion was a horrible mistake. Both love jihad and ghar wapsi have become a part of public discourse, that further promotes a certain mindset.[127] The 2015 Dadri mob lynching and the manner in which four Dalits were stripped and mercilessly beaten in Una, Gujarat, for allegedly trading livestock, are all symptomatic of caste and communal schisms. Whether these instances are engineered or not is an open question. However, such instances of lynching disturb the nation's peace and harmony.

Whenever the BJP fights a state election, its ministers are more than willing to blatantly make communal remarks in order to polarize the people for electoral gain. Modi quietly espouses this since he never comments on remarks made by Yogi Adityanath or his minister Sanjeev Balyan, or Sadhvi Prachi and several others within the BJP. Yet, the Prime Minister chooses not to condemn all those making such inflammatory statements. This does not reflect any change of heart, but merely a change of tactics by the PM.

---

[127] http://www.sabrang.com/news/2015/ReportModi300days.pdf

The Intolerant Hindu

Another aspect of Modi's strategy is to be regarded as a symbol of the essence of Hindu culture which, to the rest of the world, epitomizes tolerance, but to Modi means an unconditional loyalty that brooks no resistance. The intolerant Hindu is Modi's mascot. This is antithetical to all that Hinduism stands for and has stood for over centuries. Perhaps that is why the RSS opposed Mahatma Gandhi. It is Gandhi's message of tolerance, coupled with an innate sense of justice, which was unacceptable to the mindset of the Hindu Mahasabha in the Sangh Parivar. They believed that the Mahatma pandered to a community which deserved no sympathy. While the Mahatma stood for non-violence, those who opposed him were not hesitant to use violence. The mindset that represents intolerance is at the helm of affairs in India today. The RSS believes in the grandeur of Hindu culture and its innate superiority to all others. They also believe in rationalizing acts of violence and intolerance by attributing the genesis to the failings of the other side.

Yet, the seeds of the decline of Modi's popularity will be sown by the attempts of such a mindset to rule India. The ordinary Hindu is tolerant, eclectic and thoughtful and believes in the live-and-let-live principle. It is the chasm between this mindset, given to intolerance, and the Hindu mind, committed to tolerance, that will cause the ultimate downfall of the Modi government. The attempt to hark back and extol the virtues of a culture that excelled in both science and technology, and, in a sense, to revel in the past without seeking to grapple with problems of the present—and future challenges—will be Modi's undoing.

The cleaving of our society along religious lines is the surest way to sow seeds of discontent, that will eventually erupt in one form or the other. This path is dangerous. The politics of hate may lead to electoral victories; but, in the long run, our battle to succeed in this unique experiment of democracy will fail. We are surrounded by nations where democratic traditions are either absent or nascent. Embracing democracy and democratic traditions is the only way forward. India today is experiencing not a clash of civilizations, but of mindsets, and the winner of this battle will ultimately determine the future of the country. What Modi promises is a future bedevilled with conflict. We need to embrace a future where conflict is replaced with dialogue and reconciliation.

By catering to an aspirational India, endearing himself to the middle class, fuelling the communal agenda and distancing himself from it after having reaped political and electoral benefits, Modi believes he will be able to sustain himself and be ready for 2019.

Where the Mind Is with Fear

The attempt to somehow validate a mindset which seeks sustenance from the past is reinforced in the government's forays into the education sector. The saffronization of institutions is the best way to infiltrate the academic world, thereby discouraging free thinking at the college and university level.

Dissent within the university system is looked down upon, and opinions that are not in sync with the ideologies of Hindu culture are discouraged. Since 2014, the BJP has tried to prop up the ABVP in campus politics, both through deception and force. The controversy around the Hyderabad University student, (late) Rohith Vemula, who was targeted because he was a Dalit and ended his life in desperation, suggests the extent to which the ruling dispensation will go to discredit a bright PhD scholar. Smriti Irani, the then Human Resources Development (HRD) Minister, mocked and belittled the tragedy by alleging that the controversy around Vemula was 'a malicious attempt to ignite passions and present this as a class battle, which it is not.'[128] In fact, the general secretary of the BJP, Muralidhar Rao, suggested that Vemula had views that supported terrorists like Yakub Memon.[129] Instead of responding with sensitivity to the endemic problem of Dalit students being marginalized and persecuted within the university system, attempts were made to project the student as a non-Dalit.

What happened in Hyderabad University was not an isolated incident;

---

[128] http://www.asianage.com/india/opposition-trying-instigate-all-charges-smriti-irani-470
[129] http://indianexpress.com/article/india/politics/for-bjp-being-dalit-not-the-issue-rohiths-support-for-terrorism-is/

the rot has slowly but surely spread to almost every university. On 22 May 2015, IIT Madras derecognized a student group called the Ambedkar Periyar Study Circle.[130] The displeasure shown to this group was directly related to the fact that it had organized a campus discussion critical of the Modi government's policies. The manner in which the HRD Ministry has been interfering in the functioning of universities is revealed by the fact that it sought comments about this student group from IIT Madras. Students were informed, without being given any chance to explain their position, that the group had been derecognized.

The manner in which Kanhaiya Kumar was arrested and sought to be prosecuted for sloganeering at JNU, demonstrates the keen interest this government has taken in targeting young minds that think and act differently. Those of us who saw covered faces shouting anti-India slogans at JNU felt that if any action had to be taken, it should have been targeted at and limited to them. Till date, no attempt has been made by the government to investigate and disclose those identities. The prosecution of Kanhaiya and others was an attempt to instil fear in young minds on university campuses. It is clear that this government, through the ABVP, or the university authorities, will not tolerate any form of dissent.

Saffronization of Educational Institutions

Another distinctive feature of the Modi regime is the undemocratic manner in which institutions are being made captive to the Hindutva ideological juggernaut. Those affiliated with the RSS, or of that mindset, find themselves comfortably ensconced as heads of both cultural and academic institutions funded by the Union.

Former IIT Delhi Board Chairman Vijay Bhatkar, who is also the president of the RSS-affiliated Vijnana Bharati, was appointed Chancellor of Nalanda University on 27 January 2017. Braj Bihari Kumar was appointed the chairperson of the Indian Council for Social Sciences Research (ICSSR) in May 2017. In an editorial in 2015, he had written,

---

[130]http://www.thehindu.com/news/national/tamil-nadu/iitmadras-derecognises-student-group/article7256712.ece

'A lesson which BJP and RSS must learn is that they can't win the overall battle by ignoring the intellectual front; their soldiers in the field are too weak. And self-hypnotism is not going to help them.' Prof. Appa Rao was appointed Vice Chancellor of the University of Hyderabad on 21 September 2015. He had outsmarted more than 35 candidates in the fray. Girish Chandra Tripathi, an RSS functionary, was appointed Vice Chancellor of Banaras Hindu University on 24 November 2014. Students alleged that Tripathi allowed RSS cadres to hold rallies within the campus and was reportedly seen hoisting flags of the RSS-affiliated student's wing, ABVP. Following the unrest at BHU, he was asked to go on leave by the Ministry of Human Resource Development (MHRD).

M. Jagadesh Kumar, a professor of electrical engineering from IIT Delhi, was appointed Vice Chancellor of the Jawaharlal Nehru University on 27 January 2016. Professor Kumar has had an association with the RSS-led Vijnana Bharati, whose aim is to create a social movement for the development of 'swadeshi sciences' through interlinking of traditional and modern sciences on the one hand, and natural and spiritual sciences on the other, and to adapt modern sciences to national needs. On 23 July 2017, he requested the Modi government to help 'procure an Army tank' that could be displayed on the campus premises to 'instil nationalism' among students.

Y. Sudershan Rao was appointed chairperson of the Indian Council of Historical Research (ICHR) in July 2014 primarily because of his close association with the RSS. He served as the head of the Andhra Pradesh chapter of the Akhil Bharatiya Itihas Sankalan Yojana (ABISY), a subsidiary of the RSS. In a blog written in 2007, Rao had said that the 'positive aspects of Indian culture are so deep that the merits of ancient systems would be rejuvenated...The (caste) system was working well in ancient times and we do not find any complaint from any quarters against it. It is often misinterpreted as an exploitative social system for retaining economic and social status of certain vested interests of the ruling class.' Lokesh Chandra, who in an interview with *The Indian Express*, had said that 'PM Modi is God and is greater than Gandhi', was made chief of the Indian Council for Cultural Relations (ICCR) on

27 October 2014. After his three-year term came to an end, BJP National Vice President and Rajya Sabha Member, Vinay Sahasrabuddhe, replaced him in December 2017.

Former editor of RSS mouthpiece *Panchajanya* and RSS Pracharak Baldeo Sharma was appointed Chairman of the National Book Trust (NBT) on 2 March 2014. In an interview to *Deccan Herald*, he stated, 'What is RSS Agenda? The RSS does not have any agenda. It only talks about patriotism, character building and our country's interest. What is wrong in it?' Vishram Ramchandra Jamdar, a professed RSS swayamsevak, was appointed head of the Visvesvaraya National Institute of Technology, Nagpur, in September 2014, even though he was not among the four shortlisted candidates. In an interview with *Nagpur Today* in November 2014 he proclaimed, 'Yes, I am an RSS man, so what?... Does it take away my technology expertise and experience in both industry and academics?' Speaking at Lucknow University in June 2016, the Chairman of the National Commission for Scheduled Castes (NCSC), Ramshankar Katheria insisted, 'Be it saffronization or sanghwad, if it is good for the country, then it will definitely take place.'[131]

Such infiltration is bound to have a long-term impact on the quality and subject matter of research papers in these institutions, in a way that caters to the objectives of the Sangh Parivar and BJP politics.

Saffronization of Constitutional Positions

The infiltration of RSS-minded people or their ideologues is not limited only to educational institutions, but also to high constitutional posts. A look at the credentials of those appointed as governors after 2014 suggests that many of them are committed RSS functionaries, or sympathizers, who are, without being cognizant of the high constitutional office they hold, involved in politics within the state they represent. This vitiates the environment in the state. Kalyan Singh, Governor of Rajasthan; O.P. Kohli, Governor of Gujarat; Vajubhai Vala, Governor of Karnataka;

---

[131]http://indianexpress.com/article/india/india-news-india/saffronisation-of-education-will-take-place-if-good-for-country-ramshankar-katheria-2863283/

Ram Naik, Governor of Uttar Pradesh; Kesri Nath Tripathi, Governor of West Bengal; Balramji Dass Tandon, Governor of Chhattisgarh; Tathagata Roy, Governor of Tripura; P.B. Acharya, who held the additional charge of Governor of Assam till August 2016; V. Shanmuganathan, former Governor of Meghalaya, who resigned from his post in January 2017 following allegations of sexual harassment—have all been associated with the Sangh Parivar. Indeed, some of them have gone to the extent of saying that their loyalty to the RSS comes before their other responsibilities.[132]

Further, most of the ministers occupying significant portfolios in this government, including the Prime Minister, belong to the RSS.[133] The so-called members of the Sangh, who wished to be regarded as representatives of a social movement, are the political masters of India. The values of the Sangh are the political values of the present dispensation. The RSS pracharaks who are ruling India today have also developed the art of selling dreams, the intent of which is to ensure electoral victories. We are not dealing with reality; we are dealing with a phenomenon that represents the confluence of the art of manipulation at the grassroots level to change social mindsets, and the art of manipulation at the political level to change the course of an electoral verdict.

A parliamentary system, to be functional and efficient, requires a fearless bureaucracy, non-political defence services and an independent Judiciary not in any way manned by those affiliated to political parties. The greatest danger to Indian democracy has emerged because key appointments in the bureaucracy are held by ideologically committed bureaucrats who are, perhaps, least concerned with constitutional objectives in the functioning of government. In that sense, commitment to self-preservation by catering to the whims and fancies of those in power, distorts the functioning of government.

In the last four years, inroads have been made in the defence services. The trend to co-opt retired chiefs of defence forces and others, and offer

---

[132] http://www.dnaindia.com/india/report-uttar-pradesh-governor-ram-naik-defends-his-report-card-after-three-months-in-office-2028517
[133] http://www.hindustantimes.com/india-news/strong-rss-imprint-in-pm-modi-s-new-cabinet/story-bPEnmRZ5Ob1epNyvRAanzL.html

them an opportunity to fight elections on a BJP ticket as well as inducting them into the Cabinet, either at the regional or at the national level, does not augur well for Indian democracy. If chiefs of staff in the armed services are being dangled a carrot after retirement, then the dangers of their doing the bidding of the government and playing into the hands of politicians is, to say the least, worrisome. The appointment of the most favoured bureaucrats is a very extreme form of bureaucratic commitment. The manner in which the Prime Minister has ensured appointment of diehard ideologically committed bureaucrats from the Gujarat cadre suggests the extent to which Modi wishes to control the bureaucracy.[134] In reality, those in the council of ministers are sidelined and the bureaucracy is run through a few bureaucrats along with a PMO, which seeks to implement the fanciful ideas of the Prime Minister since the Cabinet is treated like a rubber stamp.

Attempts have also been made for those lawyers affiliated with the RSS to be elevated to the higher judiciary which, in the long-term, will also politicize the judicial system. This government has tried to destabilize the carefully crafted balance embedded in our Constitution. By trying to set up a Memorandum of Procedure (MoP) in the appointment of judges to the higher judiciary through which it can somehow get a foothold into the process of appointments, this government has made its intentions clear. The government wishes to have a say in the appointment process even though judges of the Supreme Court have resisted such attempts. In fact, the tenure of Chief Justice T.S. Thakur witnessed a complete breakdown of dialogue between the Executive and Judiciary. There seems to be no meeting ground between the two constitutional bodies. The appointment of judges by the hundreds has been held up. The matter is yet to be settled, and in the bargain, it is the people of India who suffer.

On 12 January 2018, four of the senior-most judges of the Supreme Court—Justice Chelameswar (who addressed the press), Justice Ranjan Gogoi, Justice M.B. Lokur and Justice Kurian Joseph—held a press conference, which in itself was an extraordinary event. The judges publicly stated that the administration of the Supreme Court was not in order and that many things 'which are less than desirable have happened in the last

---

[134]http://dailyworld.in/rise-gujarat-cadre/

few months.' They went on to say that the preservation of the values of the institution of the Judiciary was paramount and that if those values were not preserved, 'democracy will not survive'.

The genesis of the problem lies in the manner in which the court has been functioning since Chief Justice Dipak Misra was appointed to the court. His tenure has thus far been riddled with controversies. Essentially, he is perceived as one who, for reasons which are not yet in the public domain, has excluded the senior judges of the court from being part of benches dealing with major constitutional issues. The heart of the problem is that Chief Justice Misra, as master of the roster, assumes to himself the complete discretion to assign cases to particular judges. There have also been instances where matters have been shifted from one bench to another. Though this is a power that has been enjoyed by chief justices ever since the Supreme Court was set up, the perception is that many sensitive matters in which the government might have deep interests are being assigned to particular benches. This has raised doubts in the minds of several judges of the Supreme Court and the Bar. The apex court, in a recent judgement, reiterated that the Chief Justice is the master of the roster and is expected to uphold the highest standards expected of the office when assigning cases.[135] The question is: If such standards are not adhered to, what is the remedy? The Court had the opportunity to provide for a solution but did not seize upon it. I wish it had. It is this lack of confidence that has resulted in Chief Justice Misra not involving the four most senior judges in major issues being addressed in court. These judges also felt that the settled MoP, which required no clarification, was sought to be derailed. We are confronted with a situation wherein a large number of seats in various High Courts remain unfilled. This negatively impacts the cause of justice. Further, Chief Justice Misra has decided to expedite particular cases, which, too, has raised eyebrows. The manner in which Justice Loya's case was taken up and heard also became a matter of controversy. This has, since January 2018, impacted the reputation of the institution.

---

[135] https://www.thehindu.com/news/national/sc-to-decide-if-collegium-is-the-real-master-of-roster/article24347937.ece

The Supreme Court giving a clean chit without taking forward the process of investigation in Justice Loya's case is, to say the least, disappointing.[136] This established a new norm, since the apex court had taken upon itself the burden to establish prima facie the circumstances in which Justice Loya died. Had the processes of law been allowed to work themselves out, the outcome, whatever it may have been, would have been subject to judicial scrutiny through the hierarchy of courts. To circumvent that process is a tragedy.

The Congress and six other parties moved a motion of impeachment in the Rajya Sabha against the Chief Justice of India, alleging misbehaviour, which sent tremors within the legal fraternity and impacted the nature and quality of discourse in court. It relates to the manner in which certain cases of admission into medical institutions were dealt with. The alleged corruption that the CBI unearthed during the course of investigation in respect of a judge of the Allahabad High Court is also referred to in transcripts of conversations of those peddling corruption, including that of a retired judge of the Orissa High Court, which are in the public domain. These conversations relate to corrupt practices in the matter of admission to medical colleges. This, along with the shifting of particular cases from one bench to another, which too is a matter on record, has resulted in deep suspicion.

Rajya Sabha Chairman M. Venkaiah Naidu, however, found the grounds for impeachment insufficient. That the Chairman, instead of allowing an inquiry, arrogated to himself the power to adjudicate, is highly questionable. A challenge to his decision in the Supreme Court was withdrawn since the Court refused to disclose the authority that passed the administrative order constituting a five-judge bench to hear the plea. Some have argued that there was no reason to believe that the bench, as constituted, would not do justice. Yet some may argue that justice must not only be done but must be seen to be done. Others may contend that since the bench was presumably constituted by the Chief Justice himself, he should not have done so, based on judgements of Constitution

---

[136]https://www.livemint.com/Politics/PhiT2HysXaYzF5vfoCbuGN/Judge-Loya-death-case-Supreme-Court-rejects-independent-pro.html

Benches since no person can be a judge in his own case. What was most curious was the fact that if an administrative order considered the matter and constitutional issues raised therein to be of such importance that it required a hearing by five distinguished judges, then clearly the matter deserved to be admitted for regular hearing with notices to the Chief Justice, the Chairman, Rajya Sabha, and others. The matter was mentioned in the list the previous evening, and the next morning, without issuing notice to any of the parties, the counsel were asked to argue it finally. Why such a procedure was adopted will never be known. We are experiencing procedures in court which have few precedents to back them.

Never before in the history of the Court has the institution been under the scanner for alleged wrongdoing. It was expected that the Chief Justice, along with the four distinguished judges, would have a dialogue amongst themselves to resolve outstanding issues; but that was not to be.

Separation of powers is the basic feature of our Constitution. Accountability of the Executive and the Legislature is tested on the touchstone of constitutional provisions. The Judiciary, which protects constitutional values and the rights of citizens, makes both the Executive and the Legislature accountable. That can only happen if the Judiciary is free from Executive interference; independent and fearless in protecting constitutional values. It must also have independence and primacy in the matter of appointment of persons to the higher Judiciary and in the elevation of judges from the High Court to the Supreme Court. Without this, democracy will be under threat. I hope our judicial system, which so far has not embraced the values of transparency and independence that it expects other institutions to display, will soon take corrective measures to assure both the legal fraternity and the people of this country that it will not allow the institution to deviate from the constitutional role assigned to it by our forefathers.

In Sync with the Nation's Values

When the prime minister speaks, people should not only believe what he says, but also believe in him. It was seldom that the statements of

Dr Manmohan Singh or the facts mentioned by him while addressing an audience or the nation could be doubted. This is true not just of Dr Manmohan Singh, but also of previous prime ministers. That is because the dignity of the office requires the prime minister's words to matter and not be a subject matter of derision. Prime Minister Modi, however, has, for reasons that are best known to him, said things in the last four years that have played truant with truth.

In the course of a recent address in Maghar, Uttar Pradesh, he mentioned that it was here that Sant Kabir, Guru Nanak Dev and Baba Gorakhnath sat together and discussed spirituality. But the startling facts are: Baba Gorakhnath was born in the 11th century, Sant Kabir at the end of the 14th century and Guru Nanak Dev in the 15th century.[137] The Prime Minister could not have been wrongly briefed.

During the course of a recent election campaign for the Karnataka Assembly, he also sought to attack former Prime Minister Pandit Jawaharlal Nehru by saying that the Congress party had treated Field Marshal K.M. Cariappa and Gen. K.S. Thimayya with scant respect, whereas historical facts do not support such a conclusion.[138] During the same election campaign, he accused Congress leaders of not meeting Bhagat Singh and other revolutionaries when they were jailed by the British. The fact is that Pandit Nehru not only met Bhagat Singh and other revolutionary leaders in jail but also wrote about it in his autobiography.[139] In September 2015, during his town hall meeting with Mark Zuckerberg at San Jose, Modi stated that the Indian economy was $8 trillion, whereas India's GDP at current prices even today stands at $2.59 trillion.[140,141] While addressing

---

[137]https://www.indiatoday.in/india/story/narendra-modi-maghar-uttar-pradesh-history-wrong-kabir-guru-nanak-baba-gorakhnath-1272424-2018-06-28
[138]https://www.oneindia.com/india/on-cariappa-thimayya-congress-hands-out-modi-a-fact-checker-and-ends-up-getting-2690018.html
[139]https://www.outlookindia.com/website/story/nehru-did-meet-jailed-bhagat-singh-modi-got-facts-wrong-says-historian/311843
[140]https://www.ndtv.com/india-news/pm-modi-at-facebook-townhall-q-a-with-mark-zuckerberg-highlights-1223623
[141]https://www.bloombergquint.com/global-economics/2018/07/11/india-overtakes-france-as-worlds-sixth-largest-economy-world-bank

a gathering of leaders at the plenary session of the World Economic Forum at Davos on 23 January 2018, Modi stated that after three decades, in 2014, 600 crore Indian voters gave a complete majority to a political party to form the government at the Centre.[142] However, according to the Election Commission of India, the electorate in the 2014 Lok Sabha polls was 83.41 crore.[143]

Such careless statements of the Prime Minister are inconsistent with the responsibility of the office he occupies. The result is that a large section of people is losing trust not just in what the Prime Minister says, but in the office that he holds. This is a matter of concern. This is not a contribution that Prime Minister Modi can ever take pride in. The fact that he is seen spinning a charkha in the calendars of Khadi Village Industries Commission (KVIC) is in direct contrast to his own pinstriped 'name suit'. The contrast presented by the two images raises suspicion about the commitment that is reflected in the images of himself, engineered to gain people's approbation.

These are some instances that suggest that any incumbent who occupies the office of the prime minister should be aware that he represents the dignity of a nation; a nation that prides itself for its cultural values and its diverse traditions; a nation which, in the years to come, will be the most populous nation in the world; and above all, a nation which passionately protects its complex social fabric. Prime Minister Modi's utterances must be in sync with what this nation stands for and the values it espouses.

---

[142] https://timesofindia.indiatimes.com/india/6-billion-indian-voters-pm-modi-commits-faux-pas-at-wef/articleshow/62621726.cms
[143] http://eci.nic.in/eci_main1/SVEEP/VoterTurnoutHighlightsLokSabha2014.pdf

Chapter 2

DEMOCRACY IN DANGER

While the people of India cherish democracy, I wonder if we are truly democratic. Even the basic premise of a democratic nation—a free and fair electoral process—is under attack. Questions have been raised about manipulation of Electronic Voting Machines (EVMs). Though such manipulations are difficult to prove, the fact is that, in most instances when EVMs have malfunctioned, the beneficiary was a BJP candidate.[1,2,3] This defies the theory of probability, making it rational to question those who swear that EVMs cannot be tampered with.

In recent by-elections held in May 2018, hundreds of EVMs malfunctioned, which the Election Commission attributed to a heat wave,[4] an explanation rather difficult to digest. Major Opposition parties want to revert to the ballot paper for casting votes. There is a compelling reason why machines should not count our votes. The process of both casting votes and counting them must be transparent. The act of voting on an EVM is clearly transparent. But the elector must know that the vote cast

---

[1] https://www.indiatimes.com/news/india/faulty-evm-in-madhya-pradesh-counts-any-vote-as-bjp-s-state-govt-removes-collector-ec-calls-for-report-274734.html
[2] https://www.business-standard.com/article/current-affairs/voted-for-coconut-but-bjp-s-lotus-lit-up-rti-reveals-faulty-evm-in-maha-117072200624_1.html
[3] https://newsclick.in/press-any-evm-button-vote-goes-bjp
[4] http://news.rediff.com/commentary/2018/may/28/evm-snag-due-to-heat-wave-ec-officials/6d2a39ceac9112b2ec0ac345ea194861

was, in fact, counted towards the tally of the candidate she or he voted for—this process of counting by an EVM is not transparent. Besides, the fact that technologically advanced nations do not use electronic voting machines in elections is testimony to the extent of mistrust in the use of such machines.

Turning India into a Hindu Rashtra

But the threat to democracy goes far beyond suspicion about EVMs. The threat is palpable and for all to see. Since 2014, attempts have been afoot to change the nature of our polity. To transform India into a Hindu Rashtra is no easy task—a dream not likely to be realized by the RSS and its pracharaks. But serious attempts have been made to awaken the impulse of majoritarianism in India. Hindutva, with its coarse display of intolerance has, on the one hand, instilled fear in the minds of those who profess a different faith, and on the other, has given confidence to the self-professed gendarmes of the Hindu faith who have both the capability and government support to make others conform to their beliefs.

While Modi silently watches, implying consent, ministers both at the Centre and the states, governors, RSS Chief Mohan Bhagwat, RSS pracharaks and others of that mindset have made communally charged public statements in the last four years. Such public statements declare their intent to make India a Hindu Rashtra while seeking to deny the minority community an identity of its own. Addressing RSS gatherings in Meerut and Ghaziabad in February 2015, Bhagwat said, 'Hindustan is a Hindu Rashtra, which is a fact. We are going ahead with this (idea)…'[5] Two years later, just ahead of the Uttar Pradesh elections in 2017, he stated that, 'everyone born in the country is a Hindu… Even Muslims are Hindus by nationality, they are Muslims by faith only'.[6] The BJP MLA

---

[5] http://www.dnaindia.com/india/report-india-is-a-hindu-rashtra-favourable-time-to-organise-all-hindus-mohan-bhagwat-2059470
[6] https://www.hindustantimes.com/editorials/bjp-must-not-lean-on-communal-polarisation-to-reap-political-benefits-in-uttar-pradesh/story-InT22Y7c6xkkAx302khXjI.html

from Bairia, Uttar Pradesh, Surendra Singh, said in January 2018 that India would become a Hindu Rashtra by 2024, a year before the RSS completes 100 years of its existence.[7]

Asking them to either assimilate with Hindu culture or go to Pakistan and blaming them for the partition of India, are some of the other ways that the members of the Sangh Parivar seek to intimidate and create insecurity in the minority community. The then BJP Rajya Sabha MP Vinay Katiyar commented in February 2018 that, 'Muslims should not stay in this country. They have partitioned the country on the basis of population. So why are they here? Muslims have been given their share. They should go to Bangladesh or Pakistan… they have no business being in India.'[8] The minority community is often denigrated by equating their religion with terrorism. The then BJP MP and present Union Minister of Skill Development and Entrepreneurship, Anantkumar Hegde, stated in March 2016 that peace and Islam were antithetical and that 'as long as there is Islam in this world, there will be terrorism. Until we eradicate Islam from the world, there will be terrorism.'[9]

On the other hand, fear is also created in the minds of the majority community about the 'danger' of demographic imbalance being caused by the allegedly high fertility rate of the minority community, thereby keeping communal hatred alive. Barely days after the 2011 Census data on religion was released in August 2015, the then BJP MP Yogi Adityanath, addressing a gathering in Muzaffarnagar in Uttar Pradesh, said, 'The Census figures have sent out warning signals. Time has come that an effective law to control population be made and Uniform Civil Code implemented to ensure national unity and integrity.'[10] From RSS Chief Mohan Bhagwat to Sakshi Maharaj and others, all have been exhorting Hindus to raise

---

[7]https://timesofindia.indiatimes.com/city/lucknow/only-those-muslims-will-stay-in-india-who-assimilate-into-hindu-culture-bjp-mla/articleshow/62497038.cms
[8]https://scroll.in/latest/867827/muslims-should-not-live-in-this-country-says-bjp-mp-vinay-katiyar
[9]https://indianexpress.com/article/india/india-news-india/hate-speech-booked-hegde-sticks-to-his-remarks/
[10]http://www.dnaindia.com/india/report-bjp-mp-yogi-adityanath-vhp-press-for-uniform-civil-code-law-to-check-rise-in-muslim-population-2119155

their population to match the growth rate of the minority community.

The constitutional office of the governor has not remained untouched under the NDA regime. Most of the governors appointed till date are political appointees having an RSS/BJP background. On occasions, their statements have the effect of polarizing communities. They have been seen to propagate the ideology of the Sangh Parivar. Some of their acts have destabilized elected Opposition-ruled state governments.

Former Governor of Assam and present Governor of Nagaland P.B. Acharya, in reply to a question on updating the National Register of Citizens (NRC), said in November 2015, 'Hindustan is for Hindus. There is nothing wrong with that. Hindus from different countries can stay here. They cannot be outsiders. There is nothing to be feared about that. But how to accommodate them is a big question and we should think about that…We shouldn't allow a single Bangladeshi to be included in the NRC list.'[11] The next day, he stated, 'They (Indian Muslims) are free to go anywhere. They can stay here (in India). If they want to go to Bangladesh or Pakistan, they are free to go.'[12]

In response to a comment on secularism, Governor of Tripura, Tathagata Roy, tweeted in September 2015, 'Whatever gave you the notion that I am secular? I am Hindu. My state, India, however, is secular since 1976'[13] (1976 was the year when the word 'secular' was added to the preamble of the Constitution through the 42nd amendment). Similarly, Governor of Uttar Pradesh, Ram Naik, while speaking at the convocation programme of Awadh University in December 2014 in Faizabad, said, 'Ram Mandir should be built as soon as possible. That is the wish of the Indian citizens and the wish should be fulfilled.'[14]

---

[11] https://timesofindia.indiatimes.com/india/Hindustan-is-for-Hindus-Assam-governor/articleshow/49876275.cms
[12] https://indianexpress.com/article/india/india-news-india/assam-governor-pb-acharya-adds-to-row-says-muslims-free-to-go-to-pak-bangladesh/
[13] https://indianexpress.com/article/india/india-others/whatever-gave-you-notion-i-am-secular-i-am-a-hindu-says-tripura-governor-tathagata-roy/
[14] https://www.deccanchronicle.com/141212/nation-politics/article/ram-temple-should-be-built-site-babri-masjid-governor

Cow Politics and Love Jihad

Open acts of violence targeting the minority community for alleged acts of trading in cows or transporting cows for slaughter are used to threaten and intimidate. After Mohammad Akhlaq was dragged out of his house by a mob on the night of 28 September 2015, in Bisada village, Dadri, and was lynched to death on the suspicion of consuming beef, ministers and BJP functionaries made inflammatory statements. Union Minister of Culture, Mahesh Sharma, while speaking to *The Indian Express* stated, 'You must have seen that whenever there is any buzz about cow slaughter, media, people, all rush (to the spot). All those who love the cow rush (to the spot). It (the murder) took place as a reaction to that incident (cow slaughter).'[15] The then Minister for Urban Development M. Venkaiah Naidu, while commenting on the incident, termed it as 'local happenings'. He said, 'Other things are happening here and there. They are not because of Central government. They are not because of the Prime Minister. They are local happenings. They are unfortunate. Some of them are condemnable also. But at the same time, you have to understand the sensitivities, the local situation, then come to conclusions.'[16]

The then Minister of State for Agriculture Sanjeev Baliyan, an accused in the 2013 Muzaffarnagar communal riots, went a step further and said, 'Akhlaq couldn't have eaten the full cow all alone. The meat would have gone to 20 families there. It's time to track them down and ensure justice is done to the other side.'[17] In an attempt to further vitiate the atmosphere, BJP MP Sakshi Maharaj said, 'If someone insults our mother, we would rather die than tolerate it…for us it is Bharat Mata, our biological mother and gaumata.'[18] In December 2017, Gyan Dev Ahuja, a BJP MLA from

---

[15] http://indianexpress.com/article/india/india-others/mahesh-sharmas-wisdom-danish-injury-shows-no-desire-to-lynch-17-yr-old-girl-wasnt-touched-in-dadri-incident/
[16] https://economictimes.indiatimes.com/news/politics-and-nation/centre-cant-be-blamed-for-local-happenings-m-venkaiah-naidu/articleshow/49272820.cms
[17] https://economictimes.indiatimes.com/news/politics-and-nation/move-over-beef-it-is-hindu-crematoriums-versus-muslim-graveyards-in-muzaffarnagar/printarticle/52611494.cms
[18] http://indianexpress.com/article/india/india-news-india/cow-mother-country-are-alike-dont-insult-sakshi/

Rajasthan, while reacting to the lynching of Pehlu Khan, a dairy farmer, over allegations of trading cows for slaughter, said, 'If one engages in cow smuggling or slaughters a cow, he will be killed.'[19]

While commenting on cow slaughter, Chief Minister of Chhattisgarh Raman Singh, in April 2017, asked reporters, 'Is cow slaughter happening anywhere in the state? Have any cows been killed in our state in the last 15 years?' adding with a smile, *'Jo gai ko marega, unko latka denge* (We will hang those who kill a cow).'[20]

The state investigating machinery is often used to protect the accused and foist cases against the victims of such violence. This, in turn, has impacted societal equanimity and livelihoods. The use of violence against Muslim boys who are in love with, or marry Hindu girls (love jihad), is yet another way of targeting the minority community. Vitriolic statements by the likes of Yogi Adityanath and Sakshi Maharaj have deepened the sense of insecurity within the minority community. The then BJP MP Yogi Adityanath, in August 2014 stated, 'If they take one Hindu girl, we will take 100 Muslims girls… The way Hindu girls are insulted, I don't think a civilized society would accept it. One community is allowed to spread anarchy. If the government is not doing anything, then the Hindus will have to take matters into their own hands.'[21] Similarly, BJP MP from Unnao, Sakshi Maharaj, in September 2014 claimed that Muslim youth in madrasas are being motivated for love jihad with offers of cash rewards—₹11 lakh for an 'affair' with a Sikh girl, ₹10 lakh for a Hindu girl and ₹7 lakh for a Jain girl.[22]

Apart from perpetrating the cult of majoritarianism, the spread of communal hatred and violence serves a political and obviously an electoral purpose. Such occurrences in large numbers happen close to elections

---

[19]https://indianexpress.com/article/india/if-you-smuggle-slaughter-cows-you-will-be-killed-bjp-rajasthan-mla-gyan-dev-ahuja-4997597/
[20]https://timesofindia.indiatimes.com/india/well-hang-those-who-kill-cows-chhattisgarh-cm-raman-singh/articleshow/57968197.cms
[21]https://www.indiatoday.in/india/story/love-jihad-row-yogi-adityanath-provocative-speech-205846-2014-08-27
[22]https://indianexpress.com/article/india/politics/bjp-unnao-mp-sakshi-maharaj-claims-madrasas-offering-cash-rewards-for-love-jihad/

in states with a fractious polity. Also, this happens in states where there is a sizeable Muslim population and the BJP's presence as an electoral force is minimal. Many of these incidents happen in Uttar Pradesh, West Bengal, Kerala and Bihar. In other states like Maharashtra and Karnataka, symbolism in the form of extolling the virtues of Shivaji or denigrating Tipu Sultan is used to create a polarized 'us vs them' discourse. The heroics of Maharana Pratap are celebrated for the same purpose. In tandem with this are the changes in children's textbooks, with a particular slant. Young minds are being influenced to think in a particular way through political diktat, rather than have history scholars decide what should or should not be taught.

Saffronization of Textbooks

Change in NCERT textbooks and other state boards, especially in BJP-ruled states, reflect this. In March 2018, it was reported that NCERT had decided to revise the contents of the Class VII History textbook to include more material on Maharana Pratap and Maratha king Shivaji. A report by *The Indian Express* detailed these revisions.[23] It follows the revision made by the Maharashtra education board in its History textbooks in 2017, reducing Mughal emperor Akbar's reign to just three lines and deleting chapters on other Muslim rulers.[24] These changes are in line with the NDA government's review of textbooks carried out in 2017. According to reports, Rajasthan board's Class VIII textbooks were restructured by a review committee in 2015. The restructured textbooks refer to the Indus Valley Civilization as the Sindhu Saraswati Culture and Aryans as natives of India.[25] Prominent leaders of the Indian National Congress find no mention, while the roles of Mahatma Gandhi and Jawaharlal Nehru in the freedom struggle have been reduced to footnotes. However, in the

---

[23]https://indianexpress.com/article/education/new-icons-in-ncert-books-bajirao-to-maharana-pratap-5196491/

[24]https://mumbaimirror.indiatimes.com/mumbai/cover-story/mughals-are-a-lost-chapter-in-the-state-boards-textbooks/articleshow/59948525.cms

[25]https://www.hindustantimes.com/delhi-news/team-to-move-high-court-against-saffronised-textbooks/story-WwmU98VAuqgDCtlxLJavdL.html

Class X Social Science textbook, Savarkar has been glorified.[26] According to a July 2017 report in *India Today*, 'The Rajasthan Board of Secondary Education has approved a change in the history section of the Class X Social Science books. The revised books will now teach students Maharana Pratap conclusively defeated Mughal emperor Akbar in the 16th-century Battle of Haldighati.'[27]

Governors as Partisan Players

Even governors proudly proclaim that they are RSS pracharaks and make communally charged statements. I wonder how such constitutional authorities can be expected to discharge their functions in a non-partisan manner. That they do not honour their oath of office is demonstrated by their constitutional indiscretion exposed during the imposition of President's Rule in Uttarakhand, when the High Court came down heavily by striking it down. It now seems clear that the said decision has cost Chief Justice K.M. Joseph his deserved seniority in his elevation to the Supreme Court. The openly partisan decisions by the Governor of Arunachal Pradesh changed the politics of that region. Even though the Union government imposed President's Rule, the Supreme Court, in a historic first, restored the status quo ante and reinstalled Nabam Tuki's government. The BJP had, by then, won over Congress MLAs and is now in power. Had the Governor not resorted to subverting democratic processes, such a turn of events might not have come to pass. In smaller states, insubstantial political outfits gladly give support to the single largest party, if called to form the government.

In Goa, the Governor did not call the Congress to form the government—it being the single largest party with 17 seats against the BJP's 13 in an assembly of 40—thereby, paving the way for a BJP-led alliance government. Governors helped the BJP form governments in

---

[26] https://www.hindustantimes.com/india-news/in-new-rajasthan-textbooks-veer-savarkar-overshadows-gandhi-and-nehru/story-NGzReSVik2uLKCRQDAsQ5I.html
[27] https://www.indiatoday.in/india/story/maharana-pratap-not-akbar-won-battle-of-haldighati-rajasthan-history-book-1026240-2017-07-25

both Manipur and Meghalaya though they hardly had a presence in either state. While the Governor in Karnataka was aware that a post-poll alliance of the Congress-JD(S) had the majority, based on official communications sent to him, he still chose to show his generosity by swearing in Yeddyurappa and giving him two weeks to manufacture a majority—an open invitation to horse-trading. The overnight decision to swear him in the next morning at 9 a.m. was to ensure that no court intervened in the matter. The Supreme Court accepted the request for a hearing in the early hours of 20 May 2018 and surprisingly did not stay the swearing in. However, it saved the day by directing a floor test on Sunday, 22 May. The BJP was left with little time to manage a majority—which they successfully could in Goa, Manipur and Meghalaya. When constitutional heads dance to the tune of the Pied Piper, democracy is, to say the least, diminished. Not that such indiscretions have not happened in the past, but not with such frequency and certainly not so brazenly.

Death of Civility in Public Discourse

The quality of public discourse is directly proportional to the health of democratic values. Since 2014 we have witnessed the death of civility in the intemperate outbursts of not only those in power, but also of those who derive strength and sustenance from them. The barriers of civility were breached during the Anna Hazare movement and thereafter when the BJP carried forward its election campaign. But no party in power has both openly and in silent support, attacked the Opposition and its leaders with such vicious abandon. This sways people from real issues that should be in the forefront of any election campaign. Even in the absence of an impending election, the nature of national dialogue is littered with verbal garbage.

While addressing the BJP leaders on the party's foundation day on 6 April 2018, BJP president Amit Shah denigrated the Opposition by saying, 'When we lost two Lok Sabha seats recently, Rahul Gandhi distributed sweets. He is the first leader I've seen who would do this.'

He also likened the Opposition to cats, dogs, snakes and mongooses.[28] When Congress Vice President Rahul Gandhi filed his nomination papers for the post of party chief, Prime Minister Modi said on 4 December 2017, 'I congratulate the Congress on their "Aurangzeb Raj".'[29] Two days later, in response to a Congress statement that the order of the Supreme Court on the Ram Janmabhoomi issue should be acceptable to all, BJP spokesperson G.V.L. Narasimha Rao tweeted, 'Rahul Gandhi has teamed up with Owaisis, Jilanis to oppose Ram temple in Ayodhya. Rahul Gandhi is certainly a "Babar Bhakt" and a "Kin of Khilji". Babar destroyed Ram temple and Khilji plundered Somnath. Nehru dynasty sided with both Islamic invaders. Travesty and perversity of dynasty!'[30]

Similarly, UPA chairperson Sonia Gandhi was described as the demonic mythical character 'Putana' and Rahul Gandhi was called a 'parrot' by BJP MP Ashwani Kumar Choubey, while addressing a BJP worker's meeting at Rajauli in Nawada district on 18 June 2015.[31] Union Minister Giriraj Singh, while speaking to journalists on 31 March 2015, said, 'Had Rajiv Gandhi married a Nigerian woman instead of a white-skinned girl, would Congress party have accepted her leadership?'[32]

Former Prime Minister Dr Manmohan Singh has also been attacked viciously. In a statement that reeked of arrogance, Modi, in his speech during a discussion on demonetization in the Rajya Sabha on 8 February 2017, attacked him saying, 'For the past 30–35 years, Manmohan Singhji has been directly associated with financial decisions. There were many scams around him, but his own image remained clean. Dr Sahab is the only

---

[28]https://economictimes.indiatimes.com/news/politics-and-nation/cat-and-dog-and-rat-have-united-amit-shah-targets-opposition/articleshow/63643087.cms

[29]https://www.thehindu.com/elections/gujarat-2017/modi-likens-rahul-to-aurangzeb/article21261871.ece

[30]https://www.financialexpress.com/india-news/bjp-leader-rao-calls-rahul-gandhi-babar-bhakt-kin-of-khilji-for-opposing-ram-temple-in-ayodhya/962667/

[31]http://www.dnaindia.com/india/report-bjp-mp-describes-sonia-gandhi-as-putana-2097093

[32]https://timesofindia.indiatimes.com/india/Had-Rajiv-married-a-Nigerian-instead-of-a-white-skinned-woman-would-Cong-have-accepted-her-Giriraj-Singh/articleshow/46768183.cms

person who knows the art of bathing in a bathroom with a raincoat on.'[33]

Leaders of other political parties have not been spared either. Union Minister of Skill Development Anantkumar Hegde, while referring to the West Bengal Chief Minister as Mumtaz, tweeted on 14 December 2016, 'No #Hindu is safe in #Mumtaz's #Bengal...'[34] In July 2016, BJP MLA from Uttar Pradesh, Dayashankar Singh while commenting on BSP Chief Mayawati said, 'Mayawati is selling tickets like a prostitute. She gives tickets for ₹1 crore and if there is someone who can give ₹2 crore then she sells it for ₹2 crore within an hour. If someone is ready to give ₹3 crore by the evening, she gives the ticket to him. She is even worse than a prostitute.'[35]

Destruction of Key Institutions

Post 2014, the calculated destruction of institutions is perhaps the most worrisome aspect of the Modi years. The RBI, always above suspicion, does not enjoy the kind of credibility that it had earned prior to demonetization. It has failed to answer pertinent questions which exercise the public mind even today. The quantum of cash that RBI received post-demonetization is still a mystery and so is its role when the decision to demonetize was announced on 8 November 2016. Authenticity of data is fundamental to decision-making. Its analysis determines policy prescriptions. Economists since 2014 have expressed doubts about the quality of data reflecting the state of the economy. Even GDP numbers are seriously doubted because of the painful reality on the ground. Institutional integrity of financial data, if suspect, strikes at the root of decision-making and subverts democratic processes.

Our Judiciary too is under attack, as I have elaborated in Chapter 1. But the most worrisome aspect of this government's disdain for democracy is the way it has ensured that central investigating and enforcement agencies

---

[33] https://timesofindia.indiatimes.com/india/only-manmohan-singh-knew-the-art-of-taking-bath-wearing-a-raincoat-pm-modi/articleshow/57043170.cms
[34] https://twitter.com/AnantkumarH/status/812664246097977344
[35] https://indianexpress.com/article/india/india-news-india/prostitute-mayawati-dayashankar-singh-haramzada-bjp-bsp-yogi-adityanath-sakshi-maharaj-sadhvi/

do the government's bidding. By selecting pliable officers and granting them unprecedented extensions, they have used these agencies to besmirch reputations. Opposition leaders are targeted and humiliated by having the agencies summon them. Charge sheets are not filed for years and investigations are kept pending only to tarnish images. When charge sheets are filed, they do not result in any conviction. The so-called 2G scam came apart with all the accused acquitted. The Maran brothers, though acquitted of the charge by the special CBI court of setting up a private exchange using the BSNL network, are required to face trial. Investigations are put on pause, opened and reopened depending on political designs and opportunistic alliances. No investigations are carried out when diaries are seized containing names of those at the helm of affairs in the BJP, who are alleged to be recipients of monies not accounted for. The excuse is that diary entries are not evidence. True, but evidence can be collected to be corroborated by diary entries. That is inconvenient for those wielding power. So, incriminating material found in the Birla and Sahara diaries are just not investigated because the agencies are caged, captive and have capitulated to the diktats of their masters. This also explains the protection of named persons in the Vyapam scam, in which those arrested are mostly parents and students, with politicians let off the hook. The U-turns by both the CBI and NIA speak volumes of the rot that has set in.

These fault lines undermining democracy could have been easily dealt with. An independent media would have exposed the government and turned public opinion against it. But a substantial part of the media has lost its credibility. Major events reflecting public angst against the government are excised by channels, as if they never happened. The media has become the government's spokesperson. Lies when spoken by politicians of significance are neither investigated nor exposed. Instead they are repeated. Channels and media persons are threatened if they don't take negative news off the screen. Sting operations that expose paid news and ideological predilections are not covered by the print or electronic media. It seems the government has some editorial control over the dissemination of news.

Coupled with the above is the social media onslaught of paid soldiers spreading fake news to polarize and incite violence. This has led to communal clashes and loss of lives—all this for political dividends. Added to this are the trolls abusing anyone saying anything negative about the government and propagating the virtues of Modi's four years in office.

All this shows that the building blocks of democracy are slowly but surely being dismantled. The destruction of democracy is afoot.

Chapter 3

BEYOND COURTROOMS

Legislation is necessary to regulate every aspect of human activity subject to constitutional protections. The plethora of statutory laws framed in this country, many of which I believe are flawed, is unfortunately implemented by agencies that seldom seek to discover the truth. The process of law-making is itself not comprehensive enough to frame laws that effectively deal with the targeted malaise. The intent of the legislator should be to follow the principle of *de minimis* interference. That is difficult since lawmakers tend to respond to public opinion and occasionally even cater to it. In recent times, laws have been framed in response to emotive eruptions in society. A tragic incident with an upsurge of sentiments leads to an environment in which the political class frames laws to respond to public outrage. The law framed might assuage public sentiment, but may not be the most appropriate framework in the current context of society. Occasionally, laws are drafted to please constituencies and gain public support for political reasons. This is a dangerous trend.

We seek to apply European liberal principles to an intensely patriarchal society even as the Supreme Court is hesitant to strike down Section 377 of the Indian Penal Code (IPC), which criminalizes sexual acts 'against the order of nature' with any man, woman or animal. It seems that the court is now inclined to decriminalize sexual choices[1]. This is a welcome

---

[1] https://economictimes.indiatimes.com/news/politics-and-nation/section-377-government-leaves-decision-on-the-wisdom-of-the-supreme-court/articleshow/ 64942825.cms

trend. This dichotomy arises because India lives at two levels. One is the educated liberal middle class, which is savvy, progressive, attuned and in sync with the global community. It has aspirations for India to embrace liberal values of the West and is obsessed with consumerism. On the other hand, rural India lives at different levels, embracing diverse cultural values which are far removed from European liberal ideas, as reinforced by the intolerance of the Khaps to accept inter-caste marriages. Practices consistent with an open, liberal society are anathema to religious communities, including the majority community. Therefore, any law that is enacted is incapable of addressing the complexity of the different shades of cultural moorings of our people. Further, its implementation is bound to sow seeds of discord and discrimination. For instance, Section 498A of the IPC, which seeks to punish a husband or the relatives of the husband of a woman for subjecting her to cruelty, has often been misused. But that section is necessary in a society where a daughter-in-law is taunted and sometimes done away with. So is the recent amendment of Section 375 of the IPC, incorporating a new expansive definition of rape—which now includes anal and oral sex without consent. Such necessary amendments for the protection of women are also used to blackmail. Without making a value judgement, the point is that, given the nature of Indian society, these laws, even though progressive, can be used by the unscrupulous as opportunities to exploit situations for personal ends. Extreme punitive provisions sometimes do not serve the ends of justice.

The Legislature cannot possibly be guided only by public sentiment, and must look at laws in the context of the situation on the ground and the balance required to ensure that such laws serve long-term ends. It is also necessary to ensure that human activity, especially economic activity, is encouraged rather than over-regulated. An overly regulated economy only breeds corruption, impacting multifarious activities of entrepreneurs, companies and individuals. If we over-regulate an economy which is struggling to survive, the results will be disastrous. Demonetization was a misplaced endeavour since it froze cash in the hands of at least 800 million people struggling to survive. A flawed GST without understanding realities on the ground is also a classic example of over-regulation. Our school systems are over-regulated, so are our universities. This is not to say that regulation is not required, but the emphasis should be on self-regulation with the creation of basic parameters that are practical and feasible.

This is also true of the revolutionary amendments that were made to land acquisition laws and some of the economic legislative measures adopted over the years. Any legislative measure must not, in the interest of national prosperity, dampen investor sentiment. Progress in society is always incremental, except in authoritarian regimes where decisions can be taken without accountability. In the democratic world, such decision-making has to be a collaborative exercise. Any disruptive decision backed by law, in a highly complex country like India, can lead to an economic downturn.

The delicate balance required to ensure that equity prevails is the task of the lawmaker. This task becomes even more difficult because the complex economic environment is not fully understood by lawmakers. This is why when any particular legislation has served its purpose and cannot deal with challenges in the present, the law requires an overhaul. Sometimes incremental improvements to legislation do not address prevailing complexities on the ground.

Ultimately, lawmakers rely on courts to smoothen creases of the law and interpret it in a manner that seeks to serve its purpose. Though we must thank the Judiciary for correcting the inadequacies of legislation, courts, when exercising judicial power, tend to take decisions that are not strictly within their domain. Sometimes, solutions to certain problems provided through judicial diktat are worse than the problems themselves. I think that lawmakers, both in Parliament and in State Legislatures, need to engage in much more deliberation when dealing with highly complex sectors of the economy.

The answer with respect to legislation lies in creating a more open and transparent system of lawmaking. Public scrutiny, through a more open process, must form an integral part of the working of every enterprise, institution or state entity. As Prime Minister Modi says, we need to create an infrastructure by which the processes and practices followed are open to scrutiny through a process of self-disclosure in the digital world. But for this we need to have a digital infrastructure in place. Even though the Prime Minister exhorts the use of technology and the rise of digital India, the implementation of these schemes on the ground is slow and inadequate, both in terms of resources and will. Our road to prosperity must be defined by the mantra of less laws and more freedom.

Real Estate

The manner in which the real estate sector was handled by successive governments in states led to a lot of anguish, especially amongst the farming community. The modus operandi of both the state and private real estate developers was to acquire land from farmers and then hand it over to real estate developers for the purposes of setting up housing and other projects. This led to the rise of competing interests. The pace at which urbanization was taking place required housing facilities to be provided for different strata of society. While low-cost housing was needed for the relatively poorer segments, there was also a rising demand for housing for middle-income groups and affordable apartments for the upper middle class. In order to serve this societal purpose, land was acquired at low cost, and then through a process of change of land use, housing facilities were provided. But there was another societal purpose that needed to be fulfilled—to ensure that fertile land was not used for urbanization. That purpose remained unfulfilled, resulting in land being lost to urbanization and farmers receiving a relative pittance. When farmers realized that the very land that was acquired or bought from them increased in value overnight because of change of land use, they felt cheated. In many instances, developers used this opportunity to aggrandize themselves.

The pace of developing colonies and housing facilities has been slow. In many instances, developers have diverted the buyers' money to other projects and thus delayed the handing over of housing facilities as promised. Several laws throughout the country have been put in place at the state level to regulate real estate development. These have benefited developers rather than farmers, and have resulted in Public

Interest Litigations (PILs) and petitions filed by farmers and farming communities. It is in this context that the UPA decided to undo the wrong done to the farming community through legislation (Right to Fair Compensation and Transparency in Land Acquisition, Rehabilitation and Resettlement Act, 2013).

The Real Estate (Regulation and Development) Act 2016 (RERA)—the bill introduced by the UPA government in the Rajya Sabha in 2013[2]—was enacted to bring clarity and fair practices, to protect the interest of homebuyers and to impose penalties on errant builders.[3] Salutary provisions of this law will certainly ensure protection to homebuyers. Further, the setting up of a regulator in the context of RERA will bring about some semblance of equity. In some instances, courts have also intervened and, apart from seeking to undo the injustice to our farmers, have also directed and, occasionally, welcomed prosecutions against rapacious builders. However, those who legislate, wish to flow with the tide on most occasions and, forgetting the complex nature of issues involved in such processes, bring about a law which does not necessarily serve the larger interest of the community. Without any doubt, real estate developers cannot be given a free run to enrich themselves but, at the same time, they cannot be overburdened with conditions that make it difficult for real estate development to take place. We need a friendly real estate environment to ensure that investment in the housing sector is not negatively impacted. It is for this reason that some of the provisions in this Act have been criticized. State legislatures have, after receiving the assent of the President, amended some provisions and exempted real estate developers from the same.[4]

Any economic activity in any state requires the acquisition, purchase, sale or allocation of land. This applies to real estate development in setting up industries, schools, hospitals, markets, commercial centres, educational institutions and developmental projects like building infrastructure. Since

---

[2]http://pib.nic.in/newsite/PrintRelease.aspx?relid=142595
[3]http://www.indiacode.nic.in/acts-in-pdf/2016/201616.pdf
[4]http://www.thehindubusinessline.com/news/real-estate/house-panel-raps-states-for-diluting-rera/article9811454.ece

land is a state subject, it is perhaps the most valuable asset of state governments. The root cause of corruption in states is, without a doubt, the manner in which real estate is managed, land disposed of and kickbacks received. The land mafia is deeply entrenched in each state and has long-standing, abiding links to the powers in command. Consequently, most of the scams emerging from states deal with the problem of distribution of this asset in one way or the other.

History of Judicial Appointments

One of the critical issues that need to be addressed seriously is the conflict over the process of appointments in the higher judiciary. Clearly, till date, no system of appointments has worked to the satisfaction of all stakeholders. A framework in which any branch of government has absolute power, and which is not exercised with responsibility, is bound to create opposition, as reflected by the Supreme Court judgement of 1993 (Second Judges Case)[5]. This was in response to the fear within the Judiciary that the Executive was imposing its will on the system by appointing judges who did not possess the required levels of excellence for discharging judicial functions. The general feeling was that those close to the corridors of power were selected for appointment. This resulted in the Judiciary, through a process of interpretation of Article 124(2) of the Constitution, arrogating to itself the power to be the final arbiter in the appointment process. This interpretation was based on the premise that only the Judiciary was aware of the quality of practitioners appearing before it as well as those in the lower judiciary working under the supervision and control of high courts. This meant overstretching the principles of interpretation with the intent to improve and bring on board only such appointees who enhanced the status of the chair. Though the objective was commendable, over the years, the system did not work as envisaged.

Those who rendered the judgement themselves lamented the process and the manner in which appointments had been made over the years.

---

[5]https://indiankanoon.org/doc/753224/

Judges too have their failings. They are not immune to playing favourites. Which is why, if one analyses appointments made over the years to the Supreme Court and high courts, one finds a pattern in which proximity to judges plays a significant role. Any such system, therefore, is bound to evoke criticism, as it did.

Further, lawyers appointed to the high courts have their own political and personal affiliations. When appointed, they carry these affiliations with them even though these may not be reflected in their judgements. Appointments made by them are also influenced by such predilections. There have been instances of lawyers being elevated to high courts not because of their appearances in court but because of their appearances outside. In addition, many chief ministers have a cordial relationship with judges of the high court in their respective states, which influences the collegium at the high court level. A party in power in a state would naturally recommend lawyers who display like-minded political affiliations. Even those promoted from the lower judiciary are considered due to factors that extend beyond the levels of judicial excellence. These are very serious flaws that bedevil the system. The closed-door process of appointment, according to some, is entirely non-transparent; there are no guidelines that are adhered to, nor does the system cater to any objective criteria for such appointments.

The entire chain of appointments of Members of the Bar, the lower judiciary, high courts and the Supreme Court is based on a system of spoils. This has not only been a source of conflict between the Judiciary and the Executive, but has also led to the legal fraternity opposing the absolute arrogation of power by the Judiciary in making such appointments. The most serious reservation is the tendency of high court judges trying to endear themselves to judges of the Supreme Court. Attempts to call on apex court judges, or otherwise to get close to them in the course of meetings and forums outside the court system, are matters of concern. When the Executive was the sole arbiter of appointments, lawyers and judges of the high courts cultivated politicians proactively. Now, they have shifted focus to the judges of the Supreme Court and the high courts. If a judge in his judicial capacity seeks to please the masters through his judicial verdicts, it compromises the independence required in the course of decision-making, and has serious implications for the independence of the judicial system.

Attempts have been made by the Executive to put in place a system in which it has a say in appointments to the higher judiciary. The premise that judges alone are aware of the levels of competence of lawyers is a myth. The reputation of a lawyer is not limited to the court premises. The clients that she or he serves are reflected in her or his reputation in society and are known to those who hold the reins of power. A competent lawyer's repute is not known only to judges, but also to civil society. Thus the Executive too is aware of the quality of practitioners in various high courts who are fit for appointment to the higher judiciary. But this does not mean that the Executive, if given the sole authority, will necessarily choose reputed lawyers for appointment. They too are influenced by factors that extend beyond the quality of the legal practitioner.

The history of appointments prior to 1993 indicates the concurrence of the Judiciary, even though some appointments were questionable. The checks and balances in the system ensured that prospective names were forwarded to chief justices who, in turn, commented on the proposed names. More often than not, their recommendations were accepted. After 1993, the power of appointment shifted from the Executive to the collegium in the Judiciary. Any recommendation of the collegium may be objected to by the Executive. In case the collegium repeats its recommendation, the Executive has no choice but to make that appointment. In almost all the cases, the Executive's reservations are overruled, leaving it with little choice but to appoint the individual concerned.

The functioning of the judicial system is not the sole domain of the Judiciary nor should it be so. At the same time, independence of the Judiciary must be regarded as a sacrosanct constitutional principle for democracy to sustain. Both the Executive and the judges of the Supreme Court and high courts should have a say in those who seek appointments to the higher judiciary.

A Flawed System

The Union attempted to set up a National Judicial Appointments Commission (NJAC), a proposed body, which was to be charged with the responsibility for appointment and transfer of judges to the higher judiciary. This commission was established by amending the Constitution of India through the 99th Constitution Amendment Act, 2014, which was passed by the Lok Sabha on 13 August 2014 and by the Rajya Sabha the next day. The NJAC set up under the Act was to replace the collegium system, giving some space to the Executive to be part of the appointment process. The NJAC Act, 2014, was passed by Parliament with this intent in mind and to regulate the functioning of the NJAC. Both the Constitution Amendment Bill and the NJAC Bill were ratified by 16 of the State Legislatures in India and were sent to the President of India on 31 December 2014. Both the amendment of the Constitution and the NJAC Act came into force on 13 April 2015.

However, on 16 October 2015, the Constitution Bench of the Supreme Court, by a majority of 4:1, struck down the NJAC as unconstitutional and upheld the collegium system. The Executive has been completely kept out of the process of appointment of judges to the higher judiciary. After the NJAC was struck down as unconstitutional, the collegium of the Supreme Court is, therefore, the final arbiter of all appointments to the higher judiciary. The Executive is neither consulted nor represented in the decision-making process. However, before the decision-making process commences, the Executive may suggest names that may well be considered by the collegium. The present system doesn't seem to be working well. Collegium meetings are not held; differences between those who are a part of the collegium (the chief justice and four senior-most judges) have stalled the process of appointment. Outstanding judges are, today, left out from the zone of consideration owing to judgements rendered by them in the recent past. The transfer of judges to high courts, too, is affected in a non-transparent fashion. The confidence in the system of appointments is fast diminishing.

This is compounded by the fact that judges of the Supreme Court are so overworked that they have no time to carefully consider the merits or demerits of prospective candidates. In-house administrative control over preparing a dossier of those who are considered eligible has its own complications. In the absence of transparent rules and guidelines, the individual in charge of collating material becomes all-powerful and subject to pulls and pressures. Further, the exercise of this administrative power is not subject to any scrutiny. We need a more effective and transparent system, through which judges of unquestionable integrity and high calibre are appointed to the higher judiciary.

We could consider establishing a constitutional body with clear-cut guidelines that consist of relevant stakeholders. Affiliation to a political party could be a criterion which excludes a person from consideration. Contributions to the development of law, appearances in court, levels of income, commitment to public causes and academic excellence could be relevant considerations for appointment to the higher judiciary. It would be appropriate to have a system of limited open hearings, a process through which we would be able to weed out candidates who should never be appointed. A person seeking appointment should be prepared to be scrutinized in every way. All this is not possible within the framework of the present system of appointment.

The words of Dr B.R. Ambedkar, while discussing Article 103 of the draft Constitution in the Constituent Assembly, reflected hope in the integrity of the appointment process to the higher judiciary. This discussion led to Article 124(4) of the Constitution which talks of the concurrence of the chief justice in appointing members of the higher judiciary. During the course of the debate, Ambedkar, though recognizing the impartiality of the chief justice and the soundness of his judgement, also stated, 'But after all, the chief justice is a man with all the failings, all the sentiments and all the prejudices which we as common people have; and I think, to allow the chief justice practically a veto upon the appointment of judges is really to transfer the authority to the chief justice which we are not prepared to vest in the President or the Government of the day. I, therefore, think that that is also a dangerous proposition.'[6]

That justices, though very eminent, have all the failings of common

---

[6]http://parliamentofindia.nic.in/ls/debates/vol8p7b.htm

people, has been demonstrated time and again. It is when judges accept their own fallibility that the cause of justice will flourish. The quicker the Judiciary distances itself from the process of appointment of judges to the higher Judiciary while retaining its role as the prime stakeholder, the better it is for the system. The level of confidence in the Judiciary is directly proportionate to the belief that democracy is alive.

Gravest Crisis Yet?

The Judiciary's resistance to reforming the collegium system emerged when a member of the collegium, who was also the dissenting judge in the NJAC judgement in October 2015, commented on the process and the manner in which names were considered at meetings of the collegium. Justice Chelameswar had refused to attend collegium meetings since 1 September 2016. Instead, he chose to submit his written comments on the process of selection of judges. He considered the entire process resulting in the recommendations made to be secretive; he particularly commented on the absence of minutes of the meetings of the collegium. He insisted that successive chief justices had 'treated members of the collegium as supplicants.' He wrote, 'It is the law of this land that no meeting can be convened without proper notice and an agenda, be it a meeting of a panchayat board or a cooperative society or a company or other bodies, statutory or constitutional. If you believed these Collegium meetings are beyond all principles of law propounded by their court, God save this country… If these discussions across the coffee table are to be treated by you as meetings of the collegium where important decisions in discharge of the obligations arising from the Constitution are to be taken, I feel sad for this country. But I am of the view that such a procedure falls short of the legal requirements of a meeting. I believe Collegium meetings are too solemn events to be conducted so casually.'[7]

However, this is not the first time that a member of the collegium has spoken out. Justice Ruma Pal, in a lecture after her retirement in

---

[7]https://timesofindia.indiatimes.com/india/collegium-meetings-follow-no-principles-of-law-says-sc-judge/articleshow/60250720.cms

September 2016, stated, 'Consensus within the collegium is sometimes resolved through a trade-off resulting in dubious appointments with disastrous consequences for the litigant and the credibility of the judicial system. Besides, institutional independence has also been compromised by growing sycophancy and "lobbying" within the system.'[8] When the Judiciary is unable to put its own house in order, can we ever be confident of our judicial system?

Of late, concerns have also been expressed about the inability of the court to stand up to the government. On 21 March 2018, Justice Chelameswar charged the government with being selective in accepting recommendations of the Supreme Court collegium for the appointment of judges to the high court. He said that the government, wherever it wished, ignored or deferred consideration of names it was uncomfortable with. This, he said, negatively impacted the independence of the Judiciary. In the letter, Justice Chelameswar demanded a full court sitting on the judicial side to discuss the turn of events. This letter was perhaps in the context of the communication sent by the Ministry of Law to the Chief Justice of the Karnataka High Court, Justice Dinesh Maheshwari, stalling the elevation of a District Session Judge, P. Krishna Bhat, to the High Court, despite reiteration by the Supreme Court collegium.

According to the law, if the Supreme Court collegium reiterates a recommendation, the Law Ministry is obliged to take the process of appointment of the judge forward, following which warrants of appointment are issued. Apparently, Bhat's name was first recommended by the Supreme Court collegium in August 2016. Allegations made against Bhat were found to be incorrect and concocted by an inquiry conducted by the then Chief Justice of the Karnataka High Court. In April 2017, Bhat's name was reiterated by the Supreme Court collegium for elevation to the high court. Surprisingly, in December that year, the Ministry of Law, contrary to all norms of propriety, forwarded to the Chief Justice of the Karnataka High Court a fresh complaint by the same judge, whose earlier complaint against Bhat was found to be fictitious. The fact that the

---

[8] https://www.scribd.com/document/75609638/5th-v-M-Tarkunde-Memorial-Lecture-2011

present Chief Justice of the Karnataka High Court reopened the inquiry against Bhat pursuant to the communication by the Ministry of Law, is perceived as an act of capitulation to the Executive since this was done without referring the matter to the Chief Justice of India. Reportedly, the Karnataka High Court's administrative committee, on 23 March 2018 decided to close the matter as it found no evidence against Bhat to support the allegations.

Yet another concern is the manner in which judges are transferred, or their transfers, if made, withheld from one high court to the other. A recent example of this reflects the crisis within the judicial system. On 25 September 2017, Justice Jayant Patel of the Karnataka High Court submitted his resignation to the President of India following his transfer order from Karnataka to the Allahabad High Court where he would have been the third senior-most judge in the hierarchy. However, had he continued in the Karnataka High Court, he would have been elevated as Acting Chief Justice upon the retirement of the incumbent, Justice Subhro Kamal Mukherjee on 9 October. There was speculation that Justice Patel was paying the price for ordering a CBI investigation into the Ishrat Jahan fake encounter case in his capacity as the Acting Chief Justice of the Gujarat High Court. The CBI probe had led to the arrest of several senior Gujarat police officers and subsequently charge sheets were filed against them. They were alleged to be involved in the cold-blooded killing of Ishrat Jahan, embarrassing the then Gujarat government headed by Narendra Modi. When Patel, who was the acting Chief Justice in Gujarat, was transferred to Karnataka, he was also passed over for elevation to the Supreme Court. In September 2016, of the five Chief Justices appointed by the President, four were junior to Patel. In February 2017, the Supreme Court recommended nine names for appointment as chief justices of various high courts. Again, Patel's name did not figure in the list, although he happened to be senior to all.[9] The refusal to appoint Gopal Subramanium as a judge of the Supreme Court, despite the recommendation of the collegium, is also attributed to his role as *amicus curiae* when he persuaded the Supreme Court to entrust the CBI with the

---

[9]http://www.caravanmagazine.in/vantage/jayant-patel-collegium-system-njac

investigation into the Kausar Bi and Sohrabuddin Sheikh fake encounter case.[10] The transfer of Justice Rajiv Shakdher in April 2016 from Delhi to the Madras High Court is attributed to his order in 2015, setting aside a lookout notice issued by the IB against Greenpeace activist Priya Pillai that prevented her from going abroad to address a UK parliamentary group. Justice Shakdher defended her right to travel and express dissent. Apparently, the collegium recommended his transfer back from Madras to the Delhi High Court.[11] He is now back in the Delhi High Court.

The arbitrary transfer of Justice Abhay Thipsay in April 2016 from the Bombay High Court to the Allahabad High Court is equally disturbing. Justice Thipsay, who was the judge of the Mumbai sessions court in 2006, imposed life sentences on nine of the 21 accused in the Best Bakery case during the 2002 Gujarat carnage. Pursuant to the order of the Supreme Court, this case was transferred out of Gujarat since the Modi-led state government was not seriously investigating and prosecuting matters relating to the carnage. Thipsay was later elevated to the Bombay High Court but unceremoniously transferred to the Allahabad High Court.[12]

In another unsavoury episode which suggests the obduracy of the Central Government in disregarding the recommendations of the collegium, Justice K.M. Joseph was overlooked for elevation to the Supreme Court. The obvious reason seems to be that Justice Joseph, Chief Justice of the Uttarakhand High Court, quashed the imposition of President's Rule in the state in April 2016, holding it to be unconstitutional. The Ministry of Law gave three specious excuses for opposing his elevation— that there are other more senior deserving judges, that the Kerala High Court is already adequately represented in the apex court and that there are no judges from the SC and ST categories serving in the Supreme Court.[13] Justice Chelameswar even questioned the collegium's decision

---

[10]https://www.ndtv.com/india-news/why-gopal-subramanium-is-no-longer-running-for-supreme-court-judge-581019

[11]https://economictimes.indiatimes.com/news/politics-and-nation/justice-rajiv-shakdher-back-to-his-parent-court-delhi-hc/articleshow/62359668.cms

[12]https://mumbaimirror.indiatimes.com/mumbai/other/Bombay-HC-judge-Thipsays-transfer-raises-eyebrows/articleshow/52058858.cms

[13]https://economictimes.indiatimes.com/news/politics-and-nation/elevation-of-km-

of not elevating Justice Joseph when five judges were elevated to the Supreme Court in February 2017.[14]

The collegium finally recommended his elevation in January 2018,[15] which the Union did not accept.[16] Why the Chief Justice heading the collegium did not forthwith send back Justice Joseph's name is a matter of serious concern. The collegium had met in May after the Union returned Justice Joseph's name, and unanimously agreed 'in principle' to reiterate his name, but it did so belatedly. It was reported that the collegium failed to agree on other names to be sent along with that of Justice Joseph to fill the existing seven vacancies.[17] This is curious, to say the least.

If we were to analyse the excuses given by the Centre for not accepting Justice Joseph's name, the only conclusion possible is mala fide intent. The seniority reasoning was flawed; firstly, Justice Joseph was elevated as the Chief Justice of Uttarakhand High Court on account of his qualities as a judge over other judges who might otherwise have been senior to him. Secondly, seniority among high court judges has never been the only benchmark for appointment as chief justice of a high court or elevation to the Supreme Court. Ever since 2014, the government of the day has never considered seniority as the only basis for elevation. When Judges Deepak Gupta and Navin Sinha were appointed in February 2017 to the Supreme Court, there were 40 high court judges across India senior to them. Similarly, in the case of Justices S. Abdul Nazeer and Mohan M. Shantanagoudar, who were also elevated to the Supreme Court in February 2017, there were 20 high court judges who were senior to them. When Justice S.K. Kaul was elevated, there were 14 high court judges senior to him. In delaying Justice Joseph's elevation, the government left itself without cover.

---

joseph-may-not-be-appropriate-govt-explains/articleshow/63927565.cms
[14]https://economictimes.indiatimes.com/news/politics-and-nation/collegium-dissenter-asks-why-justice-joseph-not-in-elevation-list/articleshow/56963025.cms
[15]https://www.outlookindia.com/website/story/centre-rejects-elevation-of-indu-malhotra-km-joseph-as-supreme-court-judges-repo/307612
[16]https://www.deccanchronicle.com/nation/current-affairs/050318/centre-snubs-collegium-advice-on-judges-posts.html
[17]http://www.tribuneindia.com/news/nation/sc-collegium-again-fails-to-take-final-call-on-justice-k-m-joseph/590305.html

Another reason given by Law Minister Ravi Shankar Prasad was that several high courts are not represented in the Supreme Court at present. This is true, but this has happened under the present regime as well as in the past. Justices K.G. Balakrishnan, Cyriac Joseph and K.S.P. Radhakrishnan were all from the Kerala High Court despite the Law Minister calling it a relatively small high court—the strength in the Kerala High Court was less than 40 judges then. Justices K.S. Paripoornan and K.T. Thomas were also elevated to the Supreme Court from the Kerala High Court when its strength was just 21. The reason given by the Law Minister, that in elevating Justice Joseph there would then be two judges from the Kerala High Court—which he considered inconsistent with the concept of adequate regional representation—was clearly specious. The Delhi High Court, with a judge strength of 60, has three judges in the top court while the Allahabad High Court with a sanctioned strength of 160, has just two. Several such instances can be given.

The third reason that there is inadequate representation from the SC and ST categories in the Supreme Court was flawed too. First, the total sanctioned strength of judges of the Supreme Court is 31. At the moment, we have a judge strength of 25. Three judges are to retire this year. Consequently, its strength will be reduced to 22. There will be nine vacancies. If the government so chooses, it can give representation to the SCs and STs consistent with its logic.

The message of the Union is loud and clear. Any judge who renders a judgement unfavourable to the government may not be elevated to the Supreme Court even if the collegium recommends her or him. Acts of such nature smack of discrimination and erode the independence of the Judiciary. If the Judiciary is perceived to be either directly or indirectly party to the vindictive agenda of the Executive, it has grave implications on the quality of independence of our judicial system. The opacity of the whole process of appointments and transfers has damaged the institution and corrective measures must be taken to resurrect the status of the institution in the eyes of the public. Institutional reform is required where such processes are conducted in a more transparent manner, and where institutions are subject to accountability.

A welcome first step to promote transparency in the system was reflected in the 3 October 2017 resolution of the collegium, which read as follows: 'The Collegium has resolved that the decisions henceforth taken by the Collegium indicating the reasons shall be put on the website of the Supreme Court, when the recommendation(s) is/are sent to the Government of India, with regard to the cases relating to initial elevation to the High Court Bench, confirmation as permanent Judge(s) of the High Court, elevation to the post of Chief Justice of High Court, transfer of High Court Chief Justices/Judges and elevation to the Supreme Court, because on each occasion the material which is considered by the Collegium is different.'[18] The honesty in making public the recommendations of the collegium must be appreciated.

However, what is really required is transparency in the decision-making process. That will not come about after this decision, for it is unlikely that such recommendations will be reviewed. What will happen is that when recommendations are sent to the government, and decisions in that regard are in the public domain, attempts will be made to influence the response of the government. It may be more appropriate if the entire process at the time of consideration by the collegium is made transparent before the formal recommendation is made to the government.

Lack of transparency is also discernible in the designation of lawyers as senior advocates. A designation reflects a level of excellence affirmed by judges, which helps in the candidate's future prospects in the legal profession and also enables him to be in the field of consideration when appointments to the higher judiciary are deliberated. In matters involving high stakes, the client also looks to engage a senior advocate instead of a person who has not been designated. Therefore, designation opens up windows of opportunity for the practitioner which otherwise may not be available or easily forthcoming. In the absence of rational criteria for the purposes of designation, we have witnessed intense lobbying with judges of the high court for their support by all candidates who might have access to them. Candidates who do not enjoy personal access to judges look for members of their fraternity to gain such access. This is a process

---

[18]http://supremecourtofindia.nic.in/pdf/collegium/2017.10.03-Minutes-Transparency.pdf

that compromises the dignity of the lawyer being designated as a senior advocate. Though there are instances of individuals designated on account of their competence, many designations made in various high courts in the past do not necessarily reflect that. There are instances of practitioners in a particular high court with no worthwhile practice to their credit who have access to judges of another high court where they have never practised and, surprisingly, have been designated by judges of that court. This leads to justified speculation and brings the institution into disrepute. The absence of clear-cut procedures means that it is left to the discretion of the court to determine the levels of competence of practitioners, and judges themselves are unwilling to give up this discretion in designating lawyers. A recent judgement of the Supreme Court attempts to make the process of designation of senior advocates more transparent by laying down a detailed procedure, required to be adopted when high courts deliberate on suitable candidates for designation. I am afraid the procedure laid down may not be practical. The stringent guidelines evolved by the Supreme Court are yet to be worked out. Only time will demonstrate the efficacy of these guidelines. I think the Court needs to have a relook at its judgement and make the process simpler.

Initiating Reforms for the Future

The exponential increase in litigation and, consequently, the inability of a practitioner to keep up with a number of decisions rendered in the Supreme Court and high courts makes it very difficult to keep pace with the law. Here, technology can be advantageous. The use of technology in the decision-making process is a major step towards legal reform. In fact, one of the most significant reforms in making court processes paperless was initiated by the UPA.[19] Several judges of the Delhi High Court do not deal with files anymore since the entire proceedings of every case pending in court is in electronic form.

There are, however, several challenges that need to be addressed. At the back end, thousands of files have to be converted to electronic mode.

---

[19]http://doj.gov.in/sites/default/files/Brief%20on%20eCourts%20Project.pdf

This is a humongous task, though the government has extended financial support for this project. The use of technology provides an opportunity for us to develop innovative software designs that will enable judges to access not only relevant decisions in relation to a particular case, but also retrieve particular issues with respect to decisions in India, and similar cases in other jurisdictions as well. Start-ups can be funded by the government, private equity or angel investors for this purpose. Tax breaks for such investments would be a boon for research and innovation and would add immense value both to the Judiciary and practitioners of law.

In future, this transformation will gather momentum as tech-savvy younger members of the Bar will possess the necessary skills and the openness to deal with electronic records in the decision-making process. A generational change will make the Supreme Court completely paperless.

The crowds that gather in courtrooms and the kind of pressure they bring to bear upon the judicial system are frightening. With the pressure of time and work, and especially when courts are clogged with cases that are difficult to manage, we need to evolve procedures in the hierarchy of courts in which a few legal proceedings take place through teleconferencing facilities without the lawyer having to visit the courtroom. This must be encouraged in arbitration proceedings. In times to come, this issue must be addressed constructively by the government and courts, as well as the members of the legal fraternity.

Unfortunately, no real reform measures have been initiated by this government since it assumed office. We have seen ministers making uncharitable remarks against the judicial system, which have become matters of discussion in the public domain.[20] There have been instances of a Chief Justice lamenting the non-cooperation of the government.[21] We are going through a period of transition. The Executive has to realize that any attempt to diminish the independence of the Judiciary weakens the democratic framework. There is a prevailing sense of fear that the

---

[20]http://www.thehindu.com/news/national/why-dont-you-trust-pm-law-minister-asks-judiciary/article20945761.ece

[21]http://www.thehindu.com/news/national/CJI-Thakur%E2%80%99s-emotional-appeal-to-Modi-to-protect-judiciary/article14257126.ece

Executive is trying to exert its influence in the appointment process. The Judiciary must ensure that its independence is not compromised in any way. The State and the Judiciary must strengthen each other's role within the parameters of their constitutional responsibilities. The intrusion of one in the exclusive domain of the other impacts the delicate constitutional balance required to ensure that the system functions efficiently. In the end, individuals do not matter, only institutions do.

CHAPTER 4

AADHAAR AND THE RIGHT TO PRIVACY

Aadhaar, the brainchild of the UPA government, was envisioned to be a technology solution. It was intended to ensure that subsidies granted to the poor and marginalized reached targeted beneficiaries of the Public Distribution System (PDS) and that such benefits were not siphoned off.[1] The unique Aadhaar number was to prevent leakages in the system. It was sought to be made mandatory under Section 57 of the Targeted Delivery of Financial and Other Subsidies, Benefits and Services Act, 2016 (also known as Aadhaar Act) which was passed and notified by the NDA government in 2016, even in respect of transactions that are unrelated to subsidies.

Today, the use of Aadhaar has been extended beyond the PDS and the delivery of subsidized benefits. Private enterprises are, as a matter of law, entitled to insist on an individual's identification through Aadhaar with respect to transactions that are purely private in nature. These include opening a bank account, buying a mobile phone, taking a flight from one destination to another and even for a railway journey. An employer is empowered by law to insist for Aadhaar identification. Therefore, biometric and iris data today is not just confined to the PDS, but is available with other government departments, non-government institutions and the private sector. That data is required for fertilizer subsidies and by

---

[1]http://www.prsindia.org/uploads/media/UID/Legislative%20Brief%20-%20UID%20Bill%202010_June%202.pdf

telecom operators, banks and other entities for providing services. Serious concerns have been raised about the leakage of this Unique Identification Number (UIN), which has implications for our fundamental freedom. Personal information, including Aadhaar identification, has been hacked and has reached the hands of those not entitled to access it. In the case of banks, if a customer's Aadhaar number is hacked, then it is possible to hack the individual's bank account, making the recovery of hacked money impossible. The hacker is incognito and hidden behind layers of secrecy which is cumbersome to unveil. In an investigation by *The Tribune* in January 2018, a correspondent, by paying merely ₹500 to an anonymous person on WhatsApp, was able to gain instant access to the Aadhaar data, including addresses, phone numbers, photographs and e-mail IDs, of individuals.[2]

A person is born with her or his biometrics. The data in relation thereto is at the heart of the right to privacy, now recognized as a fundamental right. Such data, in the context of the right to privacy, should not be disclosed without the consent of the individual. That consent, if and when given, should be informed consent. Once Aadhaar is made mandatory, the concept of consent is given the go-by in respect of the biometrics of a person, which is his or her personal property.

Challenges in Implementation

The process of implementation of the Aadhaar scheme has also thrown up issues that need to be addressed seriously. The first issue relates to the potential misuse of the data collected by the State—data which is mandatory to share not only for subsidies for which money flows from the consolidated fund of India, but also in reference to private transactions. Why should the State, in the context of 'metadata' collected under this Act, get to know when and in which bank I opened an account; which flight I took on which airlines and when; which ticket I bought for a journey and at which railway station?

---

[2] http://www.tribuneindia.com/news/nation/rs-500-10-minutes-and-you-have-access-to-billion-aadhaar-details/523361.html

In the digital world, data is property. Information about an individual is central to targeting her or him commercially or otherwise depending on the use to which data is put. An individual's choice for a particular product amongst the range of products offered is a choice personal to the customer. The exercise of that choice is known to the platform on which it is exercised. A range of individual choices made in the context of these platforms in dealing with commercial transactions gives a window of opportunity to enhance user experience in order to lure the customer. Since that choice is personal to the customer, any information related to it should be protected from third parties. However, there are some digital platforms, especially Facebook, where individuals share information about themselves in multifarious ways. That amounts to voluntarily sharing information with third parties, not necessarily known to the individual.

Once data is in the public domain, we cannot retrieve it. The largest multinationals in the world—Facebook, Google, Amazon and Uber—own no physical assets. They only manipulate data. It is the most powerful tool today, and like any other technology, can be misused. Corporations collect and use data, which in turn, can be leaked or sold. We have seen how Cambridge Analytica harvested data for electoral benefit. There have been charges that Russians sought to interfere in the 2016 US presidential election. Data can be a threat to democracy, especially in the hands of a government. This is an affront to the fundamental values of democracy. So, the question that we must ask ourselves is: Should we allow this data to be stored in the hands of the State?

Then there is the issue of those receiving biometrics. In the process of taking biometrics, the concerned entity can store biometrics without the knowledge of the individual concerned. Thereafter, that information can be used or misused if and when it enters the public domain. The use of an individual's biometrics without her or his knowledge could mean that a benefit intended for a particular individual could be diverted to someone not entitled to it.

Over and above, there is the problem of change in biometrics on account of ageing, injury, illness or manual labour. A large part of the Indian population is involved in manual labour—women working in tea plantations, people employed in brick kilns, quarrying and farming. The multifarious ways in which manual labourers use their hands to earn a daily wage impacts their biometrics. These beneficiaries, therefore, are suffering as Aadhaar has been made mandatory for availing benefits under State Dispensation. Many people, it is reported, have died because of their inability to receive benefits to which they were entitled. Imagine a widow being deprived of her pensionary benefits, vital for her survival. This is also true of the entitlement to food grains for the marginalized. The government insists that if a person seeks an entitlement in the form of subsidy by the State, the said person is required in law to part with data relating to his or her biometrics. The fallacy in the argument lies in the fact that a person's entitlement has no relationship to her or his biometrics, but relates to her or his status to receive that entitlement. A widow is entitled to pension because she is a widow. Similarly, a person living below the poverty line is entitled to subsidized foodgrains because of that person's economic status. This has nothing to do with a person's biometric data. This logic applies equally to subsidized LPG and other benefits. The question then is, why prescribe only one form of identity for entitlement to such benefits when entitlements relate to the social or economic status of individuals? It would be unreasonable not to allow the person entitled to such benefits a proof of identity other than Aadhaar. The Act, which recognizes no other form of identification other than Aadhaar, makes for a highly iniquitous, discriminatory framework.

The Constitution recognizes only one identity—that of a citizen of India. But a passport of a person, even though it is the most authentic document proving a person's status as a citizen, is not recognized under the Aadhaar Act as an appropriate document for establishing identity. Since the name of a person who is not a citizen of India cannot be included in the electoral roll, therefore, ideally, a voter's identity card should be an acceptable document for establishing identity. That, too, is not recognized by the Aadhaar Act. This makes the functioning of the Aadhaar Act oppressive and, in a sense, disenfranchises those entitled to subsidies even though they are citizens of India.

Principle of Proportionality

The recent judgement of the Supreme Court holding that privacy is a fundamental right is of great significance. The Court insisted that privacy is an inalienable right and is a part of the right to life and personal liberty.[3] It is also a part of the right to move freely throughout the territory of India and other rights enshrined in Article 19 of the Constitution. With this judgement, the manner in which that right is protected will again depend on how different courts in this country, especially constitutional courts, resolve contentious issues of privacy in different situations as our democracy chugs along.

The Court also held that an individual's relationship with her or his family and activities within the individual's home are sacrosanct, and cannot be invaded without cause. The Court went further to hold that the fundamental right to privacy is also protected in public places. Just as no right is absolute, the Court struck a balance, and rightly so, holding that the right to privacy is subject to larger interests of the community. For a just cause, privacy cannot be a defence; the State can interfere and intrude into an individual's privacy, but it must justify that on the basis of a valid law. The extent of intrusion must be proportionate to the need. This is what the Court held.

This principle of proportionality is exceptionally significant. At the same time, the Court also gives protection to informational privacy in respect of data that is voluntarily shared with non-State actors. Cab aggregator services are aware of the pickup point and destination of individuals accessing the service. Airlines are privy to flights individuals take to various destinations. Banks are aware of our personal and business transactions, while hospitals know our ailments. Educational institutions are aware of the activities of our children and have information about us. E-commerce allows for information to deliver products and services. All this information that non-State actors are privy to needs to be protected, considering that it is based on confidentiality. That data must be protected as a part of informational privacy.

---

[3]http://sci.gov.in/supremecourt/2012/35071/35071_2012_Judgement_24-Aug-2017.pdf

Any leakage of personal information to a third party could compromise an individual's rights and ability to live freely and with dignity. But if such information is to be protected, how secure is it and what measures can be adopted to ensure its security? What commitments are expected from a service provider to give confidence to the customer? What laws must be put in place to ensure that the data is secure? These issues will arise with reference to every non-State actor who uses digital technology to facilitate communication between individuals, between entities, between individuals and entities and between communities, which, in times to come, will be the norm in which communications take place. Parliament and non-State actors will have to address these issues when enacting a law for data protection.

A Bumpy Road Ahead

The Supreme Court mandated the government to legislate a data protection law so that privacy of information is protected. A committee under the chairmanship of former Supreme Court Judge Justice B.N. Srikrishna has been set up and, hopefully, the government will take into account the recommendations of the committee to put in place an appropriate legislation.[4] Of course, legislations by themselves are incapable of preventing misuse of data, but they can mandate institutions and authorities, state and non-state actors, to implement appropriate mechanisms for the purposes of protecting confidential information. The legislation should also incorporate punitive measures for violations.

I do hope that unlike the half-baked policies forced on the people of India, like demonetization and an ill-conceived, poorly implemented GST, the government will think through a data protection law. The government will be well advised to appreciate that what might work in other countries may not work in India because of the nature of the State and in particular, the stakeholders in our economy. The informal sector is the backbone

---

[4] http://meity.gov.in/writereaddata/files/meity_om_constitution_of_expert_committee_31072017.pdf

of our economy and most of it does not have either the capacity or the wherewithal to put systems in place.

The government could begin by narrowing down areas in which Aadhaar should be mandated, while making it voluntary for availing other services. This will allow an individual to exercise her or his right to choose. There will be situations in which non-State actors will require it for their convenience, but their convenience cannot be mandated by law. In the context of mandating Aadhaar, citizens' concerns are justified—the State can keep track of every activity of an individual, making its presence all-pervasive.

A fine balance will have to be drawn between the larger interest of the community and an individual's right to privacy as declared by the Court. The issue of proportionality will arise if the extent of intervention by the State is disproportionate to its need. There again, the adjudicatory authorities, in particular constitutional courts, will have to do a fine balancing act.

Another issue that will arise in times to come is whether one department of the State is entitled as a matter of law to share an individual's information with another department of the State and, if it does, what are its parameters in the context of the right to privacy.

Today, informational privacy and the level of confidentiality expected of individuals stands diluted. Principles will have to be evolved in times to come, about the different levels of protection for diverse activities on various platforms. This will require to be evolved through legislation, policy prescriptions, statutory enactments, rules and by-laws and through Executive decisions.

Declaring the right to privacy is, thus, the starting point of a journey. The road ahead will be bumpy owing to the highly complicated issues that will arise. As democracy flowers and democratic traditions are on firmer ground, principles will be evolved to balance the interest of the State with the inalienable right to privacy. A solid beginning has been made by the Supreme Court. Time will tell if that verdict will be diluted or the right to privacy will be zealously protected.

Given the track record of this government, my worry about Aadhaar is that data generated will be used for electoral purposes. Data regarding Aadhaar is collected by both private players as well as government agencies. We have witnessed very disturbing instances of vital data being leaked, with individuals and entities willing to part with it for commercial or other reasons. This is worrisome because the whole concept of Aadhaar is based on improving the quality of services, subject to the constitutional right to privacy. Technology and advanced computing open the gateway to collecting and collating data for public good. Use of such data may also subvert democracy. Agencies may use this data for political purposes. The National Population Register does not indicate the caste or religion of individuals. But that is not difficult to determine given that the names belonging to certain castes and associated with certain religions can easily be identified and targeted during elections. Data and metadata collected through Aadhaar can, and is likely to, be misused. It can benefit political parties who are in power both at the Centre and the states. This should worry us all.

Chapter 5

FOREIGN POLICY: HITS AND MISSES

For a nation's foreign policy to be successful, continuum is necessary. What has happened in the past is perhaps the key to understanding what might happen in the future. In the context of foreign policy, nations do not change course quickly since their interests are conditioned by both history and geography. Consequently, no nation should expect quick breakthroughs. One cannot fool the people of another country, though one may attempt to fool gullible people within India.

Diplomacy should not necessarily be accompanied with fanfare and drumbeats. One can carry forward a relationship with quiet maturity, ensuring that those unhappy with our position within the country and outside are not disenchanted. The hallmark of successful diplomacy is to be seemingly equidistant and tactically opportunistic—protecting our national interests at any cost without overtly ruffling feathers; making symbolic statements yet leaving others guessing; and moving forward carefully instead of meandering without a well-planned course of action. Modi's diplomatic moves, since he came to power, have unfortunately not followed any of the above.

Neighbourhood First Policy

The legacy of this government in the area of foreign policy is mismanagement and inconsistency in dealing with key players, particularly in the immediate neighbourhood. The bonhomie that we had with our neighbours prior to 2014 has been soured.

Pakistan

At his inauguration ceremony, Modi wanted to make a spectacle; he invited prime ministers and presidents of neighbouring States to send a signal that he was ready to do business with them and strike a bond with each of the world leaders. This was an immediate turnaround from the vitriol that we had seen Modi spout at Pakistan.

Prior to 2014, he would castigate the UPA government for its diplomatic initiatives while our soldiers' heads were being severed.[1] A few days after five Indian Army soldiers were killed by Pakistani troops in Poonch, he said, while addressing a rally in Hyderabad in August 2013, 'Indian Foreign Minister went to Jaipur and fed guests from Pakistan biryani...he said it was protocol. What protocol should we follow with people whose countrymen have cut off the heads of our soldiers?'[2] Addressing another election rally in Trichy, Modi wondered why we had been forced to bear all these atrocities silently by keeping our eyes closed.[3] BJP cried revenge. It did not want the UPA to engage in a dialogue with Pakistan. The then Leader of the Opposition in the Lok Sabha said that if the head of one of our soldiers was cut, we should avenge ourselves by severing the heads of ten Pakistani soldiers.[4]

I remember vividly Modi's critical comments in Mumbai in the midst of the terrorist attacks in November 2008. Despite being advised against it by the state government, he visited Trident Hotel, a site of the terror attacks, on 28 November—the attack occurred between 26–29 November—and

---

[1] http://www.sify.com/news/modi-attacks-upa-on-pakistan-china-news-politics-niltzLccbbcsi.html
[2] http://www.sify.com/news/mission-2014-modi-mocks-upa-s-foreign-policy-rakes-up-telangana-issue-news-national-nilsIBejegbsi.html
[3] http://www.livemint.com/Politics/XKAAteS4ivwBMSDW3gLJiL/Narendra-Modi-questions-need-for-SinghSharif-talks.html
[4] http://www.ndtv.com/india-news/if-hemrajs-head-not-returned-bring-10-heads-from-pakistan-says-sushma-swaraj-510339

had accused the then Prime Minister Dr Manmohan Singh and the UPA government of being soft on terror.[5] He perhaps thought that it was his right and duty to criticize the government while it was involved in dealing with an act of terror which shook the whole world.

In an interview with Rajat Sharma in 2011, Modi called Pakistan an 'enemy country' and a nation of expert liars, and insisted that it was a shame that the UPA chose the path of peace with Pakistan. He stated that had he been at the helm of affairs when the Mumbai attacks of 2008 happened, he would have responded with the use of force. He said, 'A neighbour hits you and in response you go to America...Why don't you go to Pakistan instead? It needs to be replied to in its own coin. Stop writing love letters to Pakistan.'[6]

As he was sworn in, the warmth with which he greeted Pakistani Prime Minister Nawaz Sharif suggested that Modi's opposition to the UPA was not based on any fundamental convictions, but was part of a strategy to vilify the then government. His statements on Pakistan, prior to 2014, fuelled feelings of antipathy within India.

After his swearing in, attempts were made to construct a bilateral dialogue to resolve outstanding issues, but that was of no use. Modi's new-found bonhomie towards Pakistan, instead, resulted in increased instances of unprovoked firing along the Line of Control (LoC) and the International Border (IB). In August 2014, Abdul Basit, Pakistan's High Commissioner to India, met Hurriyat leaders in New Delhi despite India's objections. This led to the unilateral cancellation of the meeting of foreign secretaries slated for 25 August 2014 in Islamabad.[7] Seven months after the cancellation of the meeting, Modi directed the Foreign Secretary S. Jaishankar to visit Pakistan and other neighbouring countries in March 2015 under the pretext of 'South Asian Association for Regional Cooperation (SAARC) Yatra' to firm up ties in the neighbourhood. Expectedly, no breakthrough followed. In the meantime, former Minister of Defence Manohar Parrikar

---

[5] http://deshgujarat.com/2008/11/28/modi-in-mumbai-lashes-out-on-pm-and-pakistan/
[6] https://youtu.be/pxn1u2OR7q0
[7] http://www.thehindu.com/news/national/india-calls-off-foreign-secretarylevel-talks-with-pakistan/article6329082.ece

and the then Minister of State Rajyavardhan Singh Rathore made some bizarre statements. On 22 May 2015, Parrikar said that India had no qualms about targeting terrorists across the border by using terrorists, and termed it *'kaante se kaanta nikalna'*.[8] In a response on 23 May, Sartaj Aziz, foreign affairs adviser to the Pakistani Prime Minister, maintained that the statement only confirmed Pakistan's apprehensions about India's involvement in terrorism in Pakistan.[9]

After the counter-insurgency operation by the Indian Army in Myanmar on 9 June 2015, Rathore, while speaking to *The Indian Express* on 11 June, reiterated that India would strike at terror hideouts at will.[10] Consequently, the same day, Pakistan's National Assembly passed a unanimous resolution which said that it 'vehemently condemns the irresponsible and hostile statements against Pakistan from the Indian ruling leadership', adding that such utterances 'called into question India's desire to establish good neighbourly relations with Pakistan'.[11] On 8 July Pakistan's then Minister of Defence Khwaja Asif claimed that the country's nuclear weapons 'were not for display alone'.[12]

Blow Hot and Cold Missteps

Modi then met Sharif on the sidelines of the BRICS Summit in Ufa, Russia. This meeting resulted in a joint statement on 10 July 2015 which paved the way for National Security Advisor (NSA)-level talks. Interestingly, the media was abuzz with reports that it was the Indian side that had asked for a meeting of the two prime ministers. The BJP in a press release on the same day described the Ufa Summit as a 'game changer' and a

---

[8] http://www.business-standard.com/article/economy-policy/we-have-to-use-terrorists-to-neutralise-terrorists-manohar-parrikar-115052200030_1.html
[9] http://indianexpress.com/article/world/neighbours/pakistan-expresses-concern-over-manohar-parrikars-remarks-on-terrorism/
[10] http://indianexpress.com/article/india/india-others/rajyavardhan-rathore-strikes-too-message-to-pakistan-56inchrocks/
[11] http://www.dawn.com/news/1187654/parliament-denounces-indias-hostile-overtures
[12] http://www.ndtv.com/world-news/if-needed-pakistan-can-use-nuclear-weapons-minister-779390

'breakthrough' and that the diplomatic agreement would bear fruit on the ground very soon.[13,14]

However, the Ufa joint statement was yet another attempt by Modi to project himself as a no-nonsense leader. When both sides interpreted the joint statement differently, it became apparent that the meeting was organized in haste and the agenda was not worked out in advance. While Minister for External Affairs Sushma Swaraj highlighted part of the statement that talked about 'a meeting in New Delhi between the two NSAs to discuss all issues connected to terrorism', Aziz pointed to the part that said, '…India and Pakistan have a collective responsibility to ensure peace and promote development. To do so, they are prepared to discuss all outstanding issues', which according to him, included the issue of Jammu & Kashmir (J&K). Consequently, the so-called 'breakthrough' and 'game changer' resulted in yet another impasse. On 13 July 2015, Aziz made it apparent that there would be no talks without Kashmir on the agenda.[15] As a face-saving measure, the BJP resorted to defending the indefensible with its spokesperson on 13 July maintaining that 'the discussion, engagement will largely happen on the lines of the joint statement'.[16]

There was nothing to suggest that Pakistan had mended its ways since the self-anointed 'strong government' came to power and a conducive atmosphere for resumption of bilateral talks had been created. The Gurdaspur and Udhampur terrorist attacks by Pakistani terror groups were testimony to this. Despite these terror strikes, the Modi government decided to go ahead with the NSA-level talks scheduled for 23–24 August 2015. In a press conference on 22 August, Swaraj set a midnight deadline for Aziz to give an assurance that the talks would be confined to terror and that he would not meet Hurriyat leaders before coming to Delhi.

---

[13]http://www.bjp.org/en/media-resources/press-releases/press-bjp-welcomes-ufa-breakthrough-as-milestone-in-pm-modi-s-vision-of-peace-prosperity
[14]http://www.bjp.org/en/media-resources/press-releases/press-bjp-welcomes-ufa-breakthrough-as-milestone-in-pm-modi-s-vision-of-peace-prosperity
[15]https://thewire.in/6281/this-is-what-sartaj-aziz-says-modi-and-nawaz-sharif-have-agreed-to-do/
[16]http://indianexpress.com/article/india/india-others/bjp-downplays-azizs-remarks-on-kashmir-says-talks-will-proceed/

However, Pakistan responded by saying that 'the scheduled NSA level talks cannot be held on the basis of the preconditions set by India'.[17]

Despite strong statements emanating from the Pakistani establishment—including those from the Prime Minister, NSA, Minister of Defence Khwaja Asif, Army Chief General Raheel Sharif and others—on Kashmir, a secret meeting of the NSAs of both countries was organized in Bangkok on 6 December 2015, following a 160-second meeting between Modi and Sharif during the COP21 conference on 30 November that year in Paris. The joint statement interestingly included the issue of J&K.[18] Thus, all the grandstanding which led to the cancellation of NSA level talks in August 2015 came to naught.

Following the meeting at Bangkok, Swaraj met Nawaz Sharif and Aziz on 9 December, while attending the Heart of Asia 5th Ministerial Meeting on Afghanistan, and announced the resumption of dialogue with Pakistan.[19] The joint statement issued on the day 'directed the Foreign Secretaries to work out the modalities and schedule of the meetings under the Comprehensive Bilateral Dialogue including, Peace and Security, CBMs, Jammu & Kashmir, Siachen, Sir Creek, Wullar Barrage/Tulbul Navigation Project, Economic and Commercial Cooperation, Counter-Terrorism, Narcotics Control, Humanitarian Issues, People to People exchanges and religious tourism'.[20]

The consistent flip flop clearly established Modi's poor track record in managing Indo–Pak relations. The Modi government didn't gain anything as Kashmir was back on the agenda, while there was no progress from the Pakistani side on terrorism and the Mumbai terror attacks.

---

[17] http://timesofindia.indiatimes.com/india/Pakistan-cries-off-pre-midnight-deadline-plays-Kashmir-card-to-wriggle-out-of-talks/articleshow/48631682.cms
[18] http://www.mea.gov.in/press-releases.htm?dtl/26127/Joint_Press_Release_on_meeting_of_National_Security_Advisers_of_India_and_Pakistan_in_Bangkok
[19] http://www.thehindu.com/news/international/india-pakistan-announce-revival-of-talks-to-call-it-comprehensive-bilateral-dialogue/article7966808.ece
[20] http://www.mea.gov.in/bilateral-documents.htm?dtl/26133/Joint_Statement_on_Discussion_between_External_Affairs_Minister_and_Adviser_to_the_Prime_Minister_of_Pakistan_on_Foreign_Affairs_in_Islamabad_December

Political Immaturity

Modi is too inexperienced to realize that foreign policy cannot be conducted as an event management affair. Dropping in at Islamabad on 25 December 2015 on his way back from Afghanistan to wish Nawaz Sharif on his birthday and participate in a family affair did not reflect political sagacity. The attack on the Pathankot air base on 2 January 2016 in which Pakistani terrorists, with the support of the ISI, targeted our defence establishment suggests that Pakistan cannot and will not abjure terrorism. That is the foundation of the policy framework of the military establishment, which controls civilian authority in Pakistan. This military–political nexus will not allow any forward movement in the Indo–Pak bilateral relationship. The conundrum is that the so-called democratically elected government in Pakistan cannot be a vehicle for dialogue because such a government in Pakistan is subservient to the military establishment. We have to find a way to deal with the military establishment, for they are the real stakeholders who may not be willing to come to terms with their neighbour.

I am sure that Modi has realized this to be the case now, but this realization has come at a price. The manner in which Pakistan's Joint Intelligence Team (JIT) was allowed to cross our borders to inquire into the terror attack in Pathankot reflects the lack of maturity of this government's foreign policy. Home Minister Rajnath Singh learned about the Pakistani JIT visit from the media[21] while the then Minister of Defence washed his hands off by saying that it was up to the NIA—set up to combat terrorism in India—to decide whom to allow or disallow access to the airbase.[22] The nation was promised that Pakistan would show reciprocity by allowing our team to visit that country, but this has not happened till date. Indeed, Pakistan has said that there is absolutely no evidence to show that there was any involvement of any Pakistani

---

[21] http://www.hindustantimes.com/india/learnt-about-jit-s-visit-to-india-from-the-media-rajnath-singh/story-1JkK2WjIJMQ4lEltagVR4J.html
[22] http://economictimes.indiatimes.com/news/defence/nia-to-decide-whether-to-allow-pakistani-probe-team-into-airbase-manohar-parrikar/articleshow/51585448.cms

terrorist in the attack.[23] On 7 April 2016, Pakistani High Commissioner to India Abdul Basit said that Pakistan's JIT visit was not based on reciprocity and announced the suspension of foreign secretary-level talks.[24]

In 2016, the surgical strikes by our security forces post-Uri turned into an act of jingoism as if this was a first in India's forays across the border. The impression given to the country was that of India winning a full-fledged war. Through the media, Modi was projected as a man of enormous determination and indomitable will, making it possible for the surgical strike to take place. The BJP put up posters to portray Modi as Lord Rama.[25] It seemed as though the surgical strikes had been conducted by Modi, and not by our soldiers, who were nowhere to be seen in the posters. The political establishment took credit for the forays of our forces and their engagement in the constant war of attrition with Pakistan. No political party in the past has taken credit for the planning, decision-making or, for that matter, the execution of a plan by our security forces.

Anyone with diplomatic experience will conclude that our Pakistan policy is in shambles, even as our NSA holds back channel negotiation. The blow hot and cold missteps of the present government have led us to a state where there is no forward movement in our relationship. The situation on the borders is perhaps worse than ever before. Every day, a jawan dies, a surviving mother is heartbroken and the family grieves. The intransigent stand of this government now allows lives to be lost with no real gain in sight. Added to this fact is the reality that the people of Kashmir are alienated, a feeling only deepened by an opportunistic coalition government—which the BJP abandoned in June 2018, leading to imposition of Governor's Rule in the state. Many Kashmiris living along the border, especially in south Kashmir, have been uprooted.

Modi has now realized that going to Pakistan is not an option.

---

[23]http://indiatoday.intoday.in/story/india-failed-to-provide-evidence-about-pathankot-attack-sources-say/1/633630.html

[24]http://www.hindustantimes.com/india/peace-process-between-india-and-pakistan-is-suspended-says-abdul-basit/story-ideKAtLQVZB3GpMz55Jd9H.html

[25]http://www.india.com/news/india/varanasi-celebrates-navratri-with-narendra-modi-as-lord-ram-and-pakistan-pm-nawaz-sharif-as-ravana-on-posters-1536141/

Irresponsible rhetoric has been met with an equally irresponsible response. This government has proved that on the one hand, it does not have the guts to take on Pakistan and, on the other, will choose not to deal with Pakistan. The fallout is loss of lives and hope. At present there is no possibility of moving forward through dialogue.

Without dialogue there cannot be any roadmap for resolving outstanding bilateral issues essential for peace and tranquility. Our relations with Pakistan have soured to such an extent that it has impacted the functioning of SAARC. Sadly, any attempt now to criticize the present government for its missteps in relation to Pakistan is termed as anti-national.

Nepal

The relationship with Nepal prior to 2014 was on an even keel. Thereafter, there has been no consistent strand in our diplomatic initiatives. Just as we have mismanaged our relations with both China and Pakistan, our relationship with Nepal is also not reflective of our historical links and affinity. Despite the fact that India reached out to Nepal during the devastating earthquake in April 2015, our relationship with the Madhesi people in the Terai region was not accorded a rightful place in the country's new constitutional framework. For India, this is an emotive issue. The Madhesis, mostly of Indian origin, have been demanding amendment of the new constitution and are concerned about their representation in Parliament.

Recent developments in Nepal that led to the victory of the Left Alliance, are seen as a failure of Indian diplomacy. Prime Minister K.P. Sharma Oli's frosty relations with the Indian government and the five-month economic blockade in 2015 that followed, increased tensions between the two countries. Pursuant to the economic blockade, which resulted in acute shortage of fuel and supply of daily essentials to Nepal, Oli signed a trade and transit agreement with China. Kathmandu squarely blamed India for this humanitarian crisis. Thereafter, Nepal began to overtly show its proximity to China. The cancellation of the visit of

President Bidhya Devi Bhandari to India in May 2016 and the recall of their ambassador was a new low in our bilateral relationship.

Our ineptness in dealing with Nepal allowed for enhanced Chinese presence. While Modi was busy with event management both within India and in meetings with dignitaries around the world, China's own brand of 'Neighbourhood First' policy was gaining ground. Oli had pledged to revive the China-backed $2.5 million hydropower project which had been scrapped by the previous government. He publicly stated that while the border with India would be open, he did not want his country to have only one option. Incidentally, Oli had to resign in August 2016 following the political crisis over the Madhesi issue.

Sushma Swaraj's visit to Nepal in February 2018 is an attempt to mend fences, after the Left Alliance once again formed a new government in Nepal in February, with Oli as Prime Minister. But Nepali Congress leader Sher Bahadur Deuba criticized the visit calling it untimely. The Maoists, too, were unhappy. Just like other initiatives of this government, which are purely symbolic in nature, Swaraj's visit was a symbolic message to Beijing that our relationship with Nepal is still cordial. India's options are now limited and we have been forced to engage with Oli and the Left Alliance to ensure that our interests in the region are secure. Mending relations with Nepal will take time.

China, on the other hand, is basking in the success of its increasingly cordial relationship with Nepal and the victory of the Nepalese Left Alliance which has paved the way for greater economic stakes and increased dependence on Chinese investors. Historically, every time the Left parties have come to power in Nepal, statements have been made by their government about reviewing the Indo-Nepalese bilateral relationship. It is in the context of increasing proximity between Nepal and China that Oli signed a 10-point agreement with China in March 2016.

The other issue that every Left government has sought to review with India is the question of recruitment of Nepalese citizens into the Indian Army. This was put in place by a tripartite treaty in 1947 with the UK as a signatory third party. This is an emotive issue, but because of the paucity of employment opportunities in Nepal, the question of recruitment has not been reviewed. The fact is that 25 per cent of government revenue is in the form of remittances, because one-third of the Nepalese live and work abroad. Forty thousand Nepalese soldiers serve in the Indian Army and more than 5 lakh Indian ex-servicemen in Nepal have strong pro-India sentiments. Attempts to break this Gorkha connection by the Chinese have been unsuccessful. But the Chinese have increased military aid to Nepal and in 2017, for the first time, a small joint Nepal–China military exercise was held.

One is reminded of the wise words of King Prithvi Narayan Shah, founder of modern Nepal, who said that Nepal was a gem between two big boulders. Despite the proximity of the Left Alliance with the Chinese and the deepening economic relationship through Chinese investments, the Nepalese are also aware of the possibility of China interfering in their domestic affairs. China's grandiose plans, including the One Belt One Road (OBOR) initiative—which aims at improving land and maritime connectivity and cooperation among Asia, Africa and Europe—would certainly be viewed by the Nepalese with some element of suspicion. Consequently, the Nepalese would not like to place all eggs in one basket and sever deep-rooted historical ties with India. But the fact remains that the Nepalese cannot be taken for granted and our policy initiatives have to be far more persuasive than in the past.

Sri Lanka

China's rise is a factor that no country in the region can ignore. No country would like to antagonize China. The recent trade war with US President Donald Trump increasing the imposition of tariffs on Chinese products imported into the US will result in instability of the global economy. China will, as a result, look towards expanding its economic presence, especially in its neighbourhood.

It is in this context that Sri Lanka's economic relationship with China has deepened. The Chinese have extended several billion dollars as loans to the Sri Lankan government for new infrastructure projects. India has been worried about the increasing bonhomie between China and Sri Lanka, taken forward by the then Sri Lankan President, Mahinda Rajapaksa (2005–15).

The new coalition National Unity government which came to power in 2015 in Sri Lanka was committed to review all Chinese projects. But unable to service the external debt, the Sri Lankan government signed the amended concession agreement in relation to the Hambantota port with the Hong Kong-based China Merchant Port Holdings Ltd. amidst opposition and controversy. According to this hugely unpopular enterprise, the China Merchant Port Holdings Ltd. secured an 80 per cent share in operating the port. Though the Sri Lankan government has stated that it will be in charge of the management of port services, like security and navigation, the project has not gone down well with the Sri Lankan people. Despite India's protests, Sri Lanka sent its Prime Minister Ranil Wickremesinghe to the OBOR Summit in May 2017 in Beijing, where Sri Lanka was offered $24 billion as additional loans.

The logic that Hambantota will be a platform to unlock the country's potential to provide a global maritime centre is an attractive rationale for Chinese investments, but India has not welcomed the concession agreement. However, we have no choice in the matter. Sri Lankans should realize that they are caught in a gigantic debt trap. We must continually caution the Sri Lankans and other neighbours with respect to China-financed projects, which we believe are initiated only for strategic reasons. Further, Chinese presence at Hambantota has security implications for India, as it will result in our geostrategic encirclement. We need to build on our historical ties with Sri Lanka and make them look beyond their economic interests.

Sri Lanka would want to follow a policy of being equidistant in their relationship with China and India. Unlike Nepal, the Sri Lankans are more conscious of a possible Chinese gridlock on account of their economic outreach. Their fears are demonstrated by the fact that just ahead of the OBOR Summit in May 2017, Colombo refused to allow a Chinese submarine to dock at Colombo port. Prime Minister Wickremesinghe had pushed for India to take charge of the development of the northern port of Trincomalee, signing an umbrella MoU listing over 10 major projects, including the development of an oil tank farm in Trincomalee. Despite India being Sri Lanka's largest trading partner with bilateral trade amounting to over $4 billion in 2016, the facts, however, show China's deepening economic stakes in that country. The country's Finance Ministry's mid-year fiscal position report shows that China accounts for 40 per cent ($170 million) of foreign disbursements in the first six months of 2017 compared to India, which released $10.5 million during the same period.[26] Of the foreign funds that are committed to the Sri Lankan economy, China's share would be 28 per cent in the years to come, while India's share would be an abysmal 3 per cent.

Our relationship with Rajapaksa loyalists and the Left parties also needs to be addressed in our foreign policy initiatives. We should not ignore the Rajapaksa faction despite the fact that the Rajapaksa government allegedly committed war crimes. They protested against Sri Lanka allowing India to develop the Trincomalee port and have also opposed the opening of the Special Economic Zone attached to the Hambantota port. We must continue our dialogue with leaders of the Opposition and persuade them that our historical ties must not be ignored and their preference for China would not be prudent in the years to come.

Bangladesh

In July 2014, after the hard work done by the UPA government, New Delhi and Dhaka welcomed the judgement of the International Tribunal for the Law of the Sea that settled a long-standing maritime dispute. With Sheikh Hasina Wajed in power, given her proximity to India, and the UPA's efforts to strengthen our bilateral ties, the ratification of the historic Land Boundary Agreement (LBA) gave a boost to our bilateral relationship. Her visit to India in April 2017 and India's announcement of a new credit line of $4.5 billion with an additional $500 million for Bangladesh's defence hardware purchase[27] exemplifies the synergy of this relationship.

---

[26] https://thewire.in/diplomacy/hambantota-china-sri-lanka-ports
[27] https://www.hindustantimes.com/india-news/india-announces-4-5bn-line-of-credit-to-bangladesh-22-pacts-signed/story-qExR2itHj3fAKsisPI3P7J.html

Bangladesh is now at the forefront of India's counter-terrorism strategy. It is a key gateway for India's sub-regional initiatives, namely the Bay of Bengal Initiative for Multi-Sectoral Technical and Economic Cooperation (BIMSTEC) and the Bangladesh, Bhutan, India, Nepal Initiative (BBIN).

The Neighbourhood First policy is a success in the context of our relationship with Bangladesh, built on our sincere efforts to resolve all outstanding issues. Yet, the sharing of Teesta river water issue is yet to be resolved. The West Bengal Chief Minister Mamata Banerjee has her reservations. Bangladesh is slated to have its general elections in December 2018. Sheikh Hasina would like to push the Teesta deal and resolve this outstanding dispute. This will help in two ways—first, showcase a strong bilateral relationship with India and, second, disarm the Opposition in Bangladesh which might otherwise have a chance to play the anti-India card.

But there are ominous signs of increasing Chinese presence. In 2016, China sanctioned a $24 billion credit line to Dhaka in comparison to India's offer of $2 billion in 2015.[28] In 2016, China supplied two submarines to Bangladesh, allowing it to patrol the Bay of Bengal, and with the Chinese and Bangladeshi navies conducting a joint drill, the attempt by the Chinese to slowly gain a foothold in Bangladesh cannot go unnoticed. In February 2018, Bangladesh's premier bourse Dhaka Stock Exchange allowed the Chinese to pick up a stake in it over and above that of India[29]—a sign of China's strategic economic footprint in Dhaka. Dhaka also acquiesced to the OBOR initiative during the President of China Xi Jinping's visit to Dhaka in 2016. Xi Jinping pledged $25 billion in investments to Bangladesh. Bangladesh's military procures 80 per cent of its equipment from China.

India must be cognizant that, slowly but surely, the Chinese presence and influence in our neighbourhood is growing. The integration of the economies of our neighbours with the Chinese, in times to come, will have a very significant impact on our Neighbourhood First policy. We must

---

[28] https://www.reuters.com/article/us-bangladesh-china/china-signs-deals-worth-billions-with-bangladesh-as-xi-visits-idUSKCN12D34M

[29] https://asia.nikkei.com/Politics/International-Relations/Dhaka-Stock-Exchange-picks-China-s-bid-for-stake-over-India-s

ensure that India builds on its economic ties and strengthens our bilateral relationships in the context of our common historic relationships. Our neighbourhood will be far more comfortable in dealing with us for this reason alone. We need to build public opinion within our neighbourhood, emphasizing our natural proximity to its people while becoming an economic powerhouse with stakes in the neighbourhood that it cannot ignore.

Bhutan

We must never compromise on our deep and lasting friendship with Bhutan. We need to constantly consult with the King because he deals with the subjects of defence and national security. At the same time, we must be ready to face any challenge in areas where the Indian Army and the Chinese People's Liberation Army (PLA) are in eyeball-to-eyeball confrontation. We must ensure that Bhutan's sovereignty is never compromised and India's security interests never jeopardized. Perhaps the building of the road on the Doklam Plateau was meant to evoke a response from India, to enable China to assess India's commitment to stand on its own. It is possible that there may be other such incidents in areas like the middle sector of the Indo–China border and in the tri-junction area bordering India, China and Nepal. We must not lower our guard and, at the same time, we must engage China in whatever ways we can to help resolve all outstanding issues.

The Maldives

The recent crisis in the Maldives erupted on 1 February 2018, which took us by surprise. The Supreme Court ordered the release of nine political prisoners, including former President Mohamed Nasheed, and the reinstatement of 12 MPs who had defected from President Abdulla Yameen's party—Progressive Party of Maldives (PPM).[30] The new session

---

[30]https://thewire.in/external-affairs/maldives-supreme-court-orders-release-of-all-opposition-leaders-president-yameen-defiant

of Parliament was to be convened with the participation of these reinstated MPs.

Yameen chose not to abide by the judgement, contending that the decision was arrived at without the government being heard. He also commented on the serious law and order situation and gave that as a reason for not abiding by the judgement. Notwithstanding international pressure, he imposed Emergency for 15 days and arrested the chief justice and another senior judge of the Supreme Court[31] as well as his own half-brother, Maumoon Abdul Gayoom.[32] In this context, the three judges of the Supreme Court went back on their judgement.[33] This is where the crisis stands today.

Our relations with the Maldives have not been smooth for some time, especially since 2012, when Nasheed was arrested and Abdulla Yameen became the President in 2013. Since then, China has become a real factor in Maldivian politics. The Yameen government cancelled Indian company GMR's contract to build an airport in Malé, just ahead of President Xi's visit in 2015. Yameen also welcomed and joined the Maritime Silk Road (MSR) initiative launched by China in 2013. Several of the Maldives' islands have been leased to China. It is possible that these islands will be used for building bases to further China's String of Pearls strategy with the intent to encircle India and reduce its influence. The Chinese have also recently signed a free trade agreement approved by the Maldivian Parliament. Despite Yameen allegedly maintaining an India First policy, the increasing influence of China will, without any doubt, destabilize our bilateral relationship.

In January 2018, Yameen sent his foreign minister to India in an attempt to reassure the Indian government of the Maldives's abiding relationship with us. Since the crisis, our government has not taken favourably to Yameen's actions and has supported the earlier Supreme

---

[31] https://www.reuters.com/article/us-maldives-politics-arrests/maldives-police-arrest-chief-justice-another-judge-under-state-of-emergency-idUSKBN1FP2XL

[32] https://www.reuters.com/article/us-maldives-politics-gayoom/maldives-police-arrest-former-president-gayoom-spokesman-idUSKBN1FP2IZ

[33] https://maldivestimes.com/supreme-court-orders-stay-on-reinstating-expelled-mps/

Court verdict. However, we should have known what was happening in the Maldives and calibrated our responses much in advance. Apart from being in touch with the US and other like-minded countries in Europe where we are likely to receive full support, we should keep track of the evolving situation. The strategic significance of the Maldives is of seminal importance to us—the increasing radicalization of the populace and the influence of fundamentalists from Islamic State and LeT, who have apparently established bases in the country, are matters of concern. Saudi Arabia and the UAE are pouring huge funds into the Maldives and they would look at their own interests in that context. We have about 25,000 expatriates in the Maldives, a large number of them being professionals; their safety then becomes a matter of concern.

India needs to reassert its influence in the Maldives. We must be cognizant of the fact that Maldivians are mainly of Indian and Sri Lankan origin and our cultural ties are deep-rooted. We cannot but face the reality that security in the Indian Ocean is increasingly in jeopardy with the deterioration of the domestic situation in that country. The Maldives contributes the highest number of fighters to support terrorist groups in Syria and Iraq. The ransacking of museums when Nasheed was overthrown is symptomatic of the turbulence prevailing there. This luxuriant island destination is embroiled in a conflict and China seems to have the upper hand for the moment.

The crisis in the Maldives is yet another event that has impacted our Neighbourhood First policy. While we were the main players in our neighbourhood a while ago, we are slowly being marginalized.

Afghanistan

Our policy with regard to Afghanistan has shown that their present establishment seeks India's support and we have done well to ensure that Pakistan does not push the country into a state of turmoil. However, attempts have been made to somehow destabilize Afghanistan. Every other day there are acts of violence which suggest that the region is still unstable. Modi has not, unlike in the context of Pakistan, indulged in any extravaganza. He has realized that the continuity of the UPA policies in relation to Afghanistan has paid good dividends.

China

Flexing of muscles in the context of India's relations with its neighbours without having the necessary economic clout leads us nowhere. It may be fodder for the domestic constituency, it may evoke a sense of patriotism and pride, but its value is of no significance since its fallout creates tension, puts a halt to the peace process and makes it difficult for resolution of matters in which there can be a meeting ground.

Modi criticized us for our consistent efforts to come to terms with the Chinese and settle the boundary dispute. The incursions made by the Chinese troops across the border in Chumar and Daulat Beg Oldie sectors of Ladakh in 2013 were met with protests in the Parliament. The UPA was blamed for extending a hand of friendship to the Chinese, especially when they were not willing to relent on issues regarding our border state Arunachal Pradesh and the McMahon Line. Modi was particularly harsh about the UPA's inability to act.[34,35]

But post 2014, his belligerent views about our neighbours changed suddenly. China intruded into the Chumar sector in September 2014, one of the biggest incursions ever, which coincided with President Xi Jinping's visit to India. However, Modi maintained a conspicuous silence. China's reaction to Modi's Arunachal Pradesh visit in February 2015—to inaugurate two development projects—was unprecedented. The Chinese foreign ministry spokesperson said that India should avoid such moves which adversely impact the settlement of the border issue.[36] While China hardened its stance on the border issue, Modi began preparations for his China visit in May 2015, which he described as a milestone for Asia.[37]

---

[34]http://www.ndtv.com/india-news/congress-has-turned-brother-against-brother-says-narendra-modi-in-hyderabad-531284
[35]https://twitter.com/narendramodi/status/366574581932244992?lang=en
[36]http://zeenews.india.com/news/india/china-objects-to-modis-visit-to-disputed-arunachal-pradesh_1550092.html
[37]http://www.thehindu.com/news/national/modis-visit-to-china/article7201072.ece

In June 2017, Chinese troops entered Doklam, a disputed area between China and Bhutan, to build a road. There was a military standoff between India and China, as Bhutan protested this military activity. The wordplay of the then Defence Minister, that India in 2017 was different from India in 1962,[38] made no impact. Indeed, he should have realized that the China of 2017 was also different from the China of 1962. The provocative statements continued. There was no quick resolution and the Foreign Minister rightly told Parliament in August 2017 that patience was the key to resolving the standoff. Both countries agreed to expeditious disengagement but the problem cannot be wished away. Of course, peace on the border is a prerequisite for further development of ties, as agreed to by Modi and Xi Jinping in September 2017. The military element in the Doklam episode was introduced because we were not prepared for a military response in the event the matter reached boiling point. Ultimately, it was the threat by China and the use of force that resulted in a temporary de-escalation.

In 2016, there were 273 transgressions by Chinese soldiers into Indian territory. In 2017, they had increased to 426.[39] Transgressions have occurred in the past as well. All that is required is constant vigil and well-thought-out diplomatic initiatives.

But the reality is that by January 2018, almost five months after India and China agreed to end their tense military face off, Beijing had taken control of the northern side of the disputed plateau, as confirmed by satellite images.[40] Apparently, there is one complete mechanized regiment of possibly ZBL-09 Infantry Fighting Vehicles (IFVs) and a large number of troops camouflaged in nets at the site. At least a two-storey-high observation tower is less than 10 metres from the most forward trench occupied by the Indian Army. The tower allows Chinese troops to observe the entire Gnathang Valley in East Sikkim from Kupup to Zuluk and

---

[38] https://www.hindustantimes.com/india-news/jaitley-responds-to-chinese-threat-india-of-2017-different-from-india-of-1962/story-zfR7xqJsphnowhcdqjeM4H.html
[39] https://economictimes.indiatimes.com/news/defence/chinese-incursions-into-india-rose-in-2017-government-data/articleshow/62793038.cms
[40] https://economictimes.indiatimes.com/news/defence/china-in-north-doklam-with-armoured-vehicles-helipads-and-observation-tower-claims-report/articleshow/62539645.cms

the movement of Indian troops beyond Kupup. It is also a matter of concern that a number of fighting posts have been created in almost every hillock on the north side of the Doklam Plateau. These posts apparently consist of communication trenches. There is also evidence of dugouts to accommodate troops, if necessary. This, along with the construction of helipads, shows the readiness of the Chinese in that area. The Indian Army Chief, while speaking at the Raisina Dialogue 2018, confirmed the development of infrastructure and the return of Chinese troops, but added that Indian forces are prepared for any exigency. In response, the Chinese military criticized our Army Chief and asserted that Doklam was a disputed territory, and even warned India to avoid similar incidents in future. The unease continues despite the fact that the Ministry of External Affairs claims that the status quo prevails in Doklam. The Ministry chose not to comment on the deployment of additional troops and the fact that the PLA had not completely withdrawn from the Doklam plateau. Further, the PLA troop deployment inside the Chumbi Valley has increased. It is time this government, and in particular, mandarins in South Block, stop being carried away by rhetoric. It is time our generals, while being prepared for any incursions, are diplomatic in their utterances.

Diplomacy is not about confrontation on the one hand and backing off on the other. It is about calibrating responses, knowing both the strengths and the mindset of the player on the other side. This is not the time for us to use coercion to solve disputes. The fact of the matter is that there are increasing Chinese incursions along our border. China is following a well-thought-out diplomatic offensive in an attempt to influence Nepal and Bhutan. It is seeking to raise the pitch in Xinjiang and Tibet. Similarly, we must also recognize China's proximity to Pakistan and its growing ties with Russia.

Consequently, the standoff has certain strategic implications, especially in the context of our relationship with Bhutan. The Chinese presence in Doklam was perhaps a result of China's geopolitical ambitions and Xi Jinping's desire to consolidate power within China. The Chumbi Valley, which is a strip of land stretching only a few kilometres at its narrowest point, is of great significance to us. Through this, the Chinese seek to annex a large part of Bhutan by enlarging the size of the valley. There is also the fear of being cut off by the Indian Army in the west as well as the east. As far as India is concerned, enlargement of the Chumbi Valley will enhance the PLA threat to our Siliguri corridor. Today, Bhutan is caught between the rise of China seeking to stamp its influence on the country, and India, a neighbour who has always stood by it and considers the relationship essential to our foreign policy. For the Bhutanese, India's security cannot be compromised and so there can be no settlement between China and Bhutan in any way at our expense. China will not vacate the area north of the Chumbi Valley and inside the Doklam Plateau. With Xi Jinping's unchallenged authority in China, challenges along the Indo–China border in the future will be even more daunting and these border skirmishes are expected to continue.

The unfolding of events has exposed Modi's mismanagement of our relationship with the Chinese. A part of the problem lies in the fact that Modi takes decisions without taking the foreign policy establishment into confidence.

Swaying with President Xi in Gujarat makes for a good photo-op, but has very little relevance to the Chinese attitude towards India. Modi seeks to bolster his own image through these photo-ops and endear himself by making unilateral announcements like issuing visas to the Chinese at the ports of entry to India. This has been happening despite the fact that the Chinese continue to issue stapled visas as they consider Kashmir a disputed territory and do not recognize Arunachal Pradesh as part of India. The External Affairs Minister even tried to justify the Chinese position by saying that the two issues were not correlated and that the stapled visa remained an unresolved issue.[41] Similarly, extravagant announcements, like an investment in the coming years, of $20 billion by the Chinese (which has come to naught), may earn Modi glory for the moment, but does not take the Sino-Indian dialogue forward in any substantial way. After more than four years, there is no

---

[41]http://www.thehindubusinessline.com/news/variety/no-link-between-evisa-to-chinese-visitors-and-stapled-visa-issue-sushma/article7268395.ece

clarity on how much of the proposed investment has come into India. The only information, sans any details, was provided by the then Economic Affairs Secretary Shaktikanta Das on 13 February 2017 when he said that it had started to flow in.[42] Chinese proximity with Pakistan, especially their $50 billion investment in the China–Pakistan Economic Corridor (CPEC) for access to the Gwadar port and their constant opposition to India's attempts to become a member of the Nuclear Suppliers Group (NSG), indicates that foreign policy requires hard-nosed diplomacy.

We must be cognizant of the fact that China's increasing investments in India and the potential of a strong business relationship developing between significant players on both sides of the border give us an opportunity to get China to recognize the enormous potential for mutual benefit in further strengthening the bonds of industry and commerce. Between April 2000 and March 2017, China invested over ₹10,000 crore in India, mostly in the telecom, power, engineering and infrastructure sectors. The Alibaba Group and its affiliates have a 40 per cent stake in Paytm, which is expected to increase. Xiaomi assembles one phone every second at a new factory in India. Other Chinese vendors like Oppo, Gionee, Vivo and Lenovo form over half of India's $10 million smartphone market. Sixty per cent of the Chinese Foreign Direct Investment (FDI) is concentrated in the automobile industry. Chinese firms such as Harbin Electric, Dongfang Electronics, Shanghai Electric and Sifang Automation either supply equipment or manage power distribution networks in 18 cities in India.

In 2016–2017, Sino–Indian bilateral trade was over $71 billion, with a trade deficit of over $51 billion.[43] In this context, we must deepen our business and commercial relations with China. At the same time, we have to be wary of the fact that just as the Chinese are making huge investments in our neighbouring countries and thereby attempting to

---

[42]http://indianexpress.com/article/india/india-making-efforts-to-increase-exports-to-china-shaktikanta-das/
[43]https://www.livemint.com/Politics/IASQhdFKA48dETW5fVc3XO/Indias-trade-deficit-with-China-dipped-to-51-billion-in-20.html

influence politics in our neighbourhood, we must not fall into that trap by allowing the Chinese to establish deep roots through trade and commerce in India. Recent statements by President Donald Trump on the trade deficit favouring India in our bilateral relationship with the US suggest that the US is rethinking in the context of bilateral trade. The Chinese have not taken any steps to bring about a balance in our bilateral trade or allowed us to enter their markets in any significant way. China, perhaps, is our most significant neighbour with the potential to increase its influence in our neighbourhood and is now, without doubt, a key global player impacting global trade. While we have our differences, we also need to build on our commonalities of interest in global warming and our efforts to reduce pollution levels in this part of the world.

Going forward, the pace at which we seek to resolve our disputes with China will be unsteady. In a foreign policy environment our forward movement has to be both cautious and strategic. We have to find a way to resolve outstanding issues with China without compromising our security. We cannot afford to be confounded and threatened with standoffs without making serious attempts to resolve these issues.

India must realize that the balance of power in Asia has changed. China is an economic power and its grand strategy is to dominate this part of the world. Back-channel talks, persuasion and quiet diplomacy by coaxing our friends to talk to the Chinese and building a relationship at the diplomatic level provide the recipe for success, not the extravaganza and event management for which Modi has a special liking. Differences should be recognized and should not be allowed to become disputes. Building diplomatic bonds is the answer, instead of throwing gauntlets that may lead to unpleasant surprises.

We need China to recognize that India, in times to come, will be a key global player, and hence, must have a place at the high table in the global order. It is already the biggest democracy and its voice will matter. The Chinese will be well advised to hear us and accept the importance of the positions we take in restructuring the world of tomorrow.

Russia

In the last four years, Modi seems to have leaned towards the US and not realized the importance of our bilateral relationship with Russia. The failure of the Modi government to maintain that balance has led to the Russians selling military hardware to Pakistan.[44] In December 2016, Russia, Iran and Pakistan conducted tripartite talks on Afghanistan, which included accommodating the Afghan Taliban in their fight against the Islamic State (IS). These talks did not include India. It is apparent that the Indo–Russian partnership has undergone dilution under Modi, forcing Russia to reconsider its diplomatic options.

Europe

In an interdependent world, economic interests provide the underlying rationale for foreign policy initiatives. Nations seek to exercise political influence through economic activity. It is difficult to galvanize nations to take didactic positions against regimes. Germany, France and other nations in the European Union (EU) would prefer to have strong ties with India, despite the fact that most nations in Europe have very strong economic relations with China. But closer relations with India would never be at the expense of their relationship with China. This also applies to countries like Australia and Canada. However, countries in Europe do not have geopolitical ambitions, and therefore, have no strategic stake in this part of the world other than to ensure that India's democratic traditions are supported through political processes which also allow for greater economic collaboration. It is in this context that our foreign policy, as far as Europe is concerned, has had no hiccups over the past many years. Our historically close ties with the UK, with whom we have a special partnership, have served us well over the years.

---

[44]https://www.rt.com/op-edge/163116-russian-embargo-military-supplies-pakistan/

Japan

Japan too would like to strengthen its ties with India, especially in the context of its tumultuous relationship with China. Despite the fact that Japanese companies have invested heavily in China, Indo-Japanese ties are on an upward curve, with Japan looking for investment opportunities in India. While the present foreign policy establishment may well have realized the opportunity India has in the current geopolitical context, not enough has been done by the Modi government to take advantage of these opportunities. The promise of $35 billion in investments from Japan has not been realized yet.

Israel

Though the Indo-Israel romance seems to be in full bloom, the credit for the relationship must go to Mrs Indira Gandhi who wanted Rameshwar Nath Kao, the first head of RAW, to replicate the working culture of Mossad. Over the years, several ministers, including those from the UPA, have visited Israel to deepen our bilateral ties in the fields of agriculture, education, defence technologies, pharmaceuticals, micro-irrigation, industry research and development (R&D), and in other areas of interest of the two countries.

As a nation, we have always tried to balance our enduring support to the cause of the Palestinian people and our growing proximity with Israel in multifarious ways. It was in the context of this balancing act that Sushma Swaraj stated in July 2014 in the midst of the Israeli-Hamas conflict that there was absolutely no change in India's policy towards Palestine. She said, 'We fully support the Palestinian cause while maintaining good relations with Israel.'[45]

Israelis are highly innovative people, but do not have either the capital or the capacity to translate that innovation into goods and services for global trade. It is for this reason that innovative solutions provided by

---

[45]https://www.thehindu.com/news/national/no-change-in-stand-on-palestine-govt/article6234699.ece

Israeli companies attract American capital. Using this lucrative platform, US multinationals produce goods and services that are exported to the rest of the world. India is in an ideal position to collaborate with such innovation. Our highly skilled human resource can collaborate with these innovative solutions and translate them into goods and services at a much lower cost than American multinationals. This will allow both Israel and India to be competitive with the rest of the world and, in that process, both countries will stand to benefit. It is the collaboration between innovative ventures in Israel and highly skilled human resource in India with the low economic cost of translating innovation into products that will pave the way for synergizing the strength of both countries for mutual benefit.

Both India and Israel are aware of the constant threat that terrorism poses. The two countries are collaborating in the area of cyber security and counter-terrorism modules. However, the two countries still struggle to add heft to their ties. No doubt, Israel is a major defence supplier to India but the overall bilateral trade in 2017 was only $5 billion. The quantum of this trade does not reflect the potential in areas in which both countries can collaborate. The bonhomie is apparent. The optics are exceptionally encouraging, especially since both countries have a shared worldview, a passion for national security and are proponents of the free market.

Yet, India cannot ignore the growing ties between Israel and China. That relationship was formally established in 1992 but it has gained momentum at a much greater pace than the bilateral ties between India and Israel. Israel is today China's second largest supplier of defence equipment. Beijing is also Israel's largest trade partner in Asia. Chinese firms have huge investments in Israel. Beijing and Tel Aviv are pursuing negotiations for a free trade agreement. Israel supports China's OBOR initiative and China has far greater capacity in wooing Israel for its technology.

There are, of course, some discordant notes as well. Our ties with Iran are on track while we are aware that Israel's position is not compatible with our ties. The signing of the pact with Iran in January 2018, allowing for locomotives to be used in the Chabahar–Zahedan railroad to accelerate the development of the Chabahar port and connect to Central Asia and

Europe, may not go down well with the Israelis. Israelis may not have appreciated the fact that India voted with the rest of the international community in the UN against the US decision to declare Jerusalem the capital of Israel.

The foundation of Indo–Israeli relations is based on pragmatism and it is this pragmatism that will serve us well. Israel's technology-oriented economy opens the door for India, which hungers for innovative solutions ranging from agriculture to healthcare. This is a relationship that emerged from obscurity and is slowly developing into a partnership where collaboration will result in dividends for both countries.

United States

The foundation of our proximate relationship with the US was laid during the course of UPA-I. The geopolitical situation prevailing at that time allowed the forging of a natural alliance between two great democratic nations. China's rise as an economic power and its growing influence in the South China Sea poses a challenge for the US, which has always sought to be a global arbiter attempting to have its footprint all over the world. The US perceived that its foothold in this part of the world depended on closer ties with India, since China was a rival and not a partner in a world that was increasingly moving from being unipolar to bipolar. In that sense, Modi, as prime minister, continued to take that relationship forward. While there are elements of political symmetry in the Indo–US bilateral relationship, there are several areas of conflict of interest, such as the opening up of the Indian economy to increasing opportunities for US investments in India. Our interests in climate change negotiations do not necessarily match. Indeed, our dependence on hydrocarbons, and their dominant future role in energy production, will be an area of concern not just to the US, but also to the global community. Though the US may push for greater opportunities for American companies in India, it is not likely to adhere to our demand for opening up the services sector to allow easy flow of investments in that sector in the US. So while Modi has changed the contours of a logistics agreement, the challenges ahead in the bilateral relationship have not been tackled in any substantial way.

Calling President Obama 'Barack' does not necessarily reflect the level of informality which Modi tried to project in the relationship. National interest is not guided by personal informality; economic interests of nations do not get diluted in this fashion. It takes constant diplomatic endeavours, both formal and informal, lobbying and the ability of nations to convince each other of converging interests to create the confluence necessary for a warm bilateral relationship. In any event, our relationship with Pakistan continues to be a matter of deep concern and the US is not willing to give up its strategic interests in their bilateral relationship with Pakistan. However, in January 2018, the Trump administration suspended $900 million security assistance to Pakistan until it took action against the Afghan Taliban and Haqqani militant groups network.[46] As the US seeks to withdraw from Afghanistan, our interests in that region are also in conflict with those within Pakistan, who consistently seek to destabilize that region. At the behest of the US, Pakistan has recently been placed on the global terrorism-financing watchlist by the Financial Action Task Force (FATF)—an inter-governmental body comprising 35 countries and two regional organizations to fight terrorism financing and money laundering—for failing to curb terrorism emanating from its soil. While India welcomes this, I doubt whether this will deter Pakistan from continuing with its policy of indulging in cross-border terror activities.

With Donald Trump as President, the challenges are even more daunting. President Trump, if his statements are converted to policy, will make the American economy more protectionist. This is a challenge Modi will have to deal with in the context of the growth of our services sector. Trump's immigration policy will also impact our bilateral relationship.[47] 'Buy American, Hire American' does not augur well for India. An insular America with restrictions on H1B visas will be a blow to our IT sector and Trump's insistence that more Americans be hired by Indian companies

---

[46]https://www.reuters.com/article/us-usa-pakistan-aid/u-s-suspends-at-least-900-million-in-security-aid-to-pakistan-idUSKBN1ET2DX
[47]http://www.rediff.com/news/interview/why-trumps-immigration-ban-should-worry-indians/20170201.htm

doing business abroad will inhibit our enterprises in their expansion plans. A new study of the National Foundation for American Policy shows that US tech companies are relying on skilled foreign workers using H1B visas.[48] Indian outsourcing firms are losing their stronghold in this area. The Trump administration has also made the application process for an H1B visa more cumbersome, time-consuming and expensive. This may also have a negative impact on American innovation. Where indigenous tech talent is not available, US innovation giants may have to shift innovation outside the US. Additionally, US corporations employed foreign nationals, paid them less and cut costs. Foreign nationals with H1B visas hold about 1 million jobs in the US, with about 12 per cent of tech jobs.[49]

The momentum in the Indo–US bilateral relationship at the political level continues without a real attempt to capture the essence of that relationship. Our tilt towards the US has made many unhappy and is reflected even more emphatically in our growing ties with Israel. The UPA was quietly building ties with Israel, as evidenced by collaboration at different levels. But that proximity was not out in the open. We were careful not to abandon our traditional friends and dealt with our relationships with an even hand, keeping our national interests in mind.

The Way Forward in a Changing Global Order

Our foreign policy needs recalibration and a fresh momentum. The global balance of power is under strain. The markets are in Asia, with China and India home to about 2.6 billion people. The two key players on the block are President Trump and President Xi Jinping. Trump, with his 'America First' and 'Make America Great Again', is attempting to change the rules of global trade. Calling off the Iran nuclear deal, imposing sanctions on countries having commercial dealings with Iran, imposing tariffs on

---

[48] https://www.axios.com/us-tech-companies-boost-their-h-1b-visas-1524068081-a3c73bc5-2cf9-4bd6-8a37-f862d7f1dfad.html
[49] http://thehill.com/opinion/immigration/364099-h1b-visa-reform-could-encourage-companies-to-hire-more-american-workers

imported steel and trying to ensure equity in the bilateral balance of trade that is skewed in favour of China and other countries, have serious global economic implications. Trump has called for trade parity, reducing levels of bilateral trade deficits in favour of other countries and abolition of government subsidies. In other words, he wants to change the terms of the bilateral and multilateral trade agreements that he attributes to the legacy he inherited. Whether he will succeed in this break from the past, only time will tell.

On our part we need to think through our strategy if Trump follows through with his unilateralism. At the end of the G7 meeting in Canada, he mentioned India and the $375 billion trade deficit with China.[50] He realizes that if the world does not come to terms with his desire for fair terms of trade with the US, it has more to lose. It is with the same logic that he seeks to renegotiate the North American Free Trade Agreement (NAFTA). If not, he threatens to negotiate separate trade deals with Canada and Mexico.[51] All this articulation is consistent with Trump's concept of defining national security in purely economic terms. 'America First' also means an insular America, wary of getting directly involved in conflicts abroad and seeking honourable withdrawal wherever possible. In this context, the US wants greater involvement from us in Afghanistan. That is consistent with our interests as well.

Trump's foreign policy will cater to his domestic audience. The perception that globalization shifted manufacturing outside the US, resulting in loss of jobs for Americans, was a significant factor in Trump's electoral success. To bring back jobs to America, he needs to change the terms of trade.

Thirty years of globalization has brought about a revolution of sorts which has impacted the world in several ways. China owes its rise as a global force to Richard Nixon, who surprised the world when he visited China in 1972. Thereafter, in 1978, the Chinese economic reform process got under

---

[50] https://thewire.in/trade/us-president-donald-trump-india-trade-tariff-relations
[51] https://www.washingtonpost.com/news/business/wp/2018/06/05/trump-aims-to-split-up-nafta-negotiations-deal-with-canada-and-mexico-separately/?noredirect=on&utm_term=.c2947af78253

way. The Chinese sought General Agreement on Tariffs and Trade (GATT) membership in 1986 and after 15 long years of negotiations with the World Trade Organisation (WTO), became a member, with favourable terms of trade that it benefited from enormously. Today, because of globalization, China is a $12 trillion economy.[52] Other less developed economies also benefited. The trade-off was that American enterprises, and those in the developed world, got access to markets which resulted in the growth of multinationals, who were enabled to leave their footprints around the world. Manufacturing shifted and outsourcing of services brought prosperity to other economies. At the same time, manufacturing capacities in the US were negatively impacted. They shifted to other jurisdictions.

Meanwhile, through mind-boggling innovation in Silicon Valley, new technologies were being seeded and nurtured, bringing about a sea change in the way the world was to trade and interact. This new paradigm bred multinationals that are seeking to globalize trade in a way that is yet to fully unfold. The nature of skills required for employment impacted lives. Those unemployed and the less gainfully employed attributed their condition to liberalization of the economies. Twenty-four years after the Marrakesh Agreement (of 1994, establishing WTO), we see that the fruits of liberal trade have had limited trickle-down effect. There is a perception that the global elite out there has been enriched and that the gap between the rich and the deprived has increased. The new species of global corporations are those whose wealth is not measured by the physical assets they possess but by the wealth of their intellectual property.

The backlash to globalization saw the rise of Trump and the vote for Brexit. Those who benefited from globalization still root for it. The EU too has benefited. But the US, to gain access to markets, according to Trump, allowed other nations favourable terms of trade, thereby resulting in a US trade gap of $556 billion.[53] Trump wishes to reverse this trend. Traditional allies of the US are upset. European nations will be badly impacted by the imposition of tariffs on imported steel. Trump's decision to impose a

---

[52] http://www.xinhuanet.com/english/2017-10/18/c_136688715.htm
[53] http://www.thehindu.com/news/international/why-is-donald-trumps-trade-war-dangerous/article23034702.ece

25 per cent tariff on Chinese imports worth $34 billion shows the US's intent for its idea of a fair-trade regime.[54] This has lessons for India too.

The rise of China and the somewhat insular outlook of the US puts us in a very delicate position. While the US under Trump views globalization through a different lens, China seeks to expand its economic footprint. The Indo–Pacific region is the new battleground of peddling influence. China has laid claim to this strategic region. It has, by building artificial islands, extended its claim to international waters. Its investments and naval presence are meant to present the world with a *fait accompli*. Claim over natural resources and control of sea lanes in this area is coveted by China. The Indo–Pacific channel of communication has huge strategic implications globally. That apart, China is successfully extending its influence in our neighbourhood, apart from becoming increasingly involved in economic activity in India. The OBOR will aid China in flooding the region with its goods and services. China has strategically financed ports in our neighbourhood, the most strategic of all being Gwadar. The CPEC makes for a level of permanency in China's strategic alliance with Pakistan.

In this changing global environment, India finds itself in an unenviable position. Both Trump and Xi Jinping, by their uniquely disruptive economic policy thrusts, are likely to change the contours of foreign policy. We cannot entirely rely on the US. Until now, it has not demonstrated how it can work with India—not in furtherance of its commercial and strategic interests, but to partner with India in its rise. China's looming presence and its increasing significance in global affairs makes us vulnerable. Membership of the Shanghai Cooperation Organisation is welcome. Our voice will be heard but as of now it will not matter for much.

The way forward is to keep befriending our neighbours, our historical and cultural ties being a cementing factor. Japan will be a steadfast partner in our development agenda. It is clear that the Quad comprising the US, Japan, Australia and India have democratic impulses and synergy. We require these democratic impulses to deliver economic prosperity for mutual benefit. With China we need to recognize both its presence and

---

[54]https://www.bbc.com/news/business-44707253

impact in the region. We too have the potential to be recognized in the same fashion. Our relationship with China and the way it pans out is most challenging for our foreign policy mandarins in South Block.

In the emerging new world order, the G7 without China and India has little relevance. Russia's increasing proximity to China and support for Iran in the ongoing conflict in Syria makes for an uneasy world order. India's reliance on imported crude from Iran, which is the second highest supplier to India, apart from our traditional ties, limits our ability to manoeuvre our diplomatic moves. Russia, our traditional ally, has no hesitation in dealing with Pakistan and supplying it with military hardware. The informal dialogue at Sochi—between Prime Minister Modi and Russian President Vladimir Putin in May 2018—is perhaps to change the course.[55] Modi tried to do the same with China at Wuhan.[56] Informal dialogues are no substitute for strategic thinking, and calibrated well-thought-out diplomatic initiatives have been woefully absent since 2014. Recognizing terrorism as a threat and resolving to combat it—an outcome of these informal dialogues—is of little significance. Such resolutions have no impact on the spiral of violence and the rise in incidents of terrorism as witnessed in the recent past in Kashmir.[57]

In this complex global order, India must constantly engage with China; be part of the Quad and address security issues collectively; start dealing with Pakistan through a more constructive process—instead of the impasse that is taking us nowhere except for flexing of muscles and loss of precious lives with no visible returns; embrace our traditional friends and ensure that the interests of our people working in the Middle East are protected. The flow of imported crude oil, the life blood necessary for our development, must always receive top priority.

Last but not the least, we should continue to build our relationship with our new-found friends and allies. Similarly, a new thrust is needed

---

[55]https://www.firstpost.com/world/narendra-modi-vladimir-putin-informal-summit-an-exercise-aimed-at-resetting-bilateral-ties-timed-for-strategic-balance-4477915.html
[56]https://indianexpress.com/article/india/informal-sino-indian-summit-in-separate-statements-meeting-points-and-pm-modi-xi-jinping-5155532/
[57]http://www.indiaspend.com/cover-story/64-rise-in-terror-incidents-in-jk-over-2-years-as-bjp-pdp-alliance-splinters-98201

to address our deep-rooted ties with countries in Africa. But in doing all this, South Block needs to be taken on board. Let not foreign policy be the domain of the PMO alone.

Part Two

THE UPA YEARS: MYTHS AND REALITY

Chapter 6

IN THE HOUSE OF THE PEOPLE

For me, contesting from Chandni Chowk was a unique experience. The mood of the constituency, gauged by the body language of the electors, was favourable to the Congress party fighting as a cohesive unit. Having failed once in 1996, I was keen to make yet another attempt to get elected to the Lok Sabha. When I was goaded by the then Prime Minister P.V. Narasimha Rao to contest from South Delhi in 1996, I was aware of my inevitable defeat pitched as I was against Sushma Swaraj, who had fought many an election. A defeat in court does not hurt as much because a lot depends on the merits of the case, but when I lost from South Delhi, I told myself that I must somehow avenge it by living to fight elections another day. I did that in 2004 and entered the Lok Sabha. While I was campaigning feverishly in Chandni Chowk, I instinctively felt the Congress had a chance. Little did I know then that the Congress would form the government and I would be given an opportunity to be a part of that government.

Heading the Ministry of Science and Technology

When it was announced that I had been given the responsibility of the Ministry of Science and Technology (S&T), I was taken aback. Prior to 2004, very few people were aware of the significance of this ministry. It was not perceived to be high-profile and on occasions in the past, especially during Congress governments, the prime minister was the minister-in-charge. My own ignorance of the extreme significance of the ministry surprised me after I got the position. As I familiarized myself with the expanse and critical role of the ministry, I realized its importance.

A scientific temper and a scientific bent of mind is at the heart of human progress. Science unravels the mysteries of nature and technology and helps us to use them for human good. Indeed, no nation can hope to benefit its people unless it recognizes the significance of science in creating wealth. I felt comfortable in a ministry in which my intellect was challenged. My interaction with highly celebrated scientists was a great learning experience. These were not the IAS officers who, having cleared a competitive examination and fully entrapped in bureaucratic rules and regulations, ran the ministry. Those who became secretary of S&T, director general of the Council of Scientific and Industrial Research (CSIR), secretary in the Ministry of Earth Sciences, and secretary in the Department of Biotechnology, were accomplished scientists and their minds were not influenced by bureaucratic impulses. Their intellectual energy was a source of stimulation. They genuinely believed that commitment to science would change the face of the nation and that solutions through technology would help in dealing with some of its most daunting challenges.

Those were the years of effervescence. The biotechnology revolution was redefining the frontiers of healthcare as well as agriculture. I realized that R&D in healthcare, especially in relation to diseases that afflict the less developed world, was not a priority for institutional research in the West. There was not enough research on tuberculosis (TB) by multinationals who were essentially investing in issues that afflicted the West. New molecules to deal with malaria and hepatitis were not being researched and it was left to the scientific community in this part of the globe to find solutions for our people. These are not lifestyle diseases. With urbanization of India, our people will face lifestyle diseases as well, but our scientists were committed to finding solutions for the diseases linked to underdevelopment, such as malaria, TB, HIV and AIDS. They realized that poor living conditions contributed to the spread of these diseases, especially TB and respiratory infections such as pneumonia.

They also realized that India would soon become the diabetic capital of the world, and considering the nature of our diets, people will suffer from coronary heart disease. In these circumstances it was extremely important for our scientific community to initiate global partnerships and programmes through which the diseases of the developing world could be addressed and new molecules discovered to effectively deal with them. We obtained a Cabinet decision to partly fund Phase-3 clinical trials for molecules addressing neglected diseases. One of the molecules for controlling malaria emanated from this initiative.[1]

Biotechnology Solutions for Critical Challenges

Another issue that constantly came up for discussion was providing solutions to highly complex environmental issues. One of the serious problems that we face as a nation is the pollution of our water resources. Our attempts at cleaning the Ganga have not resulted in any significant change, mainly because of untreated effluents being discharged into the river by small industrial units located in towns and cities along it. To deal with pollution caused by tanneries, a PIL was filed in the Supreme Court. Tanneries along the Hooghly river were required to be shifted.[2] A CSIR institute was asked to find a solution to ensure toxic wastes are treated before being released. This was a massive enterprise and I remember Dr T. Ramasami, who was the head of the Central Leather Research Institute (CLRI) at Chennai, committing to find such a technological solution. Tanneries were indeed shifted from a particular location and the problem of toxic wastes was resolved. CLRI also developed a technology plan for implementing 'Do Ecology' solutions for the tanneries in Tamil Nadu. By adopting a 'Zero Liquid Discharge' programme based on it, all the tanneries of the state have stopped discharging any waste water onto public land for over a decade now.

With depleting resources of water for human consumption, we need

---

[1]https://www.biospectrumindia.com/news/18/540/indian-lead-molecule-for-malaria-bags-us-patent.html
[2]http://www.ebc-india.com/lawyer/articles/718.htm#Ref28

to find solutions through technology; otherwise water stress will lead to social conflicts. At present, almost 70 per cent of water meant for human consumption is used in agriculture. This is a very inefficient way to use a vital resource. We all know that paddy cultivation is water-intensive and most of the water meant for human consumption goes into its production. The Prime Minister recently made a trip to Israel. We have much to learn from the scientific community there. Israel suffered from water stress but by using technology it enjoys a water surplus today. Despite our slogan 'More crop per drop', not much has been done in India through scientific and technological solutions to reduce the quantum of water used for paddy cultivation and save it for human consumption. Israel has done so through the processes of desalination and precision agriculture that delivers water at the root of plants. These technologies can be adopted along the vast coastal areas in India.

During my tenure in the ministry, we laid much stress on setting up desalination plants in these areas. Our experiment in Lakshadweep, which has very limited water fit for human consumption, was successful. We set up an on-shore desalination plant which converted saline water of the ocean into potable water.[3] This was a great boon to the population of Lakshadweep. We in the ministry also planned to set up desalination plants along coastal regions. One of the problems the ministry was facing at that time was the stability of the desalination unit away from the coast when the sea is turbulent. We had a plan to set up a desalination unit in the ocean for supply of drinking water to Chennai, which suffers from water stress.

The possibility of setting up such units all along the coast of India has huge potential and can, if addressed seriously, deal with many of the problems that our population will face in times to come. Of course, such solutions are not possible in the hinterland. But for paddy cultivation in the hinterland, the solution will emerge through biotechnology when we are able to develop seeds which can produce the same amount of rice without using the quantum of water now being used.

---

[3] http://pib.nic.in/newsite/backgrounders.aspx?relid=161296 (last accessed on 11.07.2017)

Technology—Boon or Bane

A few months into the ministry and I realized how we take technology for granted. It touches our everyday lives. From the time we get up to the time we sleep, we are seldom cognizant of the use of technology. While technology has the capacity to further our well-being, it also has the capacity to hurt us.

Somewhere down the road, while I was deeply impressed by the enormous strides the world had made in providing technological solutions which touch our everyday lives, I realized that much that we do in some of our state-funded research organizations has to do with highly sophisticated solutions. They might relate to the launch of satellites or to components in a weapon system or, for that matter, to high-end technological solutions that require enormous inputs of capital which the private sector might be hesitant to invest. The reason is simple—private capital will only embrace ventures which are likely to earn returns at the earliest. Private capital cannot afford idle investments in which profits might either elude it or take years to realize. I admire the wisdom of our forefathers who decided to set up State-funded labs with the objective of building a scientific base for national advancement. A lot of the State-funded labs which produce solutions today were set up in the initial years of our independence.

I also realized that for private capital to invest in science and technology, we need private industry to have surplus funds. Maybe the way forward is to incentivize R&D in the private sector through tax breaks, to lay the foundation of a strong private sector venture capital infrastructure. Today, of the 0.9 per cent GDP investment in science and technology, almost 0.6 per cent is funded by the State.[4] I would like to add that after 2004, conscious efforts were made to ensure that gross expenditure on R&D met the best global norms. Indeed, India's investment on R&D is the sixth largest in the world, as per 2015 World Bank data.[5] It represents nearly 88 per cent of the total investment of 35 low income

---

[4]http://www.swaminathansivaram.in/media/data/INDIA%E2%80%99S%20SPEND%20ON%20SCIENCE,%20TECHNOLOGY-May-2016.pdf
[5]https://www.iriweb.org/sites/default/files/2016GlobalR%26DFundingForecast_2.pdf

and 55 lower middle income group countries. This is the direct result of the government's initiative.

Having said that, I lament the inability of the scientific community to provide solutions for the common man. Very few realize how the lives of millions of people are touched by the ability to know when the monsoon will set in. That prediction too is a marvel of both science and technology. To predict the monsoon is perhaps one of the most complex technological tasks. We need to have the tools to compute prediction of temperature changes and thereafter analyse the movement of currents and their relevance in predicting wind patterns. Highly powerful supercomputers are necessary tools for such computing, along with highly complex software systems for their analyses.

Very soon after I took over, I was shocked to learn that much of the measurements of basic weather parameters, like temperature, humidity, wind and rain, were being done in analogue mode. Till then, we had never even attempted to use digital technology. All our rain gauges were not digital and, therefore, we could not get online information on rainfall. I also realized that though we had a supercomputer, we did not have the necessary software to analyse the data it could provide. It is in this context that I decided to push the ministry to digitalize our entire weather measurement system and simultaneously sought the advice of the scientific community about forging an alliance for accessing software which could predict not just the advent of the monsoon, but also its continuous progress as it moved across terrain. We forged an alliance with a French company and received the necessary capacity to analyse data for a more accurate prediction and visualization of the monsoon and other climate events.

I remember that the Meteorological (Met) Department was not considered very reliable before we used these technology solutions. Indeed, people would say that if the Met Department predicted rain, the sun would surely shine. That has completely changed. The Met Department can now predict, well in advance, not just the onset of the monsoon but the day it will shower. It can predict the extent of the monsoon in the long term and on a weekly basis. What does that do? It helps farmers to know when to sow their crop. Untimely rains can destroy a crop while timely rains and their prediction can lead to a good harvest. The extent of a torrential downpour during a freak climate event can also be predicted but this can only happen if we use even more sophisticated technology.

When I took over the ministry, just a few of the 54 Doppler radars, required to detect weather-related events accurately, were in place. A Doppler radar is a device which enables the scientific community to accurately measure speed and direction of wind currents at a particular height which, in turn, helps in predicting a natural event that might endanger lives. With adequate Doppler radars in place, lives can be saved and public inconvenience reduced. We put in place a procedure through which we could acquire more Doppler radars.

Understanding the Business of Science

The problem with our bureaucratic system, especially in the scientific world, is that intellectual stalwarts who are not 'bureaucrats' find it very difficult to deal with the world of commerce. Their mind is not accustomed to bureaucratic intricacies of acquisition. It is also true that many in the scientific community have set up or joined enterprises for manufacturing such equipment post-retirement and attempted to persuade their in-service colleagues to help their enterprises. But when it comes to selecting the best possible technology for public good, we need to trust our scientists' decisions.

One of the peculiar problems that often confronted us in the ministry was acquisition from a single vendor. We know that in a competitive commercial environment we may float a tender for acquisition of products for which there is open competition. It is easy to compare between a Samsung and a Whirlpool air-conditioner. But at the high-end of technology, there are no similar products. A highly sophisticated software computing system cannot be compared with any other. Each software system is unique. And, therefore, a decision to acquire any such unique system hits the wall of the single-tender rule—which, in normal circumstances, does not allow government agencies to invite or

In the House of the People ▸ 143

accept bids from a single entity. Faced with such a hurdle, scientists, by and large, hesitate to take decisions and, therefore, acquisitions are delayed for years.

This is also true of acquiring defence equipment. The acquisition of an aircraft, whether it is a Sukhoi Su-30MKI or an F-16 or a Mirage 2000, is not an easy proposition. Each particular aircraft will have its unique capabilities. What has to be measured from the point of view of the buyer is the need of a particular acquisition in the context of our overall strategic requirements. That, in turn, depends on the defence capability of India and our neighbours. Is it good only to rely on one supplier of highly sophisticated aircraft or should you diversify your acquisitions from several vendors? Complete reliance on one may result in glitches in times of conflict because of short supply of spares. And so, diversity of acquisitions in the context of aircraft has strategic implications too.

Delayed acquisition can have serious security implications, especially in the context of defence hardware—be it high-end helicopters, sophisticated tanks, armoured equipment, guns of a particular range or night vision equipment. Very few of us, especially politicians, are fully aware of the nuances involved in taking such decisions.

We must also be cognizant of the fact that a competitor who senses that its offer may be rejected is bound to spread misinformation, which further muddies the water. It is, therefore, extremely important, especially for acquiring sophisticated strategic equipment with hardware or software tailor-made to the needs of a department, that the application of the single-vendor rule should not be an impediment in the acquisition of technology for public good.

Nature in Its Multifarious Manifestations

Natural phenomena are unpredictable. Just as we constantly attempt—with the use of technology—to understand the onset of the monsoon and its intensity, we can similarly try and understand other natural phenomena which have the potential of destroying human lives.

A phenomenon that I had not heard of since my childhood—nor

was it taught in our geography classes—the Tsunami—occurred on a Sunday, 26 December 2004 at 7:58 a.m. It was caused by the subduction of the Indo–Australian oceanic plate under the Eurasian continental plate, 240 km off the coast of Indonesia. Essentially, this caused an earthquake which involved the uplifting of the seafloor over a 1,000-km fault line by 20 metres. This, in turn, resulted in billions of tonnes of water being displaced, causing a disturbance called tsunami, which, in simple terms, is a huge wave that can cause unimaginable damage.

That was what happened when the coast of Indonesia was hit within half an hour of this earthquake. The earthquake was of the magnitude of 9 on the Richter scale. It caught millions unaware and brought them grief, especially in the coastal areas of Indonesia, since they had no warning of such an event. We in India also did not have a tsunami warning system in place, nor was it in place for any of our neighbours, including Sri Lanka.

Nature has a way of both destroying and protecting itself. Our mangrove forests provide natural protection from phenomena of this nature. But as we destroy our mangroves in the name of tourism, we also expose those living in our coastal areas to dangers of such a cataclysmic event. The result was that at least 2,26,000 people died, around 5 million were either rendered homeless or had no access to food and water and 5 to 6 million needed emergency aid due to the 2004 tsunami.[6] Apart from this, the disruption of sewage systems mixed up with salt water created a health hazard with the spread of disease and pestilence. Almost 60 per cent of fishing fleets were destroyed along the coastal areas of India and Sri Lanka. Crops and farmlands were ruined and coral reefs damaged. The devastation was heart-rending. Its impact was felt along our eastern coast and the coastal areas of Indonesia, Malaysia, the Maldives and Sri Lanka. In fact, the tsunami was of such magnitude that it also impacted some coastal areas of east Africa.

It was then that I realized how inadequate we were in protecting our people from such events. We in the ministry immediately decided to set up a tsunami warning system to provide for timely alerts to allow for

---

[6]https://www.newscientist.com/article/dn9931-facts-and-figures-asian-tsunami-disaster/

evacuation of people from coastal areas.

The task of the ministry—and we committed ourselves to it—was to set up perhaps the most modern tsunami warning system in the world. While countries like Indonesia, in the context of such an event, would hardly have any response time given the fact that dangerous seismic fault lines are in very close proximity[7], the Indian coastal region is so situated that we have enough leeway between the occurrence of such an event and its impact on the eastern coast. As a result, we can warn our people to protect themselves and mobilize local administrations to minimize damage.

We dedicated the most sophisticated tsunami system to the people of the country in less than three years of our promise at a cost of ₹125 crore.[8] I was amazed at the quality of the product. We had software in place by which we could predict such an event, depending on its origin along the fault line abutting the ocean and the coastal areas it might affect. This, of course, would vary depending on where the tsunami event occurs. We can today, in fact, predict, depending on the intensity of the earthquake, the amount of dislocation that it would cause in the water body of the ocean and the likely impact areas on the eastern coast. We can calculate the extent to which the waters will travel inland and the devastation that might result.

Today we have a reliable system that could warn of a tsunami within 13 minutes of tsunamigenic activity. Our system has been so designed that we can help our neighbours with advance information. We have also integrated our tsunami information system with those of neighbouring countries that are likely to be affected.

Now that we have such a system in place, our people can rest assured that we are sufficiently empowered to protect them in any such eventuality. Scientific solutions can be great benefactors to our everyday problems.

---

[7]https://news.nationalgeographic.com/news/2014/12/141226-tsunami-indonesia-catastrophe-banda-aceh-warning-science/
[8]http://www.livemint.com/Industry/En84n1VNz6BBAn7vCACMjK/India-unveils-tsunamiwarning-system.html

Innovation through Disruptive Technologies

The Indian scientific community is deeply involved in translational research at the high end but not so much in those areas that may help people at the bottom of the pyramid. I remember a programme adopted by the CSIR called Project 800, a unique project for improving the quality of life of people in rural areas and small towns.[9,10]

I have been troubled by three things for which I wanted CSIR to present some solutions. Having travelled on trains in my younger days, I was extremely disturbed that a coolie had to carry someone else's burden. Some of them were old, some young. The image of an old coolie straining to carry heavy luggage on his head, climbing stairs for his daily living disturbed me. Why can't technology provide a solution so that he doesn't have to strain his physical being? Technology should be developed to have a contraption where carrying that luggage is not a physical challenge. We don't have a technological solution for that till date, nor could the CSIR provide one.

I was also troubled by the fact that we don't treat our dead with dignity. I still see dead bodies being brought on a vehicle and then carried to the cremation ground. Why can't there be a vehicle with a contraption which slides the body out, giving the entire movement of the dead some dignity? No solution for that too.

The third most troubling thing was the sight of a rickshaw puller physically straining to carry the weight of a fellow human being. In the modern civilized world, this should not be allowed. As of 2013, there were 6,00,000 rickshaw pullers in the city of Delhi alone. They suffer from poor nutrition and lack of preventive healthcare. To pull two or three times their weight results in injuries and chronic conditions. They suffer from TB from exposure to air pollution and low nutrition, leading to immunosuppression. They start with bronchial infections and in three to four years, contract TB. So many families of rickshaw pullers see their breadwinners die young because of TB, and the paltry money they earn

---

[9]http://www.niist.res.in/english/out-reach/csir-800-program
[10]http://pib.nic.in/newsite/PrintRelease.aspx?relid=97658

is not enough for the constant medication needed.

The CSIR provided a solution for that. Rickshaw appeared in India around 1880, first in Shimla. At the turn of the century, it was introduced in Calcutta (now Kolkata), and by 1914, it became a popular mode of conveyance for hire in the city.[11] It provided for intra-city transportation of goods and an easy mode of travel for the elite. But for 80 years, no innovation had taken place for these cycle rickshaws. Remember, most rickshaw pullers are migrant workers from rural areas looking for employment in urban areas. These migrants don't have the wherewithal to get into the formal sector and so become a part of the informal workforce. First these rickshaws were hand-pulled and then with the coming of the bicycle, they became cycle rickshaws. It's interesting that the seemingly small industry of rickshaw pullers supports nearly 4 per cent of India's population.

The CSIR developed a low-cost technology—a solar-powered electric rickshaw christened Soleckshaw.[12]

They initially started with a prototype, which was launched in Delhi in October 2008 for trial and testing. The Soleckshaw was launched at an initial price of $670 but efforts were made to reduce it to $450 so that it would be affordable for rickshaw pullers. It was officially launched in October 2008 at Durgapur in West Bengal, Chandni Chowk in Delhi and Ghaziabad in Uttar Pradesh and it has now been successfully deployed in Ahmedabad, Chandigarh, Delhi, Durgapur, Faridabad, Gurgaon, Jaipur, Kolkata, Ranchi, Bokaro, Pune and Shillong. To ensure that the benefit of this technology reached the rickshaw puller, a Soleckshaw licence was distributed as a non-exclusive licence. The CSIR retained the intellectual property rights so that technological innovations and improvements could take place. The technology was transferred to several companies through licensing. The Central Excise Tariff Act allowed for duty exemption on

---

[11]Ashish Verma and T.V. Ramanayya, *Public Transport Planning and Management in Developing Countries*, CRC Press, 2014; Frederic C. Thomas, *Calcutta Poor: Elegies on a City above Pretense*, M.E. Sharpe, 1997

[12]http://www.livemint.com/Politics/937DlXpuBjgRrvh7dsmQlL/The-humble-cycle-rickshaw-gets-a-solarpowered-makeover.html

important components of battery-powered road vehicles so that the imported components of electric rickshaws could be easily used for their manufacture.

Soleckshaw has transformed the cycle rickshaw industry. It disrupted the market through the intervention of technology. Through a liberal technological transfer agreement with a non-exclusive licencing policy, there was rapid proliferation of such soleckshaws. Easy commercialization helped reduce the drudgery of rickshaw pullers and exposure to health hazards. It has also put more money into their pockets and helped millions of families.

This is an example of the kind of innovation that is required, through disruptive technologies, to change people's lives. What our scientific community needs to do is to find simple solutions for everyday problems. If a solution is expensive, it is unaffordable and its imprint on public good, limited.

India is known for generic drugs. In the field of healthcare, the industry has provided drugs at affordable prices to millions. Simple solutions for providing clean drinking water can save millions of children who die of contaminated water sources. The scientific community will also have to develop houses for the poor made of fire-resistant material which are not swept away during the monsoon.

Technological solutions for sustainable development are essential not just to combat poverty but also climate change. For agriculture, the CSIR provided domestic tractors for the Green Revolution.[13] They developed Streptokinase as a low-cost domestic clot-buster for heart attacks[14] and Terafil water filter as an affordable, simple, no-power, portable water option.[15] That should be the focus of our scientific community—innovate, and at the same time, use technology to provide solutions for the common man.

In an interconnected world, new platforms of research have to be set up and R&D scientists across the world should be persuaded to come

---

[13] http://www.nrdcindia.com/english/index.php/success-stories/65-swaraj-tractor
[14] https://www.imtech.res.in/achievements/technologies-commercialized/natural-streptokinase
[15] http://www.immt.res.in/TERAFILWaterFilter.aspx

on one platform for drug discovery. The IT network allows minds to function together and interact with each other without travelling long distances. Dialogues can take place through technology networks. Of course, the key to such interaction is security for these platforms. In a sense, it is like WhatsApp, in which communications are encrypted and secured from outside prying. Protocols also have to be developed for the purposes of sharing IT. This can only happen if those conducting key research across the world in certain specialized areas come together. This, in turn, requires our scientific community to travel across the world, connect with key scientists known for their research and persuade them to come on board on such IT platforms. We have the advantage of Indians working in key global academic institutions and research organizations. They should be our sounding boards for locating R&D fellow travellers who could join us in this enterprise.

The CSIR did an experiment that created an open-source drug discovery platform. This was done for the purposes of bringing global researchers together for discovering new therapies for neglected diseases like TB, malaria, etc.[16] Doubts were expressed on the nature of the collaboration and the sharing of intellectual property rights, but those were unfounded. Global research could now be shared in conversations taking place on that platform. The web-based platform, called SysBorg 2.0, allowed independent researchers to freely share their work and collaborate through the Internet.[17]

This open sharing platform allowed multifaceted approaches and shared advances on different fronts for new drug discoveries. It involved students, scientists, researchers, academicians, institutions and corporations. This experiment in integrative science through collaboration has the potential of sustaining itself by generating a storehouse of alternatives for the pursuit of drug discovery.

It's interesting to note the number of participants in this programme—7,900 from more than 130 countries.[18] This is particularly

---

[16]http://www.osdd.net/about-us/What-is-OSDD
[17]http://www.osdd.net/about-us/how-osdd-works/sysborg-2-0
[18]http://www.osdd.net/about-us/how-osdd-works

useful and critical for India because multinational pharmaceutical corporations make minimum investments in R&D for tropical infectious diseases in the absence of a market in their own backyard. Tropical diseases tend to affect the poor more, and drug discovery being an expensive process, corporations feel the poor may not be able to afford manufactured drugs and are, therefore, reluctant to invest.

The open-source drug discovery platform relies on the generic industrial business model. This way, the cost of research can be minimized through collaborations. The best minds can interact through this platform and corporations can associate themselves to pick out such possible molecules that may have the potential for commercial success. We should replicate this model with the government, supporting and encouraging a consortium through partnerships for collaborative models of research.

India must look at such innovative solutions for path-breaking discoveries in the field of agriculture, safe drinking water, and affordable healthcare. Exploration of the ocean is needed to discover its hidden wealth for public good. We must identify frontier areas of research and ensure a directional shift in innovation and enterprise.

Successive governments have to realize that the key to creating wealth is not profits through industrial production. Wealth is also created through ideas, and ideas take shape through research.

Investment in R&D

For quality research we need to get the best minds together. Governments must ensure that enough investment is made in R&D. Much of the success of the private sector in the US is due to the federal government's funding of R&D projects. A larger number of R&D projects in the university system are government funded. It is when multinational corporations associated with these R&D experiments realize the possibility of commercialization of new discoveries, that they fund further experiments. In India, public funding of such projects is minimal compared to the billions of dollars invested in R&D in the US.

In our corridors of power, I am yet to see a commitment to R&D and a realization that it is the scientific community in India that can deliver us from the scourge of poverty. Without that realization, our country will forever remain an arid land where what we will see are oases of prosperity surrounded by vast tracts of poverty. During my stint in the ministry, I realized that R&D funding in India is subject to bureaucratic controls. To overcome this, we set up the Science and Engineering Research Board, through legislation in 2008, which is currently funding research in the frontier areas of science and engineering.[19]

Pushing New Frontiers of Knowledge

Today India is one among a handful of nations that are capable of deep sea mining. National Institute of Ocean Technology (NIOT), the technical arm of the Ministry of Earth Sciences, took up this challenging area of developing technologies for harnessing ocean resources. India was elected as a member of the Legal and Technical Commission (LTC) of the International Seabed Authority (ISA) for a period of five years (2007–12).

Towards this end, the Technology Demonstration Vessel 'Sagar Nidhi' was launched in June 2007, during my tenure as S&T Minister. It was dedicated to the nation on 3 March 2008. This multipurpose vessel harnesses various non-living resources from the ocean in a sustainable manner. This vessel also caters to shallow water survey, and acts as a supply and support platform for various coastal and deep ocean activities and is capable of conducting multidisciplinary studies in the sea continuously for 45 days with 30 scientists onboard.

Setting Foot on Antarctica

Antarctica is a unique continent, 98 per cent of which is covered in ice. It is key to our understanding of global and environmental concerns. It provides scientists with unique opportunities to investigate the origin of continents, the phenomenon of global climate change and issues related

---

[19] http://www.serb.gov.in/home.php

to meteorology that are crucial in forecasting weather patterns, to name a few. India, through its three research bases, conducts studies in the areas of biodiversity and environmental physiology; solar terrestrial processes and their coupling; medical physiology, adaptation techniques and human psychology; environmental impact assessment and monitoring; enabling low temperature technology development; and studies on earthquakes, among others.

In February 2005, I led a high-level delegation to take stock of the various operational and scientific activities in the region and evolve a plan for strengthening our Antarctic Programme. To experience the harsh working and living conditions of our scientists, I chose to visit 'Maitri', India's second research station in Antarctica, as well as our research sites in the region. During the visit, I announced modernization plans for Maitri and other research sites. The objective was to make the stay of our scientists in the continent more comfortable.

India was privileged to host the 30th Antarctic Treaty Consultative Meeting (ATCM) in May 2007, at which India's proposal for a new Indian Research Base at Larsemann Hills, East Antarctica, was accepted. A third research base station was accordingly established in Antarctica for carrying out multidisciplinary research and observation studies. Christened 'Bharati', this research base was commissioned on 18 March 2012.

First Indian Expedition to Arctic

The Arctic Ocean and surrounding regions are one of the most important areas that not only govern the Earth's climate but have also faithfully recorded its past climatic history. The region is also an excellent harbinger of future change, because signals or clues that signify climate change are much stronger in the Arctic than elsewhere. This region has been significant to the Indian subcontinent due to the probable teleconnection between the northern polar region and monsoon intensity in India.

India embarked on Arctic research by launching the first ever scientific expedition to this region in August 2007, using the international research facility at Ny-Alesund on Spitsbergen island, Norway. In the second phase initiated in February 2008, an Indian Arctic Station, 'Himadri', was set up at the base camp in Norway. India's first permanent research station was inaugurated in July 2008. The research base is equipped with state-of-the-art facilities for conducting round-the-year scientific research in contemporary fields of Arctic science with special emphasis on climate change. With the inauguration of this station, India joined a select group of 10 countries that have established full-fledged research stations there. The other countries are—the UK, Germany, France, Italy, China, Japan, South Korea, The Netherlands and Sweden.

Technology for Public Good

Technology is a great benefactor, but there is a downside to it if we are not alert.

Digital platforms, for instance, have brought a communications revolution in India, but they are being misused by some individuals to incite people and disturb communal harmony and peace. We have seen that happen in the past. These platforms are likely to be used for polarizing India in the future. Fake news is the new weapon of offence for such individuals. Taking alarming images from the past, either from India or from outside, and making them go viral through digital networks by portraying them as events happening here and now is perhaps the most insidious way of inciting passions. It is also unfortunate that the State itself has used fake news to claim non-existing achievements. No less than the Home Ministry has published photographs of other countries to falsely showcase great progress being made in India.[20] It is time that this country wakes up to the dangers of such misuse of digital platforms.

One can use certain provisions of the Indian Penal Code for individuals inciting violence through fake news, but then someone can set up fake accounts for doing that. There must be a law to ensure that fake accounts are not allowed and punitive actions follow if such accounts are used for criminal activity. Certain provisions of the Penal Code—like Section 153A,

---

[20]https://www.altnews.in/home-ministry-annual-report-uses-picture-spain-morocco-border-show-indian-border-floodlighting/

etc. cannot ensure peace and tranquility in the present context. We need stricter punishments and procedural laws in which the burden of proof shifts to the accused, as in the case of activities relating to terrorism and drugs. Special legislation for tackling fake news should be put in place as soon as possible, after due consultation with all stakeholders.

Another issue that has to be looked at globally is the concept of anonymity on digital platforms. Anonymity is protected in other jurisdictions and, therefore, criminal activity is perpetrated under the cloak of secrecy. This is unacceptable and all digital platforms operating in India—Facebook, Google and others—must operate on the condition that in the event of any request for information on an anonymous account involved in criminal activity, the veil of secrecy will be lifted and the individual traced within a particular time frame. This is of fundamental importance to India, a cauldron of diversity which can potentially be set on fire if such platforms are allowed to be misused through anonymous accounts.

One of the key game changers in the future will be the marriage of Geospatial Information Systems (GIS) with information on the IT network. GIS allows for mapping of the terrain on the ground. This can happen if our data on the ground is shared with the private sector so that GIS can be developed with reference to any region and to the extent desirable. We can focus on a village through GIS data and figure out the problems that villagers may face with respect to drinking water, sanitation, placement of schools and health facilities like primary health centres, the possibility of flooding, the nature of the soil and its composition, the availability of water for agriculture, etc. and provide solutions where required.

GIS can be used in the field of education too. Litigation floods the Supreme Court every year at the time of admission of students to medical colleges. One of the problems that confronts courts is the skewed method of assessing private medical institutions for the facilities they provide when admitting students. The method used for this is to send professors in universities to private institutions. They are called assessors. These assessors are known to submit reports which are, more often than not, in conflict with the claims made by private institutions. Private institutions are charged with providing substandard service, not having enough faculty and not enough patients in the hospital meant for clinical research—which is a fundamental requirement, apart from other benchmark conditions.

We could have a GIS system which connects every institution to a central server and at any given point in time, a professional body, independent of the government and unconnected with institutions, assesses the quality of private as well as government medical colleges, having the necessary wherewithal to admit students. This can easily be done by setting up cameras in each part of the college connected to a central server located anywhere in India. This has issues, of course, of privacy and allowing a watchful eye to monitor institutions in an invasive manner. The Union of India can formulate rules to protect the right to privacy of institutions and individuals working there, if such an infrastructure is to be put in place.

As for the necessity of excluding discretion and arbitrariness of assessors, I have found that in many of the assessments, the heart of the problem lies with the Medical Council of India (MCI)—an elected body with many of the heads of private medical colleges at the helm of its affairs. Inbuilt in the system is a conflict of interest because the heads of colleges will be inspecting their competitors in the field, which is unacceptable in any democratic set-up. While the principle of conflict of interest seems to be of great concern to the Supreme Court in the field of cricket, the same concern is absent in the context of the nature of assessments of private medical institutions.

What is required is a GIS system which looks at the facilities provided by these medical institutions so that litigation can be reduced. It will help the private sector and the professional body to monitor quality, and ensure transparency. This can't possibly be a platform through which a watchful eye monitors the functioning of individual doctors and the day-to-day functioning of institutions.

We did an experiment in the ministry to collate all data on Delhi in respect of its roads, underlying sewage systems, educational institutions, built-up structures and others and put it on a GIS platform.[21] Through this process we can monitor traffic and watch construction activities in any part of Delhi to figure out whether it is authorized or unauthorized. Through this GIS platform, we can also calculate the extent of property tax in reference to any building. Of course, if we use this system on a daily basis, it will cut at the root of corruption. No stakeholder in the system was willing to use it for public good.

We invested a lot of money in collecting data. We set up a monitoring system near Delhi Gate and demonstrated to corporations that the system was available for them to deal with multifarious issues. We could, in fact, map in advance all the areas in Delhi where water would collect at the time of the monsoon and identify the sources of mosquito breeding. The latter would allow us to take measures to prevent dengue and malaria. We can, by putting sensors in our water systems—which are underground— figure out which pipe in a particular water system has broken and carry out quick repairs. By mapping electricity distribution systems and wiring, we can also figure out the unauthorized use of power and check theft on a daily basis.

GIS technologies can also be used for planning purposes. This is possible after mapping infrastructure on the ground. That will help identify requirements in situ and become a developmental tool.

Geospatial technologies, therefore, provide an interface between government and citizens. This requires a vast network of fibre optics. The pace at which that network is being laid on the ground today will not meet even our basic needs by 2019. A fibre optic network is like a highway where instead of cars, information will flow. That will happen only if there are private players creating content. What we need is quality content. That is only possible if we liberalize our regime and allow all players—public and private—to operate on that fibre optic highway. At the moment, the fibre optic highway will connect only gram panchayats. That is not enough. We need this connectivity from the gram panchayats to the village schools, hospitals and public utilities. Unless that connectivity is established, information flow will not empower our citizens. Such an

---

[21] http://www.ciol.com/sibal-unveils-gis-technology-aid-realtime-monitoring-delhi/

outcome requires enormous capital which no private player is willing to invest because of low returns. Governments in turn do not have adequate resources at their command to realize this vision.

Lack of Vision

The recent statement by the Junior HRD Minister Satyapal Singh, that Darwin's theory of evolution by natural selection lacked scientific basis and, therefore, must be withdrawn from the school curriculum, left the scientific community shocked and dismayed. Three thousand scientists from prestigious institutions signed an online petition refuting the statement.

It is important to realize that unless we increase funding for science and education, delineate priorities in our policy and ensure that the genuine concerns of the scientific community in S&T education are addressed, our commitment to scientific research and innovation in national development would come a cropper. For a population of 1.3 billion, this is the need of the hour. The UNESCO Science Report of 2015 compliments India for building capacities in science and technology. Over the years, our scientific publication output has increased from 62,000 scientific publications to 1 lakh. As compared to 4 per cent global rate of growth in scientific publications, ours is 10 per cent. Our per dollar spend on research output is as good as that of the developed world. Because of our low-cost, high-quality human resource, one rupee spent on research in India is equal to ₹3 spent in developed countries.

However, we are still woefully lagging behind in innovation, which alone will transform our economy. Surprisingly, the number of patents sealed in India has fallen from 40 per cent in 2001–02 to 15 per cent in 2015–16. However, the patents granted by the US Patent Office to Indian applicants, mostly MNCs, have been on the rise. The 'Make in India' policy seems to have failed. Data suggests that 'Make in India' is, in fact, 'Made by MNCs in India' who control patents for their innovation. I hope, this was not the intent behind the Prime Minister's policy. In fact, in the last four years, we have not seen any substantial steps being taken on the technology transfer front. There is no policy in place by this government, unlike in China, that ensures that those who invest in India, especially in the manufacturing and strategic sectors, must transfer technologies as a precedent condition. In fact, indigenous technology development has been successful in some strategic sectors such as space and missiles. The fact that we import electronic goods worth $40 billion annually is evidence of technological decay in the absence of self-sufficiency. In 2008–09, India's R&D spend as share of GDP was 0.83 per cent. In 2016–17, it fell to 0.69 per cent. This is because private sector spend has gone up and the government's commitment is not in tandem with the private sector. In fact, funding in research is being cut down or stalled. Students are not receiving fellowships from CSIR and the University Grants Commission (UGC). Emphasis on Yoga, Ayurveda and Panchgavya seem to be the flavour of this government. While these projects do require enthusiastic support, it should not be at the expense of our national priorities. In fact, autonomous research bodies are in severe financial emergency. Though CSIR got an allocation of ₹4,000 crore in the last budget, funds available for research in the year were a little over ₹200 crore. This reflects on the poor vision of this government in the field of S&T. Whatever has happened is incremental but the dream sold by Prime Minister Modi that *desh badal raha hai* (the country is changing) does not reflect in policy initiatives of this government in the area of S&T.

Chapter 7

TRANSFORMING INDIA'S KNOWLEDGE LANDSCAPE

Education reforms during the period of 2009–12 tried to bring about a sea change in the established processes of learning. The idea was to free children from the dreary processes of formal teaching. We wished to phase out the class X board examinations to alleviate students' stress and provide a certain element of autonomy to schools by asking them to undertake school-based assessment. This, of course, would have burdened teachers because they would now have to assess the quality of each student and monitor their progress. As experience showed later, the teaching community was not entirely ready to adapt to this system. But phasing out Class X board examinations and making them optional gave the kind of freedom to children they were longing for; it was extremely popular in a lot of schools. However, a fair number of parents wanted it to be made compulsory to ensure that their children did well in Class XII.

A section of the parent community was against Class X board examinations being made optional. A section of the teaching community welcomed it while the rest found it difficult to cope with school-based assessment. We also tried to introduce a grading system to substitute marks-based assessment. We wanted to grade students to reduce the undesirable comparison of small differences in marks. In 2013–14, we tried the open text-based assessment which the board introduced for a component of about 10–15 per cent of the Class IX and XI students to help learners demonstrate original thinking. The Central Board of School Education (CBSE) also introduced the system of online marking of answer sheets to reduce paperwork and the requests for rechecks.

Another aspect was an attempt to connect school education with higher education. The MHRD decided to assign 40 per cent weightage to marks scored in the Class XII board examinations in determining eligibility for various institutions of engineering and technology. It was a challenge for the CBSE to design an appropriate method to normalize marks. The CBSE completed this process in record time. The board was also engaged in the in-service training of teachers and principals as a part of its mandate of supporting continuous professional development, which made it compulsory for all schools affiliated to it to organize at least one week of training programme every year in association with a teachers' training institute recognized by the government or by any agency identified by the CBSE. The annual reports of the MHRD reflect the thinking that education is not just an instrument to enhance efficiency, but an essential tool to augment and widen democratic participation and improve the overall quality of the young who will become proactive members of society in the future and hopefully be contributors to civil society.

The time has come for a lot of us to realize that—I think we're a bit late—if we wish to utilize the enormous potential of the demographic advantage that exists, we must not look at the number of children who go through the education process but at the quality of education imparted. The nature of education all over the world is changing fast. Literacy needs a new definition. We have to make a national effort to enhance the status and quality of teachers in this country. This cannot be done without having quality teaching institutions and programmes. With the paltry salaries of teachers throughout the country—in the exclusive domain of state governments—the teaching profession is not something that those who pass out of school opt for as their preferred option. It will never be so until we give a reasonable salary to teachers and accord them the status they enjoy in many parts of the world where they are perceived to be the architects of future generations.

Right to Education Act: A Model for the World

Between 2009 and 2012, some valiant attempts were made to bring in some structural reforms in the school education system.

When we introduced the Right of Children to Free and Compulsory Education Act (RTE) in 2009, the idea was to get all our children to school. Many opinion makers criticized us, contending that people preferred to send their children to private schools and, therefore, the proposed legislation would be counterproductive. Perhaps they were unmindful of the fact that private sector investment will happen only when there is the possibility of getting a substantial return on investment. It was our thinking that the private sector will hardly find it attractive to build schools in rural areas where people have limited capacity to pay and where there may not be enough students to make setting up a school a viable proposition. The solution that private enterprise must be given a freehand in setting up schools, we thought, was not the way forward. So, we introduced the legislation with the intent to ensure that every child must reach school and must be provided free education up to class VIII. This was not easy. It required setting up new schools to ensure that all children had access to education. Of course, parents in rural areas, who had their children helping them in farming, had to be persuaded to send them to school instead. There was no penalty for not doing so but the message was clear that we wanted to give all our children access to education.

The RTE gave an opportunity to our children between the ages of 6 and 14 to receive education for free. At the time the Act was enforced (1 April 2010), the Gross Enrolment Ratio (GER) in higher education—the ratio of students who enter Class XII and then move to the university system—was an abysmal 15 per cent, that is, out of every 100 students who passed Class XII, only 15 went into the university system. With the RTE Act, the GER today stands at about 25.2 per cent. This is a huge jump. This suggests that the Act, in terms of giving access to students to enter primary and secondary education, has been a great success. We should be supportive of the efforts that have been made since 2010 to ensure that enough number of students actually move into the university system.

The Act also attempted to address the issue of quality of education. I'm afraid consistent reports by renowned organizations who analysed its working on the ground informed us that our objective to enhance quality was not working and that children in Class III were unable to read Class I texts and children in Class V were unable to comprehend textbooks of Class II. That problem continues.[1] We tried to ensure that there were no single-teacher schools. That is why the Act provided for a student-teacher ratio—one teacher for every 30 students. However, when I went around the country, I still found schools in which there were 90 students with only one teacher. There are two problems here: One, that we need more teachers and two, teachers must be so trained that they can impart quality education. To have more teachers, we need more teacher training institutions, but the government does not have enough resources to set them up. Private teacher training institutes are few and their quality is doubtful. Some even give bogus degrees. Of course, with the technology revolution, and a fibre optic network in place, we could have one teacher providing lessons to millions, but ultimately, we need teachers on the ground. This is a real problem, the resolution of which is difficult. We tried to create an architecture of a public-private partnership in which investment was made by the private sector and a certain percentage of children were charged appropriate fees to pay for those who would get free education. There were huge complications in implementing such a model. The only way, perhaps, is to give huge incentives to the private sector in terms of tax breaks and make it a part of their Corporate Social Responsibility (CSR) to set up teachers' training institutions. We will have to address this issue seriously if we want quality education for our children.

The third element in the RTE Act was to ensure equality. The children of the rich have access to the best schools in the country; the children of the poor, as always, are left behind. They can't get admitted in these schools because private management will not admit them, and if admitted, they can't pay for their education. We decided that we would make it mandatory for private schools to admit 25 per cent of their students from

---

[1]http://www.livemint.com/Education/WgtUkpjlzUPGhMMTgepGQM/One-in-two-Indian-students-cant-read-books-meant-for-two-cl.html

the weaker and marginalized sections of society free of charge.[2] This has economic implications for private schools. It also has a social impact. A lot of parents in some schools were not happy with it. Children of that age, we thought, had no biases. A child at age 5 or 6 is not aware of caste, creed or religion and is not perhaps aware of poverty issues. We thought this is one step forward in making private schools more egalitarian and providing some of the poor children quality education.

Despite these tensions, many of the children coming from weaker sections have benefited enormously. I think, in the process, children of the rich also start to understand issues of poverty. Further into the process, this will instil in their minds the necessity for equity. That may not happen but it's a hope. The worry is, what will happen after Class VIII? I believe that the State must commit itself to free and compulsory education till Class XII. We also must cater to the children of the poor from all communities, including children of minorities who have been left behind. A nation that does not prioritize education, does not invest in its children and fails to understand that the fundamental foundation of any progressive society is based on quality education cannot possibly hope to bring prosperity to its people.

Any government committed to education must recognize the abysmal state it is in. The 2016 Annual Status of Education Report (ASER) by Pratham highlights the shortcomings in educational outcomes in India. It's interesting to note that the problem of out-of-school children between the ages of 6 and 14 has increased between 2014 and 2016 in some states. In Madhya Pradesh, it increased from 3.4 per cent to 4.4 per cent, in Chhattisgarh from 2 per cent to 2.8 per cent and in Uttar Pradesh from 4.9 per cent to 5.3 per cent and in three states—Rajasthan, Uttar Pradesh and Madhya Pradesh—out-of-school girls between ages 11 and 14 remain more than 8 per cent.[3] This shows lack of commitment of the regimes in these states.

---

[2]http://www.thehindu.com/news/national/Children-from-weaker-sections-can-now-have-access-to-private-schools/article12957998.ece
[3]http://img.asercentre.org/docs/Publications/ASER%20Reports/ASER%202016/aser2016_nationalpressrelease.pdf

In September 2009, we launched the Saakshar Bharat programme with the objective to achieve 80 per cent literacy at the national level, reduce the gender gap and minimize social disparities. We tried to target about 60 million beneficiaries who were women, and 60 per cent of the target group comprised of SCs, STs and minorities. We also tried to formulate a policy framework for Public-Private Partnerships (PPPs) in setting up schools, which did not really take off though we spent a lot of time trying to build an architecture for it. With the laying of the fibre optic network, our objective was to ensure the use of information and communication technologies in secondary schools and allow for open distance schooling. So, a draft policy on ICT in school education was prepared and posted on the ministry's website. This was also sent to various states and union territories for feedback. We evolved the National Curriculum Framework (NCF) for teachers' education in accordance with the NCF 2005. We also thought that it was important to set up an independent accreditation mechanism for school education. It is very important to accredit institutions for quality and I think if we give this task to independent agencies, it would be of great value to parents. They would be able to distinguish between institutions of quality and decide which to choose for their children. At the same time, it would also result in competition amongst schools. All schools would wish to be high on the accreditation framework. We also tried some examination reforms, making continuous and comprehensive evaluation an important element in ensuring that teachers get more involved in the progress of their students.

Radical Changes in Higher Education

We tried to bring about some fairly radical changes in higher education as well. We set up the Yashpal Committee to advise us on its renovation and rejuvenation. The recommendations of the committee were extremely important and should have been taken into account to charter the future course of education. We also set up a National Knowledge Commission, which recommended some basic structural changes in the functioning of higher education. Through these recommendations, we wished to establish an autonomous overarching National Commission for Higher Education and Research to prescribe standards of academic quality and define policies for advancement of knowledge in higher educational institutions, enhancing autonomy of such institutions. In fact, a draft legislative proposal to establish such a commission was placed on the website of the department for initiating consultations with stakeholders across the country.

Unfair practices are rampant in our educational institutions. In order to prevent them we actually formulated a draft legislation named, The Prohibition of Unfair Practices in Technical Educational Institutions, Medical Educational Institutions and University Bill, 2010, which aimed at curbing malpractices in matters relating to charging of capitation fee, making admissions dehors merit, making false claims of availability of infrastructure, faculty or about recognition of institutions. With the Supreme Court making the National Eligibility cum Entrance Test (NEET) mandatory for medical education, the problem of admissions dehors merit was substantially taken care of in this discipline. Of course, there are other challenges with respect to medical education. The oversight of the MCI has proved to be a nightmare. Every year, litigations are filed in the Supreme Court to bring some sanity into the process of medical admissions. But that sanity will never come about as long as the MCI has the responsibility of inspecting institutions. As a result, the Supreme Court is asked to decide on issues for which it doesn't have time, with allegations and counter-allegations becoming the order of the day. Because of pressure of time, justice eludes some deserving institutions. As far as medical education is concerned, we need to transform the entire system for quality through a structure which is radically different from the one that exists. We need to use the ICT framework to set it right.

It is imperative that in the field of higher education, assessment and accreditation of institutions be made mandatory. This should be done by an independent regulatory authority. We do have a National Assessment and Accreditation Council (NAAC) but it does not possess the wherewithal to manage accreditation on a national scale. We need to bring on board private authorities of unquestionable integrity to accredit institutions. Legislation to that effect—for setting up basic criteria for these accreditation authorities—could be a way forward.

Another attempt at an important reform was to establish a national education finance corporation to fulfil the need for an institutional mechanism to nurture philanthropic traditions in the education sector, and provide a means to access comparatively low-cost funds which could develop into a self-sustaining spiral for improving access and quality and enhancing the expansion needs of the sector. A corporation could also act as a refinance agency for educational loans for higher education. A PSU under the MHRD was requested to prepare a detailed project report to establish the viability of such a proposal.

We also proposed establishment of a national database of academic qualifications created and maintained in electronic format for an identified registered depository, to ensure that data in demat form is easily available as and when required by employers, students and institutions. This is of immense benefit as it eliminates the need to approach educational institutions for verifications and reduces the need for institutions to preserve academic records in physical form. The system could also eliminate fraudulent practices, such as forging certificates and marksheets.

Addressing Issues

We also need an alternative dynamic structure to address issues of quality. While elite institutions like the IITs, IISERs, NITs, IISc and others absorb the best of students after Class XII, what the nation needs is quality higher education institutions which serve students in general. Our education system and the courses we run are least suited to the demands of the workforce.

We need a three-pronged approach to address some of the issues of higher education: First, a commitment and emphasis on research not only in areas of science but also in humanities. Research alone provides the bedrock of knowledge which is fodder for the young. It is through research that we are able to think through issues that contemporary India faces. Our quality institutions in the medical and health sector should impart not just knowledge to acquire a degree but start addressing healthcare issues. Diseases that mostly affect the poor, which multinational pharmaceutical companies are not addressing, need to be tackled through our own institutions. Scholarships should be set apart for high quality students and incentives given for research in these areas.

One of the biggest roadblocks in taking healthcare to our rural folk is the lack of commitment of young doctors to serve in those areas. A part of the problem is lack of basic amenities—schools, clean water, appropriate infrastructure, healthcare and an efficient transport system. Without this, it is difficult to persuade young people to serve there. The problem, therefore, needs to be addressed holistically. State governments must identify areas where healthcare is most needed and create an ecosystem which will persuade young doctors to serve there. Christian minority institutions have had a tradition of service to the poor. Their admission processes are such that students are picked out for their sense of commitment and passion to serve even in far-flung rural areas. This has worked very well so far. But the NEET examination and some of the orders of the Supreme Court give no room to educational institutions to admit students of their choice even though all of them have cleared NEET.[4] This has created a roadblock which does not serve the national interest.

It is important to ensure that institutions do not provide backdoor entry by holding their own tests. To that extent, a uniform testing system has served the cause of equality and reduced levels of nepotism. Having done that, once a student qualifies through NEET, state counselling and admissions pursuant to the test leave no room for institutions to develop their own personality and focus. In the marketplace, unless institutions are able to show results, they will not attract students in the future. Instead of counselling, institutions should be free to admit students of their choice so that they can compete with each other in the hope that those who adopt bad practices will not be able to deliver and fall by the wayside. In this process, quality institutions will survive and the ones that do not meet the aspirations of the student community will fail. It is very

---

[4]http://www.dnaindia.com/india/report-neet-issue-supreme-court-says-no-to-separate-medical-entrance-tests-for-mbbs-bds-by-states-2210816

important to recognize that uniformity breeds mediocrity—any attempt to ensure uniformity will destroy the spirit of innovation and will be counterproductive. It is, therefore, necessary for courts to realize that while addressing the issue of equality, they should not destroy quality and suppress impulses for innovation.

The second issue that needs to be addressed is the prime need for accreditation. It is my belief that accreditation in terms of quality of every educational institution in India is imperative. Accreditation for quality must, of course, be in the hands of independent professional entities. We may even allow the private sector to provide for accreditation of institutions. This can be done by legislating on the subject and allowing entities to seek governmental recognition for being empanelled to provide accreditation facilities. Standards for such entities should be very high and must consist of professionals of high standing with an appropriate infrastructure and human resource to provide for quality service. The NAAC has, to some extent, the wherewithal to perform this function, but it neither has the vast human resource required nor the capacity to accredit all educational institutions in India in the fields of engineering, medicine, law and research institutions as well as universities and colleges. This is a humongous task and must be thrown open to others if we wish to put in place a transparent system which will allow students and their families to look at accreditation scores.

An attempt was made when the UPA was in power to introduce and pass such legislation. But again, the then Opposition led by the BJP was adamant not to allow any reforms in the education sector to pass muster in Parliament. In this context, I must add that the use of geospatial technology would also enable students to look at accreditation scores of individual institutions sitting in their homes and deciding which institution to go to. If this happens, it will be a dream come true, but I'm afraid the present dispensation is not even looking at these issues in right earnest.

The third issue is the highly regulated structural dispensation in the MHRD. The UGC is both a funding and a regulatory agency. As a first step, these two functions should be separated. Funding should be divorced from regulation and a separate funding agency should be set up which looks at the needs of institutions in the context of societal priorities and concerns.

Recently, the MHRD has proposed to restructure the UGC.[5] This government suddenly seems to have woken up to the reality that the education sector needs fundamental reforms. After being a dog in the manger by opposing the agenda of reforms of the UPA and having wasted four precious years since 2014, the government has suddenly fired a salvo by proposing to repeal the University Grants Commission Act, 1956 and hoping to replace it with the Higher Education Commission of India. The proposed legislation has incorporated some of the features of the National Knowledge Commission and the Yashpal Committee recommendations in attempting to set up this new Commission—a regulatory body dealing with multifarious issues relating to academic standards, setting up of higher education institutions, supporting academic operations, etc. The worrisome aspect of the proposed legislation is to allow government to control funding of all educational institutions. The ministry will now have the power to make allocations to institutions. The Bill's hidden agenda is perhaps to control institutions by controlling their purse strings. The absolute and unilateral powers given to the Commission to authorize, monitor and shut down higher education institutions expose the sector to ideological manipulations. In the desire to impose uniformity in the sector, it will kill the spirit of innovation. Power concentrated in the hands of the ministry may be used as a weapon of coercion. We have, in the last four years, seen universities being manipulated through appointment of vice chancellors of a particular ideological mindset. If the government has the power to fund or withhold funding of educational institutions, it may jeopardize academic freedom. Even more worrisome is the proposal that the chairperson of the Commission be selected from among functionaries of the Central or state governments. This strikes at the very root of academic independence. With bureaucrats assigned to be the driving force, universities will henceforth function at the pleasure of the government. Even though, presently, the UGC controls both setting

---

[5]https://indianexpress.com/article/education/hrd-ministry-proposes-to-restructure-ugc-repeal-act-5235463/

up of academic standards and funding, at least there are systems in place, with the involvement of academics, which allow the relatively independent functioning of the UGC. Conceptually, the UPA was opposed to the UGC being both a funding and a regulatory agency. Both the Yashpal Committee and the National Knowledge Commission sought to set up an independent agency, removed from the government, to decide on funding processes. This did not allow for governmental interference. That salutary principle has been discarded. What we have is a solution which is much worse than the malaise. The spirit behind this commission is not academic reforms but subjugation of the academic community.

The government should not hesitate in funding private institutions. The regulatory mechanism must allow institutions to grow and receive corporate funding. We must ensure that just because an institution receives corporate or private funding, government contributions and funding are not reduced.

The management of institutions should be left to the institutions. Appointments even in the IITs should be made by the IIT itself through a process they may themselves evolve. We must assume that the desire to improve is embedded in the institution's structure itself. Unfortunately, instead of giving freedom to institutions to flower, we are making them subservient to those who sit in the corridors of power. It is a matter of great disquiet that many of the IIT directors are chosen for their ideological affiliations, and the constitution of panels for selection is so manoeuvred that the candidate to be selected is already determined before the committee sits for interviews.[6] Not only is this extremely destructive of the autonomy of the institution, it makes the institution—through its director chosen in collaboration with the government—subservient to the government. The fact that the government funds IITs cannot be the basis for controlling them. The logic that since public money is expended and provided by the government, therefore the government must have control, is flawed. The government has a societal obligation to fund these institutions. The taxpayer's money is used to set up high-quality

---

[6]https://www.ndtv.com/india-news/selection-process-of-iit-directors-like-running-lottery-anil-kakodkar-765354

institutions. The government is a mere repository of trust with money spent for public good.

IITs, IIMs, IISERs, NITs, NIITs and all other such institutions should have complete freedom to manage their affairs, to appoint faculty at different levels without constraints and to have a roadmap for their own future depending on their priorities, which will represent the collective wisdom of those who are at the helm of affairs in these institutions. It is only then, and then alone, that education will serve larger societal ends. Institutions should be free to decide on the courses of study, the nature of curriculum and the manner in which it is to be taught. Let each institution develop public recognition of its unique qualities. Then alone will children have a real choice. Public interest will be best served if we allow such institutions to discover their own genius. The kind of controls that the UGC and the All India Council for Technical Education (AICTE) exercise are antediluvian. In a country where urbanization has led to the spiralling prices of land, it is impossible for any institution to meet the parameters set by the AICTE. That, of course, does not mean that institutions may be allowed to mushroom in every city without complying with quality standards, but let that be done through appropriate agencies and not under the direct control of the government. Let those systems be made transparent. Here again, the use of information and geospatial technology can serve the ends of transparency and ensure that institutions, through a self-disclosure process, can be both accredited and allowed to function without government surveillance.

Recently, the NDA has taken a policy decision to give autonomy to some institutions of higher education. This will enable those institutions to devise their own curriculum. They are also given the freedom to introduce new courses which do not come within the regulatory supervision of the ministry. While this autonomy is a welcome step, the problem lies in the ability of those very institutions to access funds. The ministry has also clarified that 30 per cent of the increase in emoluments of teachers under the 7th Pay Commission will have to be borne by the institutions themselves through resources that they will have to raise. The attempt to grant autonomy allows these institutions to hire faculty at salaries which need not comply with the norms laid down by the UGC. The policy prescription, however, is not clear about the applicability of the reservation policy of the Government of India.

The problem with this initiative is that many of these universities may not be able to raise funds to finance the upgradation required in respect of education infrastructure as well as liabilities consequent upon change in curriculum and faculty salaries, without all of which the institutions can never achieve global standards. It is yet to be seen how these institutions seize this opportunity to transform the quality of education. The cost of this transformation will ultimately have to be passed on to the students.

Many of the students who have access to these institutions do not necessarily belong to families who have the capacity to meet any substantial increase in fees. The possibility of seeking loans from public sector banks to finance higher expenditure by a student is unlikely. Public sector banks are already overburdened with non-payment of educational loans by students on account of their inability to find jobs. With the current state of NPAs in public sector banks, it is unlikely that there will be any scheme for financing university education in such institutions. This will be yet another Startup India scheme that will fail. There will, of course, be some institutions which get financed by the private sector and benefit from this scheme. The daunting task that faces India is that the demographic dividend we expect from our young population entering into the university system can only be achieved if the quality of higher education is enhanced throughout India. In its absence, an oasis in a desert will only increase disparities and lead to angst and dissatisfaction.

The MHRD has also failed to realize that, today, education is being transformed at such a fast pace that we need to think of innovative and transformative ways to ensure that quality education reaches students in higher education across the country without investing too much in physical assets and without paying faculty from abroad. First, very few teachers across the Atlantic or from the UK will be motivated to shift residence. They will be facing many problems, such as lack of facilities like healthcare and education for their children, and other issues qua their families. Besides, very few faculty would like to shift permanently, committed to the cause of higher education in India. The salaries they may be offered may not be commensurate with their earnings, in the event that we wish to access the best faculty in the world. This is not a well-thought-out initiative, and it is likely to create more problems for the institutions.

This government, perhaps, does not have either the commitment or the resources to improve the quality of higher education. Nor has it, in the last four years, conceived a policy framework within which quality upgradation could be achieved. The changes that the UPA had conceived of were an attempt to improve quality by making structural changes. That is why the National Knowledge Commission sought the bifurcation of institutional funding from regulatory control and made other systemic changes. But at that time, the NDA opposed every reform that was sought to be initiated in the education sector without any rational basis. Massive funding is required, apart from commitment, if higher education is to be reformed.

The UPA had conceived the idea of setting up 14 innovation universities with global standards. These universities were to be set up in fields which would seek to solve problems confronting society. These were not to be run-of-the-mill institutions, which, in today's India, emphasize rote learning and have no direct connection to the problems faced by people. The UPA was also attempting, through academic reforms, to persuade universities to give an impetus to research mandated under the Central Universities Act, 2009. The UPA believed that the semester system, choice-based credit system and regular revision of syllabi, if mandated after consultation with all stakeholders, would be a positive step in transforming higher education. It is with this intent that the ministry had taken up the matter with 24 older central universities to raise the reform agenda before their statutory authorities so that the changes suggested could be adopted for facilitating academic reforms.

In the new digital world, we need fresh ideas to empower our students. The digital world allows innovative solutions which will not necessarily raise the cost of higher education. These are solutions that will allow access to foreign faculty without them having to travel to

India; solutions that will give access to courses of high quality from outside India.

Innovative syllabi involving universities around the world could be the basis of accessing new knowledge and interacting with the best students and faculty around the world. We have seen the spectre of mafias operating in the education sector, which we believe are linked to political establishments, allowing for exams to be taken by persons other than the candidates. This happened in the case of Vyapam (Madhya Pradesh Professional Examination Board) in Madhya Pradesh. As long as governments turn a blind eye and a deaf ear and show no commitment to dismantling such mafias, this transformation is going to be a mirage. The recent paper leaks in the CBSE examination, the mafia operating in the Staff Selection Commission (SSC), etc. are all examples of a government unable and unwilling to transform the education sector.

It is sad that almost four years down the road of this government, the MHRD has not thought of reforms. I wonder what this government has been doing. It is more obsessed with controlling institutions by installing vice chancellors in universities and heads of institutions of higher education who are closely linked to the ideology of the RSS. The dismantling of the academic culture in India is for all to see. This is the transformation that they have attempted to bring about. That is where they think they have succeeded. But it has nothing to do with education; it has everything to do with politics.

State of Secondary Education

Empowerment of our children and future generations depends ultimately on three factors: first, access to education; second, ensuring that this access provides for quality education; and third, that no child is left out of the system to ensure equity. These are the three pillars on which the education structure must stand.

In 2009 during UPA-II, I was cognizant of the challenges ahead in the field of education. The Union government has somewhat limited powers for implementation of the three pillars that I listed. Education being a state subject, responsibility for implementation rests on state governments. The launch of the Rashtriya Madhyamik Shiksha Abhiyan (RMSA) catered to providing state governments with financial support to ensure access to quality and equal education.[7] Through this scheme, the MHRD could and did monitor both the need and the extent of funding required in various states. To some extent, therefore, the ministry attempted to ensure that the money allocated was spent, but on many occasions, the states did not have the capacity to spend the sums allocated.

It is a challenge to ensure that education imparted at the secondary level subscribes to norms, removes socio-economic and disability barriers and addresses gender concerns. We must ensure that the gross enrolment ratio in secondary schools is as near to 100 per cent as possible. The Rashtriya Madhyamik Shiksha Abhiyan (RMSA) aimed to achieve an enrolment rate of 75 per cent—from 52.26 per cent in 2005–06—by providing a secondary school within a reasonable distance of any habitation. The other objectives included improving quality of education by making all secondary schools conform to prescribed norms, removing gender, socio-economic and disability barriers, providing universal access to secondary level education by 2017—by the end of the 12th Five Year Plan—and achieving universal retention by 2020.

The scheme provided for additional classrooms, laboratories, libraries, art and craft rooms, toilet blocks, drinking water and residential hostels for teachers in remote areas to improve physical infrastructure. There were quality interventions by way of appointment of additional teachers to reduce pupil-teacher ratio to 30:1; focus on Science, Maths and English education; in-service training of teachers; science laboratories; ICT-enabled education; curriculum reforms and teaching-learning reforms. The scheme also included equity interventions like giving preference to Ashram schools for upgradation, preference to areas with concentration of SC/ST/minorities for opening of schools, special enrolment drive for the weaker sections, more female teachers in schools and separate toilet blocks for girls.[8]

---

[7]http://mhrd.gov.in/rmsa
[8]Ibid

The 2017 ASER report which focusses on the age group of 14–18 reveals that about 25 per cent of students cannot read basic texts fluently in their own language and about 57 per cent struggle with solving basic arithmetic problems.[9] It suggests that the demographic dividend that we keep talking about will turn into a demographic nightmare if this issue is not addressed immediately.

As far as the dropout rate of students at the secondary level is concerned, the dropout rate amongst ST students is 19.2 per cent while for SC students, it is as high as 26 per cent, compared to the all-India average of 17.8 per cent.[10] However, this rate is asymmetrical and varies from state to state. In a state like Odisha, the dropout rate is as high as 30 per cent. All this suggests that in the less prosperous states and states with a large SC and ST population, dropouts from these communities are high—an indication of why, in public services, enough candidates from those categories are not available either at the entry level or at the promotional level.

The high cost of education is a serious concern. The Economic Survey 2016–17 notes that 31 per cent of those who move up to Class XII do not access higher education. For women, the dropout rate is around 30 per cent because of domestic activities. While about 16 per cent of those who reach Class XII do not move higher because they are not interested in doing so, 15 per cent cannot because of financial constraints. The problem that our kids face, even those who move up to Class XII, is the cost of education, which has made education burdensome for the marginalized and the less privileged. This cost has gone up because of the increase in input costs. It is estimated that the average annual private expenditure on general education per student through schooling has increased from ₹2,461 in 2007–08 to ₹6,788 per student in 2014.[11,12]

---

[9] http://img.asercentre.org/docs/Publications/ASER%20Reports/ASER%202017/aser2017nationalfindings.pdf
[10] http://www.indiaspend.com/cover-story/why-merely-fixing-schools-will-not-bring-back-children-to-classrooms-35647
[11] https://www.indiabudget.gov.in/es2016-17/echap10_vol2.pdf
[12] https://www.business-standard.com/article/current-affairs/available-but-unaffordable-story-of-higher-education-in-india-116123100779_1.html

Another element of cost is the attractiveness of private institutions that provide coaching. At the level of secondary education, such coaching represents 30 per cent of the total expenditure incurred and in urban areas it is around 45 per cent. Consequently, cost has become a key element in the choice of parents and students in accessing education.

The Rot in the MCI

I think the biggest scandal in recent years relates to the functioning of the MCI, which sends inspectors who are required to give their reports on the wherewithal available in medical institutions seeking recognition both at the time of entry and every year thereafter for a period of five years. The scandal, despite data available, has not been recognized even by the Supreme Court.[13] The mafia operating this system includes the MCI, its officials, a few chosen professors who inspect most frequently and the central government, which often favours institutions set up by those close to it. The Vyapam scam itself, and the fact that till date no meaningful investigation has taken place despite the death of over 50 people connected with it, is a telling example of the levels of corruption that have permeated a sector which is meant to serve the healthcare needs of society.[14] That outsiders were allowed to sit for exams in collaboration with the authorities, and politicians were involved in the subversion of the processes of admission into medical institutions, are not just matters of great concern, but are symptomatic of the malaise that we are confronted with in the admissions process.

The rot that has crept into the MCI cannot possibly be removed without structural surgery. Elected bodies of professionals, given their past track records and their own deep interests in those institutions, are wholly unsuited to regulate medical institutions in India. Though a Bill has been moved in Parliament seeking to put an alternative structure in place, I'm afraid that there will be vested interests that might impede

---

[13]https://www.outlookindia.com/magazine/story/its-inspector-vs-inspector/297990
[14]https://timesofindia.indiatimes.com/city/bhopal/vyapam-scam-probe-2-years-on-cbi-yet-to-make-a-major-breakthrough/articleshow/59568554.cms

the process of change.[15] The merits of the Bill are also highly suspect.

The extent of the rot cannot just be attributed to the MCI. The political establishment must share a part of the responsibility. Those closely associated with the corridors of power can get relief through the MCI. Alternatively, if the MCI stands up to oppose approval of substandard medical institutions in the hands of the private sector, the central government, which is the final approving authority, overrides these recommendations. This creates societal heartburn. Institutions which are allegedly marginally deficient on certain parameters get left out while those which are abysmally substandard get a green flag to move ahead. What is even more surprising is that when such scandalous approvals are brought to the notice of the court, even the court turns a blind eye. This is even more troublesome since courts give somewhat unconvincing reasons for not interfering—opining that there is no petition pending to challenge such unconscionable approvals while facts stare them in the face. In a sense, what's happened in the MCI is symptomatic of the entire culture of education with a nexus among politicians, the statutory approving authority and the government. This is insidious. It is unfortunate that there are no rules or norms which are either set in place or otherwise accepted and adhered to when dealing with approvals of institutions. The admissions process in these institutions is equally flawed and where demand far outstrips supply, the consequent aberrations in terms of capitation fee come into play.

The architectural structure under which educational institutions function needs to be looked at afresh. Regulations need to be reduced and court interference restricted. For the court to take an ideological position by opining that education is not a business but an occupation, and thereafter regulating all aspects of it, is a matter of concern. While the court's intervention may be justified when confronted with rampant corruption and discrimination, it should hesitate to provide policy prescriptions in this regard. The genesis of the problem, of course, is public pressure, when a vast majority of students are incapable of meeting

---

[15]http://medicaldialogues.in/national-medical-commission-bill-to-replace-mci-finalized-with-changessent-to-cabinet/

the demands of the costs of higher education. To provide quality medical education, there is a price to be paid. The cost is determined on the quality of infrastructure, capital costs necessary to provide education of high quality and continuing revenue costs in terms of salaries and other such expenditure. Since the financial capacity of a vast majority of students is inadequate to meet the demands of high quality private institutions, a lot of students compete to seek admission in government institutions in which education is subsidized. It's this tension emanating from the capacity to pay which is the genesis of the crisis that prevails in professional institutions of higher education.

The other problem is that many of those who are meritorious are so because of the advantage of the quality education they received during their schooling. They have a natural advantage in maintaining higher ranks or merit and availing of subsidized professional education in government institutions. Here again, the poor, who have unequal opportunities in their schooling, are occasionally lower in rank, and not having succeeded in getting admitted to government professional institutions, don't have the capacity to pay private institutions who do not subsidize education. The cost of professional education in private aided and unaided institutions ranges between 1.5 to 2.5 times of that incurred in government institutions.

In responding to this endemic problem, courts have allowed states to set up fee fixation committees, which in turn, impact the quality of education.[16] Regulation of fees is also the result of public pressure when politicians cater to the community seeking lower fees while demanding high-quality education. In many cases, that's not possible, especially in professional education. Consequently, state governments ensure, through subtle mechanisms, that the fee fixation committees do not adequately compensate institutions for the costs of high-quality professional education, and this impacts the economics of running these institutions. It leads to litigation and a large part of the institution's time is spent in seeking orders from courts, which are cognizant of the public pressure to lower costs. These complex issues can only be resolved if the political

---

[16] https://ccimindia.org/downloads/21%20to%2024%20Commentary%20on%20admission%20&%20fee%20Committees.pdf

establishment does not pander to populist demands and recognizes that if you want quality doctors and engineers, then costs will have to be paid. Systems will have to be devised for students to meet such costs if they are meritorious and do not have the means to pay for their education.

And last of all, the courts must not take an ideological position to state that education cannot be perceived as a business for profit. We must appreciate the fact that any educational institution which caters to quality must ultimately be competitive in the marketplace. It must be ahead of others and perceived to be providing high-quality education. Those institutions which do not do so and are short on infrastructure and quality faculty, will naturally not be attractive to students and these will eventually fall by the wayside. It's important to allow market forces to operate. On the other hand, the government must ensure high-quality infrastructure and quality faculty, along with other requirements necessary for quality education in its own institutions. These are issues which require public debate; if not during parliamentary sittings, then in committees looking into education. We need to be accommodative and yet not jettison quality. I hope we find the right solutions.

We find that there are a large number of institutions which have shut shop over the years. Engineering colleges have vacant seats in thousands because of the overcapacity created at the time when a lot of students were attracted to engineering courses. Around 5,000 seats in medical institutions will go vacant this year itself because of the highly unprofessional way in which the MCI deals with assessing these institutions on the anvil of the norms set up by it.[17]

National Knowledge Commission

Employment and skill development are other areas in which the State has not been able to make impressive strides. Policy interventions in the past have not borne much fruit. In fact, we do not have appropriately accurate figures on the levels of unemployment or underemployment in

---

[17] http://indiatoday.intoday.in/education/story/5-000-seats-vacant-in-medical-and-dental-colleges-across-the-states/1/796970.html

India. The informal unorganized sector absorbs most of the workforce in India. The employment landscape represents exorbitantly high levels of underemployment. Educational institutions don't prepare students for the labour market. Quite apart from that, on account of rigid labour laws, entities are hesitant to give regular employment because of increasing costs involved. Consequently, contract labour is the only way to reduce costs and survive in a highly competitive environment. The National Skill Development Corporation (NSDC), concentrating on 24 high-priority sectors, was hopeful of skilling 150 million young men and women by 2022.[18,19] Accordingly, short-term as well as long-term skill training is imparted through ITIs and model skill centres are being set up in every district. Part of the problem is that skill development is not a priority for young men and women. Those who access such institutions are the ones for whom this is not a choice of their preference. Institutions have also not been able to skill candidates suited to the demands of the market. That requires appropriate investments which are not visible. There is also a prime need for an appropriate academic structure by which a student can move from a regular academic course to a skill-development course or vice versa. A lot of individuals have acquired skills over the years even in the absence of academic training for which there is no means of recognition. Attempts have been made to build a framework within which prior learning and experience can be recognized and benchmarked. We have yet to grapple with the multifarious problems relating to skill development and the education system is yet to provide answers for the above.

The UPA tried, through the report of the National Knowledge Commission, to radically change the structure of higher education. The commission was constituted on 13 June 2005 with a time frame of three years, from 2 October 2005 to 2 October 2008. It attempted to provide a framework to build excellence in the education system, focussing on the need to meet the knowledge challenges of the 21st century. Attempts were made to promote knowledge in science and technology laboratories,

---

[18]https://www.nsdcindia.org/New/vision-mission-0#
[19]https://www.nsdcindia.org/New/faqs

improve the management of institutions, create intellectual property and promote applications in agriculture and industry. The core concerns of the National Knowledge Commission were easy access to knowledge, creation and preservation of knowledge systems, dissemination of knowledge and better knowledge services.[20] What is needed is breaking down the walls between research bodies and universities. IITs and IIMs are perhaps oases of knowledge but they exist in silos. We need to break down this isolation. We need to make sure that students who pass out of institutions of higher learning obtain skills that are aligned to those required in the real world. This is because academics is no longer problem-oriented. It does not integrate different branches of knowledge into a holistic framework. Private industry must work with academic institutions in the field of engineering and management.

The curriculum framework of higher education must be broadened to give choices to students who are interested in multidisciplinary education. We must move away from the entrance examination system and look at outcomes. Evaluation of knowledge through a highly rigid examination system is hardly the way forward if we wish to produce young men and women who have the capacity to confront the real world and provide solutions for the challenges ahead. Knowledge must be used to study local issues and problems. Local data, wherever the institution finds itself, must be accessed and, within that framework, problems confronting society in that area must be resolved. There should be compulsory exposure and engagement with different kinds of work. Such occupational exposure is necessary to prepare a student when she or he steps into the real world. Syllabi must be designed with that objective in mind. Partnership amongst institutions should be encouraged, especially institutions which are proximate to each other. Faculty must find creative ways of ensuring that such institutions engage with each other. The State must bring in a framework through which complete autonomy is available to institutions of higher learning, which is fundamental in any attempt to pursue knowledge. The institution should develop its own framework of control without any government interference. Such institutions must breed

---

[20]http://knowledgecommissionarchive.nic.in/downloads/report2009/eng/report09.pdf

a culture of independence; they must be allowed institutional protection to prevent any form of intervention from outside players.

The proposal to set up a commission for higher education and research and give it constitutional status was intended to achieve the objectives of autonomy, transparency and freedom from government control. The present government, in March 2017, gave the nod for the Higher Education Empowerment Regulation Agency (HEERA) which sought to replace existing higher education regulatory bodies like the UGC and the AICTE, but it has been reportedly put on hold.[21] It is important that accreditation norms be universalized and vocational education be assimilated within the university and college system. Alienation of this sector has resulted in a lack of skill development. A holistic view of education is, therefore, necessary. Existing regulatory bodies in the education sector must be subsumed into an apex regulatory body. This will ensure that there is no fragmentation of knowledge. All knowledge must be treated in an integrated manner.

Unless the present establishment sheds its obsession with the past and deals with the challenges of contemporary India, unless it recognizes that those who step out of the university system must be fully equipped to meet the challenges of a world where knowledge is at the centre of all human conundrums, we will remain a static, stratified society with the youth themselves ill-equipped for an India that needs innovation to meet the challenges of a highly competitive world.

Completing the project of laying the fibre optic network and connecting it to schools and hospitals and centres of municipal services will be a great boon for the community, especially for our children's education. It is in this context that I had conceived of the Aakash tablet, which in the hands of our young, could have perhaps become the most empowering tool for educating themselves and accessing information in tune with their interests. One wonders why this government has not moved forward in this direction. Instead, it is seemingly committed to changing the content of our textbooks, not with the objective of empowering our children but

---

[21]https://economictimes.indiatimes.com/industry/services/education/plan-to-replace-ugc-aicte-with-heera-on-hold/articleshow/60146472.cms

to use this as a vehicle to propagate personalities and mindsets akin to the RSS ideology and extol the virtues of our Prime Minister and the decisions that he has taken. Obviously, this government has no understanding of the purpose of education. Education is a constant endeavour to discover. That is true not just of children but of adults and all those who seek to enrich themselves. Tailor-made textbooks with the objectives of the kind sought by this government are the very antithesis of education.

It's important for our children to discover the concept of virtue and, through their journey of discovery, become responsible citizens. Inculcating virtue is something that needs to be discovered through interactions within a classroom amongst excited young minds dealing with problems of contemporary society, so as to impress upon them the value of resolving differences and conflicts through dialogue and understanding. That is why a programme like Swachh Bharat has a positive impact as we teach our children to embrace cleanliness as a way of life. This is because children will be able to associate themselves with such a national campaign. What we need to teach them is the virtue of cleanliness. We need to teach them the virtue of togetherness, of peace, of the strength of our commonality, our multifaceted culture, respect for language and, most of all, the importance of opinions, which cater to debates and resolutions. Education needs to inculcate these values; not include chapters on demonetization or GST and, thereby, extol the virtues of the Prime Minister and the party in power.[22] Values need to be understood, not thrust on young minds.

The Aakash tablet would have given our children access to all kinds of information to discover the path of rectitude. The internet, therefore, is perhaps the greatest highway for empowerment ever conceived by man. It'll be a pity if our children are not provided access to that highway. There can be alternative ways of achieving the same end and one can't be didactic about a particular mode of doing it, but at least there should be thought processes at work in the MHRD to achieve this end. I don't see that happening.

This highway of information can also be used for targeting bogus

---

[22]https://thewire.in/147887/rajasthan-textbooks-revised-glorify-modi-government/

degrees. We in the UPA wanted all degrees to be awarded in demat form also and stored in a repository which could, with payment of a nominal fee, give information as and when needed. A lot of work had been done in this area. All that we needed was to mandate all universities and institutions of higher education to uplink degrees in demat form. Finally, the National Academic Depository (NAD) was launched on 9 July 2017 by the MHRD and UGC by appointing NSDL Database Management Limited (NDML) to facilitate academic institutions to digitally issue certificates and degrees.

The politicization of education will ultimately be detrimental to the growth of young minds and would be subversive, in that our young will be influenced not by information but by propaganda. With the laying of the information highway, quality lectures could flow to millions of young minds desirous of acquiring knowledge. This would also be a great equalizer.

One of the impediments to equality, especially in the field of education, is that quality of education differs from institution to institution and there is a hierarchy of institutions in which those at the top end are inaccessible for the poor and marginalized students. However, one could develop a host of lectures, a series of learning programmes in any field of knowledge and have the best of our teachers provide the content and make them accessible on the information highway. Such content would reach every inquisitive mind for self-empowerment. There could also be lectures where students could access the content by payment of a nominal amount. An outstanding teacher in mathematics could, through such lectures, teach every student in schools around the country. Even interactive sessions could take place. That should be the focus. Through such sessions we can discover the best of minds. How is it that in cricket we now have the most talented cricketers emerging from rural India? Cricket could reach rural India and give talented young people a chance. A similar attempt through information technology will allow the marginalized access to the best minds in India.

On the other hand, we have discovered how information technology perpetrates inequality when misused. We are an ideal example of how the rich, the powerful and the connected abuse the network to allow students to gain admission to medical and engineering institutions. Recently, the Delhi Police arrested three people for running a pan-India fake degree racket. They had been running this racket since 2002 and had sold around 50,000 fake degrees and certificates.[23] The discovery of this scam is at a nascent stage. We know that the investigating authorities will not catch the big fish which might lead to political bigwigs being implicated. There may be many more such scams which have not yet been exposed. What we need is a mindset ensuring that technology is used constructively for salutary ends.

---

[23]https://www.outlookindia.com/newsscroll/delhi-police-busts-fake-degree-racket-3-arrested/1241352

Chapter 8

DECLINE OF THE UPA GOVERNMENT: WHEN PERCEPTIONS OUTPLAYED FACTS

In the 2014 general elections, we not only lost, but lost badly. In boxing terms, one could say that we were mauled. It is difficult to surgically assess the reasons for this loss. It would be unfair to attribute it to the prevailing cross-currents over which we had no control. The bottom line is that people wanted change.

Change, in normal circumstances, should be welcome. There cannot be a way forward without change. It is a fact that with almost 1.3 billion people in a highly complex political, economic and social structure, it is difficult to resolve overnight the problems of large sections of the population. There are communities in this country which, in terms of statistics, could constitute another nation. The nation does not have enough resources at its command to cater to all the needs of the masses, who constantly want change for a better tomorrow.

It was not that the UPA-I and II did not make genuine efforts to improve the lives of those at the bottom of the pyramid; we introduced some path-breaking legislation to cater to their needs, especially in the context of their daily tryst for survival.

MGNREGA helped families living at subsistence levels and provided support to those who needed jobs within the localities in which they lived. The minimum job guarantee for 100 days under MGNREGA served as social security, which had two definite implications: One, that it halted the exodus from the rural to the urban centres, and second, it also resulted in the rise of wages due to scarcity of labour in some parts of the country. Clearly, MGNREGA was a beneficial legislation which positively impacted the lives of millions.

Yet, the scheme was vilified by the Opposition as wasteful expenditure involving diversion of funds and massive corruption. So why did a programme, the outcome of which was beneficial to the community, become a punching bag for the Opposition? One possibility is that we in government were not savvy enough to convince people that it was a great programme. Our ministers did not talk about it on a daily basis. Neither the electronic media nor the print media gave it the prominence it deserved. Within the system, the forces of change somehow got the better of us, and we as a party and as individuals contributed to it.

Even though Prime Minister Modi castigated the programme on the floor of the House, today, having realized the inherent significance of its outcomes, it is one of the programmes carried forward by this government, but without the kind of funding it deserves.

Battle of Perception

The notion of presumptive loss, created by the then CAG, in the allocation of spectrum and coal blocks gave rise to allegations of scams of the highest order. Right decisions, even if there may have been individual aberrations, were portrayed as acts of vandalism by the Opposition. We were painted by the media as a corrupt lot, frittering away valuable national resources, benefiting specific entities, and were charged with crony capitalism. I believe all of this could have been defended. We should have stood up collectively to the decisions that we made. A few of us unsuccessfully attempted to justify our position. Unfortunately, we did not use the tactics which the present dispensation adopts. Today, when any news adverse to the government is placed in the public domain, the media refuses to pick it up. There is no explanation for this. Those in power can very well say that the media, in its wisdom, does not consider such adverse reports as valued news items, but the more probable explanation is the control this government exercises on both electronic and print media, which in turn, is owned by industrial houses, who constantly seek the help of government in their business and industrial enterprises. To my mind, this is the most quintessential form of crony capitalism because it creates a situation in which favours are granted if news is kept under wraps.

We could not halt the tide of misinformation because we chose not to exercise that kind of control and arm-twist those who disseminate news. The democratic fabric of this country and its sustenance is far more important than either the acquisition or the sustenance of political power. We cannot denigrate and stymie institutions which are pillars of democracy for the crass, political objective of self-aggrandisement of power.

This was not all. In the aftermath of these alleged scams, we witnessed the rise of a phenomenon that has now been eclipsed—Anna Hazare and all those who joined the bandwagon in an attempt to put in place a law that everybody has now conveniently forgotten. Hazare's rise was facilitated by the universal belief that corruption was an issue that needed to be addressed immediately. There is no doubt that corruption is a major menace that needs to be dealt with on a war footing. But since the UPA government was already perceived to be corrupt in the public eye, the anti-corruption crusade, encouraged by its constant presence in the media, especially in the electronic media, created a situation in which Hazare and those who wished to ride on his shoulders sought from the government the creation of a committee to formulate a model law to deal with corruption. The government succumbed, which I believe was a mistake. The committee was set up and the outcome was ultimately reflected in the formulation of a model law by the Sense of the House Resolution in Parliament. During the course of the agitation, Hazare threatened the government and went on a fast unto death. The government relented, and the fast was broken. Hazare was taken into custody and the drama that followed in Tihar jail resulted in his release. All these events portrayed the government as weak, unsure and defeated in its responses. No government can afford to portray that kind of image. This, along with the dramatics of Baba Ramdev, made the government look like it was not in control of the situation.

Our meeting with Ramdev at the Delhi airport was a big mistake. Our intent was different, but it was interpreted as if the functionaries of the government were afraid of Ramdev entering the capital and, therefore, sought to negotiate with him at the airport. The optics were hurtful to the government's image and the outcome was worse. Ramdev reneged on the promise that he had made to the representatives of the government. Much was made of the events that followed at Ramlila ground. It was made to look as if the government was persecuting Ramdev.

The unfortunate Nirbhaya incident of December 2012, and the candlelight marches and skirmishes with the police that followed, again, portrayed the government as unresponsive. In a sense, the government was blamed for the dastardly act of brutal rape and murder of a young girl.

Finding Our True Strength

Our defeat can also be attributed, to some extent, to the fact that in many states in India, our committed cadre had moved away to other political parties; perhaps not entirely, but in large measure. We still have a strong cadre in Kerala and in some other states, but the cadre in Uttar Pradesh, in particular, is all but non-existent, especially since we have not been in power in the state for over 20 years now. In Madhya Pradesh and Rajasthan, too, we do have an organizational structure on the ground. The fact is wherever the Congress and BJP are the only rival parties in the state, the cadre does exist, but wherever there is a triangular contest or where a third political party has made its presence felt, we see the cadre diminishing.

At the booth level, people get attracted to cadres because they need help to address their everyday concerns. If a party has not been in power for over 20 years, the worker is inclined to transfer her or his loyalty to another political party. This did not happen prior to independence since the entire Congress party was committed to India's freedom. The position has radically altered post-independence. But for those who are committed to the Congress party, they will never dissociate themselves from it, which is why even today we find a Congress loyalist in every part of India.

Families over generations have been committed to the Congress party.

That, indeed, is the strength of the Congress. But over the years, the party leadership at the regional and local levels has not concentrated its energies and focussed on strengthening the party at the booth level. The local cadres are not provided with the leadership that they need for strengthening their bond with the party and for the commitment required to spread the party's message. Pradesh Congress Committee (PCC) chiefs, on many occasions, have not been appointed for long periods of time. We need to develop a bond with the grass-roots-level worker. In this, the Congress satraps play a crucial role since they are the ones who are heard by the leadership. With tensions developing at the local level, workers get alienated and look for greener pastures on the other side, where they hope to get recognition. Inability to strengthen the party's organizational base and spread the core of our ideology is one of the most important reasons for the party losing strength over the years.

Our inability to attract youth is another area of concern. Those who have reached the age of 18 and are entitled to vote, have witnessed several allegations against the Congress party, in their growing years. They have grown up in the midst of the Anna Hazare movement, and witnessed the rise of Arvind Kejriwal and the venom and vituperation with which he attacked the defenceless leadership of the Congress. They have witnessed the era when Parliament was stalled for prolonged durations and heard the fiery speeches of the Opposition alleging not just corruption against the Congress but charging the then UPA government with policy paralysis for which, in fact, the Opposition itself was largely to blame.

All the issues raised from October 2010 onwards have now been forgotten by the present government because they were only meant to castigate the then UPA government. The Lokpal is still not in place. Aadhaar, which the BJP opposed, is now their flagship programme as if its virtues were discovered by them. MGNREGA is now openly supported, though with insubstantial allocations, and a delivery mechanism which is questionable. The concept of Digital India was, in fact, the idea of the UPA, groundwork for which was prepared with the laying of the fibre optic network. The CAG no longer interferes with policy prescriptions as the erstwhile CAG did in the years before 2014. Stalling of Parliament is no longer a strategy that can be legitimately used by the present Opposition. Ramdev is silent about black money. Corruption as an issue has died down despite its potent presence in every activity involving the government. Big scandals are not allowed to erupt because of the kind of control this government exerts over the investigating agencies. Courts seem to be less concerned about corruption than they were ever before. The corporate sector is vulnerable to pressures of the establishment, which was largely absent during the UPA years as the then government seldom made industrial houses feel vulnerable. There was a conspiracy of disparate forces committed to defeating the UPA government by supporting Modi. We were not ready for the polls in the manner that Modi was in the run-up to the 2014 election.

Finally, we cannot underestimate the impact of the extensive use of social media platforms and the false propaganda spread through them. Professional teams were set up to vilify the Congress. There was no opposition, indeed, no preparation, to counter such insidious attacks. Modi was somehow projected as larger than life, as if the solution to all problems confronting India were known to him alone and, when elected, he would revive the economy, make India a power that would be respected and feared in the world, confront China with aggression and teach Pakistan a lesson. All this appealed to those who wanted change.

Time to Reconnect

We failed to connect with the people of India and demonstrate how we were not inept and that our government had done much more than any government in the past. Despite the meltdown of 2008, our rate of growth was not abysmally low. Our neighbourhood was peaceful, our reform processes were on track, our relationships with both China and Pakistan were much better and the economy was on the rebound by 2014. Our stimulus package for revival of the economy was working. We were focussed on the travails of the poor. Our emphasis on education, healthcare and poverty alleviation showed that we as a government were concerned for the marginalized and all those at the bottom of the pyramid. But somehow, we could not deliver this message to the people of India.

If people fail to connect with you, it is the beginning of the decline of any political party. It is time for us to reconnect with the people of India and recent electoral outcomes have shown that the process is afoot. We need to be clear in our policies and strategies. We need to encourage our cadres at booth and block levels to spread the message that Modi has failed miserably. The only party that is truly national in its perspective and has the talent to take this country forward and bring prosperity to ordinary folk is the Congress party. We are perhaps one of the few parties committed to communal harmony, without which we can never aspire to create the future that we imagine for our country.

Chapter 9

2G: A 'SCAM' OF MONUMENTAL PROPORTIONS

Communication is perhaps the most lethal of all weapons. It has the ability to persuade, disturb and radicalize. Totalitarian states have come about because of the power of communication. It is said that communication can empower as well as disempower; can create as well as destroy. Nothing exemplifies this better than the manner in which the UPA government was destroyed by visual images on television channels.

News in the contemporary world, especially in the electronic and social media, is not about facts, it is about perceptions. Facts, by their nature, are malleable; they can be woven into a fabric to suit the message you want to deliver. Unlike the world of print where you need to read, pause and absorb, the electronic media is a feast for the eyes where visual images supplant the printed word. You can excite, edit, juxtapose and, in a sense, create the subject of your target and then eulogize or expose her or him, depending on the point of view the channel wishes to project. The cacophony of sounds drown each other out even as the anchor takes over to carry the debate forward and deliver the message meant for the consumer.

The electronic and social media sensationalized the 2010 CAG report 'on the performance audit of issue of licences and allocation of 2G spectrum by the Union government' and made people believe that a scam of monumental proportions had been unearthed.[1]

---

[1] http://www.cag.gov.in/content/report-no-19-2010-performance-audit-issue-licences-and-allocation-2g-spectrum-union

Shared Benefits beyond Territorial Boundaries

The survival of the human race depends on natural resources that it has inherited, like the rich flora and fauna, coal, oil and airwaves. A nation's natural resources and their optimum utilization determine the future of its population. Every citizen of this country has a stake in these natural resources. The State frames policies for the optimum use of each natural resource to deliver benefits. If the State enriches itself but does not pass on the benefits to consumers, it fails in its duty towards people. These benefits must accrue to its consumers at a cost that is affordable. Pricing, therefore, will depend on the consumer's capacity to pay. But pricing policies and objectives will differ from time to time. And, neither the policy framework nor the rollout of its benefits can be static. Apart from the importance of the cost factor, the benchmarks against which a particular policy framework must be tested include high-quality outputs in the form of services provided at reasonable prices.

Freeing of the airwaves and allowing uplinking and downlinking from satellites brought about the communications revolution, and the resultant increase in the use of mobile phones. Mobile signals are carried on airwaves of a particular frequency, a band of which is known as spectrum. In 1991, the second generation (2G) wireless technology was invented, which basically delivers voice calls and SMS along with slow speed data services. 2G operates in several frequency bands—800, 900 and 1800 MHz. A mobile operator is allotted its separate bandwidth within the range of frequencies to ensure that signals of different operators do not get mixed up, making sure there is no interference while providing services to the consumer. 3G, referred to as the third generation wireless telephone technology, was first offered to the world in 2001. This can carry voice calls, SMS, high-speed Internet, video calls and mobile television. On mobile handsets, this premium service operates in the frequency band of 2,100 MHz.

A government can deal with spectrum in two ways: Either it can invest in infrastructure on its own, without any private sector participation, by laying down the fibre optic network, or allowing the private sector to do so. Apart from China, no other government in the world has invested in building the entire telecom infrastructure since they do not have the resources to do so. Hence, they allow private sector participation not only because it would have to make the investment, but also because the private sector is far more efficient in laying down infrastructure. But once infrastructure is set up, tariffs are not subjected to price control. This is possible in the developed world because the per capita income is sufficient to pay for relatively high tariffs. But in India, where the per capita income is very low, there is public pressure to keep tariffs low. Further, it is not possible for operators to earn the kind of returns necessary to plough them back into improving infrastructure and increasing efficiency.

Understanding the National Telecom Policy

The National Telecom Policy (NTP) of 1994 was designed to open up the sector to private investment. At that time, there were no telecom operators in India with any experience of exploiting spectrum nor were they aware of the manner in which the telecommunications revolution would transform the nature of communications in India.[2] The rapid transition that took place in later years happened by virtue of the architecture of the regime that was put in place by the government, which made it possible for tariffs to be affordable. Auctioning spectrum would have enriched the treasury but would not have enabled the operator to invest in quality service. This became the subject matter of controversy in later years.

The initial telecom policy of 1994 had to be replaced by the NTP of 1999, which was framed by the NDA. It allowed existing cellular telecom players to migrate from a 'fixed licence fee' to a 'revenue sharing arrangement'.[3] The reason for the change was that, in terms of their contracts, the first and second Cellular Mobile Telephone Service (CMTS) licencees of 1994–95 had to pay ₹10,040 crore for 10 years for 18 circles. Basic licencees (of 1997 licence) had to pay ₹27,862 crore for six circles

---

[2]http://www.dot.gov.in/national-telecom-policy-1994
[3]http://pib.nic.in/focus/fomar99/fo3103991.html

for 15 years, which they claimed they would not be able to pay because of the low density (3 per cent) of consumers in the telecom sector. The NDA's caretaker government allowed them to shift from a fixed licence fee to a revenue sharing arrangement and, thereby, wrote off their dues, which at that time amounted to ₹3,708 crore.

Teledensity increased from 3 per cent in 2001 to 18 per cent in 2007.[4] Telecom tariffs came down from ₹16.99 per minute in the 1990s to as low as 30 paise per minute, thus benefiting the ordinary consumer. Through that policy prescription, low tariffs resulted in India's socio-economic empowerment. This happened because operators worked in an environment where spectrum was allocated to a licence holder who paid an entry fee of ₹1,658 crore. The operator paid an additional amount calculated on the gross revenue earned by the licencee in the preceding year. Apart from that, the operator licencee also paid on a 'per subscriber basis' after the government introduced a revenue sharing formula in 2003. Operators now functioned under a unified licence scheme and received spectrum up to 4.4 MHz. Operators claimed that they were entitled to another 1.8 MHz as contractual spectrum since operator licencees could exploit and utilize spectrum by paying an entry fee of only ₹1,658 crore and thereafter sharing with the government the revenues earned by them as their business expanded. This enabled the operator licencee to invest in infrastructure development to provide quality service at a reasonable cost to the consumer. In the initial years, this policy was exceptionally successful. Teledensity increased to 61 per cent in 2010.[5]

In 2003, the Unified Access Services Licence (UASL)[6] provided the roadmap for a uniform licencing regime.[7] In January 2008, there were problems related to the issuance of 122 new licences for Unified Access Services in one day. Questions were raised as to why the government allowed the allocation of spectrum at ₹1,658 crore as determined in 2001

---

[4]http://indiabudget.nic.in/es2007-08/chapt2008/chap97.pdf
[5]http://pib.nic.in/newsite/PrintRelease.aspx?relid=68025
[6]http://dot.gov.in/access-services/introduction-unified-access-servicescellular-mobile-services
[7]http://pib.nic.in/newsite/PrintRelease.aspx?relid=93289

instead of a market-discovered price which would have been higher. Questions were also raised regarding the manner in which licences were granted and spectrum allocated, which ultimately led to serious allegations about an alleged scam to the magnitude of ₹1,76,000 crore.

CAG—Transgressing Its Traditional Role

A quasi-federal constitution, which has overwhelming unitary features like ours, can only function if each wing of the State recognizes its own responsibilities and seeks to exercise its obligations within the contours assigned to it by the Constitution. Of late, there has been a tendency amongst constitutional authorities to transgress the contours of their powers and responsibilities in the name of larger public interest.

Parliament has the primary responsibility to frame legislation after consulting all possible stakeholders in our society in order to realize the objectives of the legislation. Legislators should not be swayed by the eruption of public sentiment. The making of laws requires a clinical appreciation of issues. Laws should also not be passed to cater to constituencies merely for political support. But on occasion, legislation is the outcome of a public outcry that pressures the government for an immediate response.

Courts have an obligation to ensure that all laws so passed do not impinge on the right to equality and are not violative of freedoms enshrined in Part III of the Constitution dealing with our fundamental rights.[8] Courts, therefore, are charged with the responsibility of testing laws on the anvil of constitutional prescriptions. But courts sometimes deal with matters which are purely administrative in nature and belong to the domain of the Executive. The rationale for such action is the Executive's failure to discharge its responsibilities. Courts willy-nilly have to step in. The Executive, too, sometimes exceeds its powers and tends to misuse the law for ends that are constitutionally prohibited.

Recognition by the State of the limitations of its powers is as important as the obligation to discharge the responsibilities assigned to it under

---

[8]http://lawmin.nic.in/olwing/coi/coi-english/Const.Pock%202Pg.Rom8Fsss(6).pdf

the Constitution. Take for example, the constitutional office of the Attorney General (AG) of India.[9] Should the AG act as the mouthpiece of the government? He may be appointed by the government, but this constitutional office was created to defend the Constitution, not necessarily the government, because actions of the government are not always consistent with the provisions of the Constitution. In the past, I have seen holders of this office stand up and address the court as defenders of the Constitution while the office of the Solicitor General of India, not being a constitutional office, defends the government and its actions. The Election Commission of India is yet another authority that must be seen to be equidistant from all political parties in the discharge of its constitutional obligations. It has, of course, over the years, ensured that elections in India are free and fair. At the same time, on some occasions it has been seen to have fallen short.

The CAG of India is statutorily obligated to look into the accounts of various departments of government, and through audit paragraphs in its report, provide its observations, which are then forwarded to the Public Accounts Committee (PAC) of Parliament.[10] It is important to understand the significance of the office of the CAG of India. Article 149 of the Constitution enjoins the CAG to perform such duties and exercise such powers as may be conferred by Parliament in relation to the accounts of the Union and of the states.[11] Article 151 stipulates that the reports of the CAG, in relation to the accounts of the Union, shall be submitted to the president who shall cause them to be laid before each House of Parliament.[12] The PAC, to which the president forwards the report of the CAG, considers the recommendations made by that office and, thereafter, places them before Parliament. In other words, the CAG's office acts as a sentinel, ensuring that the money allocated under the Appropriation Bill to various departments of the government is spent in accordance with the allocations economically, effectively and efficiently.

---

[9]https://indiankanoon.org/doc/1985537/
[10]http://www.cag.gov.in/menu-links/our-mandate
[11]http://www.cag.gov.in/content/duties-and-powers-comptroller-and-auditor-general
[12]http://www.cag.gov.in/content/audit-report

The purpose behind audit reports is to ensure that public money is not frittered away, resources are used in a timely and appropriate manner, and the outputs delivered in terms of quantity and quality are such as to meet the objectives and intended results.

The CAG is not concerned with policy and yet, of late, it seems to be guiding policy under the misconception that it can do so by hiding under the cloak of a performance audit. Performance audit, the latest guidelines for which were framed in 2014,[13] is an independent assessment, or examination of the extent to which an organization, programme or scheme, operates economically, efficiently and effectively. Were resources available with the State acquired, held and used economically in appropriate quantities and quality, and at the best price? A performance auditor examines whether the means chosen represent the most, or at least a reasonable, economic use of public funds. In terms of efficiency, it investigates the relationship between resources employed and outputs delivered, in terms of quantity, quality and time. Ultimately, have the resources as expended met the objectives and the intended results?[14] A performance audit is meant to promote governance by contributing to accountability and transparency.

Can the CAG opine on and decide policy or attempt to guide it? That is the domain of the Executive. Once the policy is prescribed, its effective, economical and efficient implementation is in the domain of the auditor. But the practice of the auditor to question Executive prescription has made the office of the CAG controversial. Adequate caution should be exercised by not going beyond the audit mandate and respecting the roles assigned to the Executive and auditor.

The 2010 CAG report on 2G spectrum allocation questioned the intentions of the government by calculating the financial loss to the it had caused to the exchequer by not auctioning spectrum. With teledensity at 26 per cent in 2008, the CAG felt that it was inappropriate for the government to have handed out 122 telecom licences on a first-come-first-served (FCFS) basis, and considered auction of spectrum as a more

---

[13]http://www.cag.gov.in/sites/default/files/cag_pdf/PA_Guidelines2014.pdf
[14]http://www.cag.gov.in/sites/default/files/cag_pdf/PA_Guidelines2014.pdf

appropriate method of allocation. According to the CAG, such auction would have fetched the government ₹1,76,000 crore.[15] Of course, the CAG termed this gigantic sum as 'presumptive loss', which essentially suggested that the government would have earned revenues to that extent; that government policy in not opting to auction spectrum was a big scam. The fact of the matter is that in many jurisdictions of the world, spectrum is not auctioned.[16] It is a limited resource and its exploitation depends on technology. Not all spectrum available in different frequencies can be auctioned or should be auctioned at one go. The nature of spectrum auction depends upon the number of operators in the field, and the nature of the band in a particular frequency to be allocated. Globally, in different environments, administrations have experimented in the way spectrum was allocated.

However, I wonder what the term 'presumptive loss' means. How can one presume a loss without calculating the gains a particular policy might have brought on the table? Loss, in the classic balance sheet of a company, occurs when outgoings—in other words, expenses—of an enterprise exceed its revenues. In the telecom sector, revenue earning is not an end in itself, neither for the government nor for the telecom operator. It is the gain to the consumer that is of vital importance. That gain can never be calculated in terms of revenue. Imagine a migrant worker in Delhi being able to get in touch with his family with a mobile call, and instantly address the concerns of his family. Though no revenue is gained, the benefits are enormous. Similarly, enabling a student to ensure that his fee is paid on time, failing which his name would be struck off the rolls. I can multiply these examples ad nauseam. How can the CAG then presume a loss of ₹1,76,000 crore without factoring into calculation the benefits of the policy? The CAG's didactic opinion has been disastrous for the sector.

Interestingly, auctions that took place pursuant to the Supreme Court verdict of 2012 in the very 1,800 MHz frequency band, fetched a higher

---

[15]http://saiindia.gov.in/sites/default/files/audit_report_files/Union_Performance_Civil_Allocation_2G_Spectrum_19_2010_exe_sum.pdf
[16]http://www.trai.gov.in/sites/default/files/3G_0.pdf

price for spectrum.[17] These licences, too, in which spectrum was allocated at market-discovered price, were for a period of 20 years. So, the old players had a great advantage because they paid less for the same spectrum that the new players paid much more for. A situation was created in which two telecom operators, having spectrum in the same frequency band, were competing with each other after paying differential rates for it. How can a policy prescription create a situation in which two operators using the same frequency band do not operate on a level playing field? It could well be that those who had paid less for spectrum were quite enthusiastic about the CAG report and were not averse to an auction, as they would have had a natural advantage over others who paid the auction price for spectrum.

Whether government should allocate spectrum without auction is a matter of policy depending on its priorities, and the CAG is not authorized by law to be an agency which enunciates policy. Clearly, the institution, in castigating the UPA government, transgressed its traditional role, which was to eventually cost both the sector and the nation.

Tumult in the Telecom Sector

In 2012, the Supreme Court endorsed the view of the CAG, and cancelled all licences granted pursuant to the FCFS policy of allocating spectrum in 2008–09. It also directed that spectrum be auctioned.[18] In a competitive environment, especially when the auction is so designed, limited supply of spectrum to be auctioned will fetch a higher price. This resulted in competing stakeholders bidding in a manner that filled the treasury's coffers but depleted their resources. This negatively impacted efficient service to the consumer. Though the government became richer, telecom operators were burdened with debt. Not enough resources were left with telecom operators to invest in infrastructure and technology for the benefit

---

[17]http://www.firstpost.com/business/2g-auctions-dot-may-approach-trai-to-reprice-spectrum-524423.html

[18]http://www.business-standard.com/article/economy-policy/supreme-court-cancels-122-telecom-licences-112020300086_1.html

of the consumer.[19] Telecom operators, especially newcomers in 2008–09, reduced their tariff to unremunerative levels in order to gain market share.[20] This was the beginning of the derailment of the success story of the telecom sector. Sadly, very few new entrants could survive the bloodbath that followed.[21]

On reflection, it can be argued that the CAG, along with courts, were directly responsible for the tumult in the sector. The court, in cancelling the 122 licences, jeopardized investor confidence. Had the court found culpability of all investors in the allocations made, then alone could such cancellations be justified. This decision was a great disservice to the sector and symptomatic of the court's proclivity in interfering in matters which fall exclusively in the domain of policy-makers. Courts cannot and should not transgress the contours of their jurisdiction by pontificating on the manner in which economic assets are distributed.

Any economic asset—be it land, minerals or the airwaves—has to be dealt with under a policy prescription. Such prescription, however, may not conform to the court's vision. Take land, for example: If every piece of land in an urban conglomeration is to be auctioned, say, to build a school or a hospital, hardly any investor would have the courage to make such an investment. It would be unremunerative in a place like Delhi for an investor to buy one acre of land through auction for setting up a school. If the annual fee charged to students is regulated by the administration, why would anyone make the investment? Such logic also applies to the establishment of hospitals. If such lands are not auctioned, and are allocated at institutional rates, can the CAG regard all such allocations as a big scam? The purpose for allocation of resources depends on the nature of the asset and the nature of the enterprise required to deal with the asset in order to serve the consumer. There may be different policy prescriptions for different assets. It is not for courts or the CAG to either

---

[19] http://www.telecomlead.com/telecom-services/indian-telecoms-debt-rs-3-8-lakh-crore-71419

[20] http://www.dnaindia.com/money/report-predatory-pricing-under-trai-lens-1328535

[21] http://www.livemint.com/Home-Page/7OVMCxGKb9SMxKe2aYVqQL/Tariff-war-cuts-short-telecom-growth-dream.html

decide on such prescriptions, or to provide their own alternatives which the government is then bound to follow.

So where does the telecom sector stand today? High upfront instalment payments pursuant to auctions has resulted in an accumulated debt of around ₹6,00,000 crore.[22] The cumulative debt of the top five telecom players—Airtel, Vodafone, Idea, Reliance Communications and Jio—stood at ₹4.59 lakh crore as of March 2017.[23] If we add industry figures of all telecom operators, including MTNL and BSNL, the total net debt of the operators stands at around ₹5.87 lakh crore in March 2017.[24]

Between 2012–13 and 2016–17, Bharati Airtel's total debt went up by around 42 per cent to ₹1.60 lakh crore and Idea Cellular's debt grew by 195 per cent to ₹68,211 crore. Vodafone,[25] Telenor,[26] Maxis and Docomo have not reported profits. Some have written off investments.[27] Idea Cellular reported a loss of ₹383 crore for the quarter end December 2016, against a profit of ₹91.4 crore during the September quarter.[28] There was consistent deterioration in the company's financial resources because of a combination of higher interest cost and Reliance Jio launching its free services, which forced all telecom operators to cut tariffs. Idea's return on capital employed declined from 7.1 per cent in the financial year 2016 to 2.7 per cent in the financial year 2017 and is expected to fall to 0.3 per cent in 2018.[29] To sustain itself, Idea would require either additional equity from its shareholders, or increased borrowings. The Vodafone–Idea

---

[22] https://economictimes.indiatimes.com/news/economy/policy/dot-finance-ministry-to-ease-burden-of-debt-laden-telecom-sector/articleshow/59745033.cms
[23] http://164.100.47.4/newrsquestion/ShowQn.aspx (last accessed on 24.08.2017)
[24] http://164.100.47.4/newrsquestion/ShowQn.aspx (last accessed on 24.08.2017)
[25] http://www.thehindu.com/business/Industry/Vodafone-loss-doubles-to-5.5-billion-due-to-India-write-down-hit-by-RJio-entry/article16448508.ece
[26] http://telecom.economictimes.indiatimes.com/news/telenor-india-q3-operating-loss-widens-due-to-impairments-and-write-downs/55067639
[27] http://timesofindia.indiatimes.com/business/india-business/DoCoMo-to-exit-India-at-1-3-billion-loss/articleshow/34218148.cms
[28] http://www.thehindubusinessline.com/markets/stock-markets/idea-puts-up-a-weak-show-owing-to-growing-competition/article9538842.ece
[29] http://www.business-standard.com/article/companies/idea-vodafone-deal-to-be-revealed-with-grasim-nuvo-voting-117022701049_1.html

merger would help the two companies to be more competitive in a highly irrational environment. Return on investment might also be helped by synergy gains from this merger. Tata Telecom has been, in a sense, gifted to Airtel, which is acquiring its assets on a debt-free, cash-free basis.[30] With the Aircel–Reliance deal having fallen through,[31] Aircel has now filed for bankruptcy before the National Company Law Tribunal.[32] Telenor opted out, bedevilled by the same problems, though its investment and network operators were limited.[33] Etisalat and Sistema have bled and exited. There is hardly any foreign investment in this sector and those who will survive will be the ones with deep pockets who cannot afford to give up their investments.[34] From the seven or eight operators in every circle, enhancing competition, the years to come will see consolidation spurred by the Jio phenomenon and survival of only perhaps three or four players in the sector.[35]

The industry has not defaulted, and perhaps may not default, but all its revenue earnings will, in future years, be substantially earmarked to pay off debt. Very little will be left for the expansion of infrastructure and efficient service. With 1,127.37 million wireless subscribers at the end of December 2016, out of which 988.14 million are active subscribers[36] (constituting 13 per cent of globally active subscribers), the global telecom revenue contribution of India is only 2.7 per cent as compared to the rest

---

[30]http://www.livemint.com/Industry/np5deDZO690meWCzkVENJK/Bharti-Airtel-Tata-to-merge-consumer-mobile-businesses.html

[31]http://www.livemint.com/Money/jV0jhKytshxHfHZoKUpW0J/RCom-without-Aircels-fig-leaf-is-not-a-pretty-sight.html

[32]https://economictimes.indiatimes.com/news/company/corporate-trends/aircel-countrys-last-small-mobile-phone-firm-file-for-bankruptcy-today/articleshow/63110441.cms

[33]http://www.dailypioneer.com/business/jio-effect-airtel-acquires-telenors-india-operations.html

[34]http://www.business-standard.com/article/companies/arpu-free-fall-makes-consolidation-look-real-in-telecom-117021100712_1.html

[35]http://telecom.economictimes.indiatimes.com/news/reliance-jio-effect-indian-telecom-market-to-have-five-players-says-js-deepak/57356397

[36]http://www.trai.gov.in/sites/default/files/Press_Release_11_17_Feb_2017_Eng.pdf

of the world.[37] Obviously, revenue earnings per subscriber are much less in India as compared to the rest of the world. Gross revenue declined by 6.79 percent to ₹66,532 crore in the October–December 2016 quarter from ₹71,378.69 crore in the July–September 2016 quarter.[38]

Our telecom sector, compared to the rest of the world, is also heavily taxed. In China, the total VAT levied is 11 per cent, whereas in India, GST is levied at 18 per cent. In addition to licence fees at 8 per cent, spectrum usage charges of 3–6 per cent make the total levy in the range of 25–29 per cent.[39] Yet, India has the lowest voice rates in the world. According to a joint report released by the Department of Industrial Policy and Promotion and Department of Telecom in November 2016, the mobile industry contributes 6.5 per cent to India's GDP[40] and is the third-highest contributor in FDI for nearly a decade and a half.[41] The sector also has the second-largest investments in infrastructure, close to ₹8,00,000 crore and a Return on Investment (RoI) of less than 1 per cent.

Despite all this, the sector has been attempting to roll out tower network sites in the various frequency bands. About 2 lakh sites have been operationalized from January 2015 to March 2016, equalling the number of all sites established in the last 20 years. The total investments of the top three telecom operators up to 2016 suggest the capital-intensive nature of the sector. Bharti Airtel has invested ₹81,528 crore in the network and purchase of spectrum. The comparable figures for Vodafone and Idea are ₹78,555 crore and ₹65,019 crore, respectively. Yet spectrum is not regarded as infrastructure investment. In 2010, spectrum constituted 10 per cent of gross investments. For the financial year 2016, despite higher levels of

---

[37]http://www.business-standard.com/article/companies/india-has-only-3-share-in-world-mobile-revenue-116081101943_1.html

[38]http://www.financialexpress.com/industry/telcomes-consumer-service-revenue-dips-10-5-in-december-quater-to-rs-37284-cr-trai/619999/

[39]https://www.thehindubusinessline.com/opinion/telecom-crisis-needs-urgent-solutions/article9865169.ece

[40]http://dipp.nic.in/English/Investor/Make_in_India/sector_achievement/Make_in_India_Telecommunications_Sector_Achievement_Report.pdf

[41]http://dipp.nic.in/English/Publications/FDI_Statistics/2016/FDI_FactSheet_OctoberNovemberDecember2016.pdf

investment in equipment, spectrum constitutes over 45 per cent of gross investment in fixed assets.[42]

The above figures demonstrate the reasons for spectrum, especially in the 700 MHz band (4G), remaining unsold in recent auctions.[43] The state of the industry is reflected by the fact that telecom players have not been able to recover the cost of capital at any time in the last 20 years. Policies as they stand today will only inflict additional cost on industry and will impair their ability to invest in infrastructure. Surely, pursuant to the CAG's policy prescription and the Supreme Court's decision, the telecom sector is in deep trouble though the government has earned revenues. Efficiency is still lagging. The consumer has not gained and call drops are rampant. Revenues from voice will not be enough to sustain the sector. Data expansion will be the only way for sustenance. Data wars will be the order of the day. Since 1994, there has been no clarity with regard to the policy prescription that would succeed in the telecom sector. Fractious court battles will continue. The telecom regulator will take controversial decisions in the light of competing interests and the raging battle among operators will not cease.

Looking Back, Looking Ahead

The CAG, through his outlandish calculation of 'presumptive loss', was a godsend for those who wished to enter politics. They made unfounded allegations and hurled abuse against ministers in the UPA. Even the Court failed to fully comprehend the economic consequences of its decision to cancel the 2G licences. Ultimately, Vinod Rai's conclusions and the Court's decision came to naught. However, by that time, those who wished to enter politics were safely ensconced in positions of power.

In December 2017, Special CBI Judge O.P. Saini, did not find a shred

---

[42]http://www.financialexpress.com/economy/call-drops-industry-body-says-3-telecom-companies-invested-rs-2-25-l-cr-in-infrastructure/247948/

[43]https://economictimes.indiatimes.com/news/economy/policy/overpriced-700-mhz-saw-government-miss-auction-target/articleshow/54744465.cms

of evidence against the accused in the 2G scam.[44] Neither was there a concept of alleged loss, nor did the CBI seek to prove a case of loss. The judge found that the prosecution had failed miserably; in fact, he referred to the charge sheet as 'well-choreographed'. Saini concluded that the CBI did not produce any legally admissible evidence to sustain its allegations and acquitted the 17 accused. Indeed, the judge held that many of the statements made orally by witnesses were contrary to the official record produced before the court. He also blamed the prosecution for not cross-examining crucial witnesses to discover the truth. The judge remarked that he was intrigued as the trial progressed. Several senior officers and the prosecutor were not even willing to sign applications sought to be filed by the prosecution, as well as replies by them towards the end of the trial. Nor was any investigator prosecutor willing to take any responsibility for what was being filed in court. In fact, the prosecution was not even willing to file its submissions to inform the accused what case they were required to meet, though counsel for the prosecution argued the matter for several months.

On the crucial question relating to the charge that former telecom minister A. Raja misled the then Prime Minister Dr Manmohan Singh, the judge found no merit in that submission, and concluded that this was only an attempt to prejudice the mind of the Court.

In relation to the procedure for allocation of spectrum during Raja's tenure, the judge remarked that the number of applications for participation in the auction became large and the ministry was confronted with the problem of plenty—a problem that had to be resolved logically. In that sense, the judge held that a policy or procedure 'cannot be set in stone', unrelated to current requirements. The procedure of departing from FCFS was changed after discussions in the department and on the basis of suggestions by the officers of the DoT. This change was ultimately conveyed to the Prime Minister on 2 November 2007. Consequently, the allegations that the criterion was changed by Raja surreptitiously and unilaterally were rejected.

The judge also found no merit in the submission of the prosecution

---

[44]CBI vs. A. Raja and others, para 1817, p. 1551 of the judgement

that advance information about the issue of letters of intent and change of procedure for allocation of spectrum was conveyed to the Swan Telecom Pvt. Ltd. (STPL) and Unitech group of companies by the accused public servants. The judge also rejected the charge of conspiracy and found no legally admissible evidence to prove it.

The trial court judgement should make us think of the dangers that present themselves when the Supreme Court, in the midst of a surcharged atmosphere, seeks to render findings without a full-fledged trial. This is the real danger in the Supreme Court entertaining PILs when irresponsible allegations are hurled without any basis and television channels hold persons guilty even before a word is said in the course of legal proceedings.

Public Policy Dilemma and Referee Institutions

In the years to come, the future of our economy will be predicated upon the level of restraint shown by institutions on issues that will be brought to court for different reasons. Occasionally, litigation is initiated not to uphold the majesty of law, but for an ulterior motive. PILs based on moral prescriptions, in a highly complex environment, may be the right prescription in a morally ideal world. If Qualcomm wishes to manufacture in India and seeks huge concessions to do so, would it be right for the government to accede to those concessions? Maybe. It depends on the priorities of the government. If the developed world clamours for India to open up its agriculture sector or demands further reduction of tariffs, should the government succumb to such pressure? In some cases, it might, depending on what it gets in return. Investors always look for profit, and unless the return on capital is assured, investment will remain a distant dream. A sector that needs investment for public good must have the flexibility to put in place a policy for that end. Such decisions do not necessarily amount to a wrongdoing or result in criminal culpability.

Policy decisions are, in their nature, temporary. A change of circumstances brings about a change in policy. Change in policy is a reflection of governments recognizing the need for change, the result of a dialogue between different stakeholders. This is an ongoing process in which policies are constantly reviewed for the benefit of the consumer. This can only be done by the government and not by courts.

The media's desire to always project the negative, and the Supreme Court's belief that it alone has the ability to set things right are dangerous trends. The 2017 Economic Survey rightly points out that 'policy making in certain areas has been heavily constrained, as a way of ensuring that decisions do not favour particular interests'. Such constraints ill serve the national interest.

New Thrust in our Policy Prescriptions

Prosperity in any sector, where the consumer is to be provided an efficient service at reasonable costs, needs a model of growth in which all stakeholders benefit. This model, based on auctions, and the manner in which they are conducted, will emasculate the telecom operator's ability to provide efficient service. Their revenues will decline and will not be enough to recover their capital costs.[45] A policy prescription that leads to these results is essentially flawed.

What needs to be put in place is a model that allows government a share in the profits of telecom operators as their revenues increase. This way, the treasury is enriched as the telecom sector prospers. This model may be regarded as an option in service-oriented sectors.

The policy of allocating spectrum at an initial price of ₹1,658 crore and, thereafter, along with a revenue-sharing method, served the industry well. Perhaps that model could have been tweaked by increasing the price of allocating spectrum to a reasonable level. The sector would have been able to make rapid investments in infrastructure and increase its revenues through expanded tele-density. Both industry and government would have prospered through a revenue-sharing arrangement. The consumer in turn would have been the beneficiary of services at affordable prices.

Take the case of China. The Chinese government, through its investment companies, holds 74.4 per cent, 72.7 per cent, and 70 per

---

[45]http://www.livemint.com/Industry/eJgsco7NaAB1dXEBtt67XI/Outlook-negative-for-telecom-industry-ICRA.html

cent of China Unicom, China Mobile and China Telecom, respectively. These investments are like the investments made by the government in BSNL/MTNL. In China, spectrum allocation is almost at no cost. They pay minimal annual fees of less than 1 per cent of revenues. The revenue of the top three Chinese telecom operators is six times the revenue of the top three operators in India.[46] Since Chinese operators do not invest anything in spectrum, their funds are available for investment in networks. Space for investments is crucial for efficiency. With overpriced spectrum and accumulated debt, this sector, in India, will be condemned to mediocrity, if this policy continues. In the ultimate analysis, we have to trust our governments except when decisions are *ex-facie* tainted. Natural resources cannot be treated as milch cows to reduce fiscal deficits.

Connectivity in a Digital Economy

The communications outreach along with the digital revolution has transformed the world. The relationship between State and citizen, between individuals, between citizens and communities, and within communities, has altered. Digital platforms have brought the world closer. In a vast country like ours, it is fundamental to ensure that for a digital revolution to succeed, a fibre optic network connects each gram panchayat. The strategy adopted by the UPA government, which in retrospect may not have been the best, required the involvement of public sector entities, including BSNL and RailTel; 2.5 lakh gram panchayats were to be connected. But as of November 2017, optical fibre and OFC pipes have been laid in around 1.11 lakh gram panchayats, and connectivity has been achieved in only 77,674 gram panchayats.[47]

What is of utmost importance is the last-mile connectivity from gram panchayats to centres where public services can be disseminated, and finally to individual households. But who will pay for this last-mile connectivity? The private sector will only do so if it can be sustained

---

[46]http://164.100.47.193/lsscommittee/Information%20Technology/16_Information_Technology_38.pdf
[47]http://www.bbnl.nic.in/index1.aspx?lsid=570&lev=2&lid=467&langid=1

economically. The states do not have the resources to do so. The economic sustenance of investment by the private sector depends on the capacity of the consumer to pay. Given the fact that 800 million people have a monthly income of less than ₹10,000—rather meagre for survival—it is difficult to imagine that such connectivity will happen in the near future.

Telecom and Social Media Platforms

In January 2011, when I took over as the Minister for Telecom and IT after the resignation of A. Raja, I realized the immense reach of social media platforms and their potential to do harm. These platforms can empower as well as disempower. As with all technologies, in safe hands, they are multipliers of public good but in unsafe hands, their capacity to harm is limitless. With the sort of images that were on the Internet, we thought that in times to come, they may inflame passions, encourage societal schisms and cause riots. Sometime in 2011, I met representatives of social media platforms and after sharing with them the content that could have had serious consequences, I requested them to recognize the potential of societal harm that may ensue. I also requested them to come back to me after a month and share their thoughts with me about interventions in the event that the images on such platforms disturb societal equanimity. This request was made with the best of intentions. However, *The New York Times* saw it as an assault on freedom of press.[48]

Those, of course, were early days and neither the government nor stakeholders in society could imagine then what we see today. My fears were proved right. Governments throughout the world and stakeholders in society realize that these platforms represent the wild west where pulling the trigger is kosher. Not only has the content shared on these platforms, with intent to cause communal disharmony, resulted in loss of lives and reputation, they provide a free hand to elements who seek to tear apart societal peace and tranquility, without which a nation cannot survive. Rumours on social media platforms led to the exodus of the people of

---

[48] https://india.blogs.nytimes.com/2011/12/05/india-asks-google-facebook-others-to-screen-user-content/

the Northeast from Bengaluru. Those in traditional vocations have lost their lives on account of rumours, morphed images and fake news, be it Mohammad Akhlaq in Dadri (Uttar Pradesh), Pehlu Khan in Alwar (Rajasthan), Junaid Khan in Ballabhgarh (Haryana), Mazloom Ansari and Imtiaz Khan in Latehar (Jharkhand) and the Dalit floggings in Una (Gujarat). Horrific incidents of lynching on suspicion of child lifting were again based on rumours spread on such platforms. The perpetrators responsible for recent lynchings are unemployed, misguided youth. It is essential for any government to take prompt action to protect the innocent and assiduously enforce the law. So far, law enforcement agencies have been laggard in their responses. This is not a problem for which handy solutions are available. It is urgent that the political class eloquently articulates that those responsible will not be spared. Courts should also think twice before granting bail to such accused. The real culprits are those who morph images and spread fake news. They must be targeted and must not enjoy the protection of anonymity on such platforms. The Prime Minister's silence on these issues is, to say the least, disappointing.

Chapter 10

ARAB SPRING COMES TO INDIA

Corruption, without any doubt, is an insidious plague that undermines democracy and the rule of law. It erodes quality of life, distorts markets and burdens the common man. In India, it has infiltrated the corridors of power.

The debate on rooting out corruption from this country has been going on for a long time. In fact, between 1968 and 2011, the Lokpal Bill was introduced in Parliament eight times but was not passed.[1] The commission to review the working of the Constitution, headed by Justice M.N. Venkatachaliah, recommended establishment of the Lokpal and Lokayuktas way back in 2002.[2] The 2005 Administrative Reforms Commission (ARC) endorsed the same.[3]

It was with this long-standing demand that the Anna Hazare movement was born in April 2011, buoyed by the mistrust and suspicion that enveloped the nation in the aftermath of the 2G scam. Events from October–November 2010, with the resignation of the then Telecom Minister A. Raja and the agitations at Jantar Mantar, suggested that it was time for people to stand up and be counted.

The movement, under the aegis of India Against Corruption (IAC),

---

[1] http://www.prsindia.org/media/articles-citing-prs/a-history-of-the-lokpal-bills-1957/
[2] http://www.prsindia.org/uploads/media/Lokpal/Pranab%20Mukherjee%20questions%20and%20committee%20recommendations.pdf
[3] http://www.prsindia.org/administrator/uploads/general/1302860449_Lok%20Pal%20Bill%20Timeline.pdf

brought together on a single platform both the middle class and ordinary folk, including the Dabbawalas of Mumbai and the farmers of Punjab and Haryana. It even caught the imagination of non-resident Indians. It was perhaps the first movement of its kind amplified by the media with 24/7 coverage, which kept people throughout the country aware of the events in the national capital. Minute by minute developments and the alleged flip flops of the government, uninterrupted sermons, and vicious no-holds-barred attacks, defamatory statements and sentimental jibes made this movement unique.[4] Mobile phones and social media also played a key role in spreading the message of the movement. Yet the focus of the movement was the UPA government at the Centre. The suffering of the common man was attributed to corruption. The UPA government was perceived to be corrupt, but more than that, it was branded as a government which was selling precious national assets to a chosen few.

In Sync with the Mood of the Times

Anna Hazare, who had failed in fighting corruption in Maharashtra, suddenly found himself at the centre of a huge emotive movement. From November onwards, he was used as a pawn by those surrounding him. Little did he know that those proximate to him had ambitions much beyond the transformation of India. The assembly of people at Jantar Mantar, the organization of multitudes swarming into Ramlila Maidan and the meticulous planning of such events were obviously the handiwork of those who had planned this movement for some time. It will perhaps be hazardous to render a definite opinion on who was behind Hazare, but those around him smelled an opportunity that they were not going to miss.[5]

As Hazare's popularity grew, and as television channels gave him a national platform on which to air his oversimplified and somewhat rudimentary views, it seemed as if the Arab Spring had come to India.

---

[4] http://indianexpress.com/article/opinion/web-edits/lokpal-how-tv-turned-the-table/
[5] http://archive.indianexpress.com/news/jantar-mantar-core-group-lost-out-last-yr-s/773844/

The UPA government did not want to use an iron hand to deal with a movement which ostensibly reflected the mood of the times. The government wilted under pressure as it knew that it was not in a position to win the battle of perception. Television channels willingly aired unsubstantiated allegations of corruption against specific ministers.[6] Media encouraged abuse, unconcerned about the damage it might cause to reputations. Sadly, nobody wished to unearth the truth. Allegations, to the public mind, represented truth and there was no space provided for any reasonable discourse.

The Jan Lokpal Bill, which the IAC had drafted in response to the UPA's Lokpal and Lokayuktas Bill, 2011 as an improvement over it, soon became a matter of national debate. Its passage was believed to be the panacea that would root out corruption. It became both politically correct and fashionable for the icons of different disciplines to support such a cause. Swamis, cricketers, and Bollywood personalities all lent their support, as did social media networks.[7] Protests spread like wildfire from Ramlila Maidan in Delhi to Bengaluru, Mumbai, Chennai, Guwahati, Shillong and many other cities. The agitations that followed became a rallying point; people took out marches in over 60 cities demanding an effective anti-graft bill.[8] A rally from Jantar Mantar to Ramlila Maidan demanded that black money stashed abroad in foreign banks be brought back to India.[9] There were also demands to set up a joint drafting committee, presided over by Shanti Bhushan, and that the text of the Jan Lokpal draft legislation in its original form be introduced in Parliament as a Bill.[10] The self-proclaimed civil society, headed by a

---

[6] http://indianexpress.com/article/news-archive/latest-news/15-upa-ministers-involved-in-graft-pm-no-exception-kejriwal/
[7] http://archive.indianexpress.com/news/cyberspace-abuzz-with-support-for-hazare-w/773135/
[8] http://post.jagran.com/Marches-on-Martyrs-Day-express-anger-against-graft-1296405375-1
[9] https://hinduexistence.org/2011/02/28/largest-ever-anti-corruption-rally-in-delhi-baba-ramdev-declared-dharmyudh-holy-war-against-corruption-from-ram-lila-maidan/
[10] http://indianexpress.com/article/news-archive/web/activists-bill-calls-for-lokpal-as-supercop-superjudge/

select few as if they represented the cause of the people of India, was the mainstay of this movement. To add fuel to the fire, the CAG, taking refuge in the concept of a performance audit, exposed yet another alleged scam—this time alleging a presumed loss of ₹1.86 lakh crore in the allocation of coal blocks.[11] It was purported that the government followed a procedure which was unknown to law and that a chosen few had been allocated coal mines without an auction, thus depriving the government of the optimum price of this resource. All this, the Opposition claimed, epitomized the extent of crony capitalism which allegedly symbolized the functioning of the UPA. A member of the Hazare movement moved the Supreme Court challenging the sale of the 2G spectrum to various recipients. Petitions were also filed to challenge the allocations of coal blocks made to various entities.

In the midst of the Hazare agitation, Suresh Kalmadi, the chairman of the Commonwealth Games Organizing Committee (CGOC), was arrested for alleged acts of corruption, which further besmirched the image of the UPA.[12] The Commonwealth Games Organizing Committee was charged with loot, and all that the Congress party could do was set up systems to inquire into the allegations and get the CBI to investigate the charges made. But the Opposition, which had coalesced, had successfully suffused the public mind with fears of rampant corruption in the government.

BJP Rides the Wave

At this point, the BJP decided to ride the wave of public resentment against the UPA. They used this movement as an opportunity for their own political resurrection. They felt it politically wise and expedient to align themselves with the movement for enactment of the Lokpal Bill.[13] They asked the government, in April 2011, to convene an all-party meeting

---

[11]https://indianexpress.com/article/what-is/manmohan-singh-cbi-coalgate-coal-block-allocation-cag-report-what-is-coal-scam-4668265/

[12]https://www.ndtv.com/india-news/cwg-scam-suresh-kalmadi-arrested-suspended-by-congress-453866

[13]Hazare achieved more in 4 days than the Oppn in 2 months' time: Advani

to discuss the gravity of the issue and demanded that the Lokpal Bill be enacted as an instrument of credible and effective action against corruption.[14] The party further insisted that both political leaders and bureaucrats must be covered within its ambit.[15] Their opportunism was evident from the fact that the party did not act against B.S. Yeddyurappa, the former chief minister of Karnataka, who was mired in corruption charges—and who became their chief ministerial candidate during the state elections of May 2018—but saw in the much publicized movement an opportunity to proclaim its concern about the cancer of corruption.[16] In fact, while the negotiations for a model Lokpal Bill were taking place and the leadership of the BJP was supporting Hazare, nothing prevented them from directing chief ministers of their party-ruled states to put in place a model Lokayukta legislation.

While these cross-currents were on display, some believe that the RSS silently supported Hazare.[17] The crowds that swarmed Ramlila Maidan, the logistics which were put in place and the movement of people represented a well-planned strategy, giving impetus to not just the movement, but creating an environment of distrust in the minds of the people about the intentions of the government. The UPA found itself on the wrong side of the public mood.

Government Wilts Under Pressure

At this juncture, there was a genuine debate about how we should deal with the situation. We could have adopted a hard-line approach and come down heavily by using the enormous powers the State enjoys. I remember discussions amongst our senior colleagues and also with our

---

[14]http://www.thehindu.com/news/national/BJP-seeks-all-party-meet-on-Lokpal-Bill/article14671758.ece?test=1&textsize=large

[15]http://archive.indianexpress.com/news/playing-graft-card-bjp-backs-anna-hazare/772188/0

[16]http://www.thehindu.com/news/national/in-a-uturn-bjp-tilts-towards-anna-hazare/article2397022.ece

[17]http://indianexpress.com/article/cities/lucknow/rss-hits-back-at-anna-was-part-of-his-antigraft-movement/

Prime Minister, wishing to deal with public sentiment instead of deciding to muffle protest. The government wished to have a dialogue, address the genuine concerns expressed by civil society and arrive at acceptable outcomes. Our accommodating gestures, perceived to be acts of weakness, were exploited by elements least concerned with democracy.

As the movement gathered momentum, Hazare announced his decision to go on an indefinite fast from 5 April 2011. It was also the date by which the Prime Minister was asked to decide on the inclusion of the self-proclaimed members of civil society (Hazare, Arvind Kejriwal and Prashant Bhushan) in drafting the Lokpal Bill.[18] The Prime Minister wrote to Hazare and invited him for discussion. This outreach reflected the essential democratic culture of the then government, willing to deal with an issue that affected the common man, so that a constructive way forward could be charted through appropriate legislation. The State coming to terms with the agitation was seen as an act of surrender by some within the government. On 7 March 2011, Hazare along with other civil society members met the Prime Minister and accepted his offer to form a Group of Ministers (GoM) that would discuss the Lokpal Bill with them. Overnight, these members became national heroes. But Hazare was adamant to fast and exhorted people all over the country to join in. On 5 April, Hazare, along with his supporters, paid tribute to Mahatma Gandhi at Rajghat, and thereafter, was joined by around 5,000 people at Jantar Mantar.[19]

The GoM received a setback with the withdrawal of Sharad Pawar from its membership following Hazare's verbal attack on him.[20] The government's image received further setback when it agreed to form a joint panel to draft the Lokpal Bill with Hazare's team, which was chaired by the then Finance Minister Pranab Mukherjee. Half of the members of this panel consisted of self-anointed members of civil society and the

---

[18]http://daily.bhaskar.com/news/DEL-anna-hazare-to-fast-for-lokpal-bill-1888120.html
[19]http://www.sify.com/news/Thousands-join-anti-graft-crusade-as-Hazare-begins-fast-news-National-lefxkhgfdfjsi.html
[20]http://indianexpress.com/article/politics/relieve-me-from-corruption-panel-says-pawar/

government committed that it would introduce the Lokpal Bill in the monsoon session of Parliament in 2011.[21]

Major differences emerged during the meetings of the joint drafting committee.[22] The main concern of the government was that Hazare and his team were attempting to create a structure which would supersede Parliament—a structure perhaps more powerful than any other in the country, with the power to decide upon the fate of public functionaries, including the Prime Minister.[23] The differences between the government and Hazare's team were quite serious, and as they could not find common ground, Hazare announced another fast on 16 August 2011, a threat that was an instrument of blackmail.

The government imposed Section 144 of the Indian Penal Code [24] before the fast. Hazare was detained and sent to Tihar jail for seven days.[25] Thousands of people gathered outside Tihar. Within a few hours, the government decided to free him. A few days later, he went on a fast again, this time at Ramlila Maidan.[26,27] The Prime Minister wrote to him requesting him to end his fast, and called an all-party meeting. In response, Hazare put forward three demands to the Prime Minister: A citizens' charter; Lokayuktas in all states with powers similar to those of the Lokpal in the central legislation; and inclusion of the lower bureaucracy within the ambit of the legislations.[28] These demands were reflected in the 'Sense of the House' resolution adopted

---

[21] http://archive.indianexpress.com/news/govt-notifies-joint-panel-anna-breaks-fast/774133/1
[22] http://www.thehindu.com/opinion/op-ed/differences-abound-both-major-and-minor-in-competing-lokpal-drafts/article2126729.ece
[23] http://indianexpress.com/article/latest-news/cabinet-approves-lokpal-draft-pm-judiciary-out-of-bills-ambit/
[24] http://indiatoday.intoday.in/story/prohibitory-orders-anna-hazare-protest/1/148156.html
[25] http://timesofindia.indiatimes.com/india/Anna-Hazare-arrested-by-Delhi-Police-ahead-of-fast/articleshow/9618768.cms
[26] http://timesofindia.indiatimes.com/india/Will-not-leave-Ramlila-Ground-till-Jan-Lokpal-Bill-is-passed-Anna-Hazare/articleshow/9660680.cms
[27] http://archive.indianexpress.com/news/annalila-begins/834561
[28] http://indianexpress.com/article/india/latest-news/lokpal-round-two-team-anna-presents-fresh-draft-govt-in-fix/

by Parliament, after which he broke his 13-day fast on 28 August.[29]

Ramdev Gets into the Act

When the Hazare movement was at its peak,[30] Ramdev catapulted himself into it with a demand to bring back black money stashed abroad.[31] He was supported by the RSS and the BJP.[32,33] He announced that he would go on an indefinite fast from 4 June 2011 on the issue of black money, within a month of Hazare's fast for the Lokpal bill. The timing suggested that the campaign against the UPA was being fuelled from several quarters. The BJP put its full weight behind this media event. What is interesting is that the issue of black money stashed abroad had been a part of the agenda of the BJP for a long time, which in 2010, claimed that between $500 billion to $1.4 trillion were stashed in overseas tax havens.[34]

The BJP, RSS and Ramdev probably believed that while the UPA government was being targeted by the Hazare-led IAC campaign, it would further demoralize the government if yet another issue was made part of the campaign. Ramdev, in fact, wrote a letter to the Prime Minister about his demands—death penalty for the corrupt; and recall of ₹500 and ₹1,000 notes.[35] It is not coincidental that after Modi came to power demonetization was unexpectedly sprung on the people of India on 8 November 2016. Back then, the UPA government did not take Ramdev's threat lightly. However, as events transpired later, he was somewhat embarrassed when cameras caught him trying to escape from Ramlila

---

[29]http://www.thehindu.com/news/national/parliament-adopts-sense-of-the-house-resolution-on-lokpal/article2403358.ece

[30]http://indianexpress.com/article/india/latest-news/baba-ramdev-to-do-hazare-to-launch-satyagraha-in-delhi/

[31]http://archive.indianexpress.com/news/battlefront-ramlila-maidan-ramdev-warns-govt-on-blackmoney-lokpal/985938/

[32]http://indiatoday.intoday.in/story/bjp-comes-out-in-support-of-baba-ramdev/1/140172.html

[33]http://samvada.org/2011/news/rss-supports-baba-ramdev/

[34]http://www.thehindu.com/todays-paper/tp-national/No-progress-in-bringing-back-stashed-money-says-Advani/article15720248.ece

[35]http://www.thehindu.com/news/national/what-baba-ramdev-wants/article2071609.ece

Maidan fearing his arrest. The government did respond to his demands and offered to form a committee to formulate law to bring back unaccounted-for wealth stashed abroad.

BJP: The Master of Doublespeak

When the Prime Minister convened an all-party meeting on 3 July 2011, there was unanimity about creating a strong Lokpal, except for the BJP, which did not reveal where it stood on the issue. The party insisted that it would reveal its stand only in Parliament.[36] This was yet another way of extracting anti-government mileage out of civil society campaigns. Its petty politicking and duplicitous conduct continued throughout the agitation. It was simply playing for votes.

One of the prominent points in the 'Sense of the House' resolution adopted by Parliament in August 2011 was that Lokayuktas would be set up in all states.[37] Hazare ranted against the UPA for not honouring this resolution, and the BJP joined the chorus.[38] The BJP passed the Lokayukta Bill in Uttarakhand on 1 November 2011, just before the state elections were called in January 2012,[39] realizing that if it did not do so, it was likely to lose the election. Today, however, it is opposed to the model legislation for creating Lokayuktas under the Lokpal law. Instead, it feels that state legislatures could, in the light of Article 252 of the Constitution, request Parliament to pass such a law for the states through resolutions to that effect.[40] Prime Minister Modi, who was then the chief minister of Gujarat, did not allow the Lokayukta to be set up in Gujarat for

---

[36] http://archive.indianexpress.com/news/govt-attacked-no-takers-for-team-anna-hazare-line/812361/0
[37] http://www.thehindu.com/news/national/parliament-adopts-sense-of-the-house-resolution-on-lokpal/article2403358.ece
[38] http://www.hindustantimes.com/delhi-news/oppn-backs-anna-hazare-but-counsels-flexibility-as-well/story-4fRrMvEjM8pkZbb3qokKeN.html
[39] https://www.outlookindia.com/newswire/story/uttarakhand-assembly-passes-lokayukta-bill/740140
[40] http://164.100.47.193/debatestext/15/IX/2212.pdf

10 years.[41] In Karnataka too, where the BJP was in power, the Lokayukta had remained headless for nearly one-and-a-half years since Justice Shivraj Patil quit in September 2011, and before Justice Bhaskar Rao was appointed as the Lokayukta in February 2013.[42]

Of course, it is ironic that the BJP government, which has been in power at the centre since May 2014, has chosen to put the Lokpal and Lokayuktas Act 2013—passed and notified by the UPA government on 1 January 2014—on the backburner. The insincerity of the cause to eradicate corruption is reflected by the fact that the Attorney General, when questioned by the Supreme Court in March 2017 about the non-enactment of the Lokpal, responded that the time was not opportune, that Parliament is yet to pass certain amendments proposed to the law (by way of the Lokpal and Lokayuktas and other related Law [Amendment] Bill, 2014, introduced in the Lok Sabha in December 2014) and that the process could not be concluded in the absence of the Leader of the Opposition.[43] The Supreme Court brushed aside all objections of the government and said, in April 2017, that there was no justification to keep the enforcement of the Act under suspension.[44] Yet, there is still no sign of the Lokpal.

The doublespeak was not just limited to the BJP. Even the Janata Dal (United), JD(U), whose representatives shared the stage with Hazare at Ramlila Maidan, committed themselves to every comma, every full stop and every word of the resolution in Parliament.[45] But when the Bill was introduced in Parliament in December 2011,[46] the party objected to the inclusion of the Lokayuktas in it.

---

[41]http://www.firstpost.com/india/after-10-years-gujarat-finally-gets-a-lokayukta-1281709.html
[42]http://www.thehindu.com/news/cities/bangalore/bhaskar-rao-is-karnataka-lokayukta/article4414463.ece
[43]http://www.hindustantimes.com/india-news/can-t-appoint-lokpal-till-law-changes-govt-tells-supreme-court/story-EeSQXIzzzL1XonTu9WKsbO.html
[44]https://indianexpress.com/article/india/cant-keep-hanging-pick-lokpal-without-leader-of-opposition-supreme-court-4631260/
[45]http://www.hindustantimes.com/delhi-news/call-special-session-to-discuss-lokpal-sharad-yadav/story-cLM2m7pBXbHuk96id8oNOP.html
[46]http://pib.nic.in/newsite/PrintRelease.aspx?relid=79168

I firmly believe that though Hazare's commitment was genuine, those who made their presence felt standing alongside him had political instincts, which emerged for all to see in the years ahead. The movement could not have caught the imagination of the people unless it was backed by forces which never came to the forefront. This anti-graft movement solicited money from the public, but allegedly kept no account of it. The money was allegedly passed on to Kejriwal's NGO called 'Public Cause Research Foundation' (founded in 2006), but nothing more was known about it.[47]

Questions were asked, such as, who paid for the media and the marketing of Hazare's fast unto death at the Ramlila Maidan? Who kept account of the money that was spent? Who brought people to fill up the Maidan and financed food that was served at the event for days? Kejriwal, Bhushan and some of the others had embarked upon this enterprise and used the movement and its aftermath to their advantage. Overnight, they became the voices that were heard, and, over the course of the movement, they found that the government continued to give them space to air their views against individual ministers. Their statements were made with impunity and lapped up by both electronic and print media. There was no way of dealing with the allegations made because those who hurled the allegations were not ready to wait for any explanation. The thin line which differentiates civilized from uncivilized discourse had sadly vanished.

---

[47]http://indianexpress.com/article/news-archive/web/iac-members-demand-details-of-funds/

Chapter 11

COAL SCAM: A SPARK THAT CAUSED A FIRE

There are moments in history when the present cannot comprehend the future impact of its actions. A spark can create a fire which can consume wherever it spreads, but the debris destroys the environment and it takes years for new shoots to spring to life.

Even as the government was reeling under the aftermath of the 2G spectrum scam in 2010, yet another report of the 'Performance Audit of Allocation of Coal Blocks and Augmentation of Coal Production, Ministry of Coal' by the CAG in August 2012 added fuel to the fire.

This report put the presumptive loss figure in the coal scam at ₹1.86 lakh crore.[1] The logic of the CAG was based on the government's decision not to auction 194 coal blocks between 2004 and 2011, thereby suggesting that the country had lost massive amounts of revenue. The report further suggested that in the absence of an auction, Tata Steel, Tata Power, Essar Power, Hindalco and Jindal Steel and Power had all benefited through allocations on a nomination basis resulting in monetary gains. Initially, the loss was estimated to be more than ₹10 lakh crore but the CAG, keeping PSUs out of its final report, brought the figure down to ₹1.86 crore.[2,3] The report insisted that precious natural resources should be

---

[1] http://www.cag.gov.in/sites/default/files/audit_report_files/Union_Performance_Commercial_Allocation_Coal_Blocks_and_Production_Ministry_Coal_7_2012.pdf
[2] Ibid
[3] http://www.dnaindia.com/india/report-what-is-the-indian-coal-allocation-scam-1828830

auctioned, and that captive mining allowed on the recommendations of the inter-ministerial screening committee was a mechanism to disburse largesse. The CAG, once again, put the government in the dock. It transgressed its role as an auditor and during the course of a performance audit, castigated past decisions to pave the way for allegedly better policy prescriptions.

The public could not appreciate the distinction between actual and presumptive loss and could not comprehend that the CAG was propounding a new policy framework in respect of precious natural resources. There was massive uproar in Parliament and in political circles. The Opposition drew blood and soon, the Anna Hazare team, the RSS, the BJP and other Opposition parties came to overthrow the UPA. The media too played the role of the Opposition.

The judgement of the Supreme Court in 2014 was the last straw. Quashing the entire chain of the allocation of coal blocks made from 1993 to 2012, the Supreme Court failed to recognize the impact of this momentous decision on industry and the economy. It led to a festival of auctions for natural resources which contributed substantially in landing the economy in the stress that it finds itself today in. The screening committee route was found to be unconstitutional and the government dispensation was regarded as arbitrary and illegal. Even joint venture agreements and other arrangements entered into by state PSUs were found to be illegal. The Court held that such agreements and arrangements defeated the legislative policy enunciated in the Coal Mines Nationalisation Act, 1973, since it allowed coal mines to be exploited by private companies for commercial use.[4] But the judgement delivered on 25 September 2014 recognized the fact that the consequences of illegality of allocations remained to be tackled.[5] Despite the fact that the Court was made aware that its decision would adversely impact the economy, the Court would have none of it.[6]

---

[4]http://www.prsindia.org/uploads/media/Coal%20Mines/SC%20judgement%20aug.pdf
[5]http://www.thehindu.com/news/national/supreme-court-cancels-all-coal-block-allocations/article6349454.ece
[6]http://www.prsindia.org/uploads/media/Coal%20Mines/SC%20order.pdf

The apex court ought to have realized that its decision to deallocate coal mines would impact the availability of coal; that loans to the tune of ₹2.5 lakh crore given by banks and financial institutions to companies which were allotted coal mines, would become NPAs;[7] that investments in existing steel and power plants would become redundant, adversely affecting public sector banks and corporations. Besides this, investor confidence was bound to suffer and cause acute distress in related industries, which depended on coal as a primary source of fuel. That this would wreak havoc on the economy was no concern of the Court. The Court also failed to realize that there would be a loss of ₹4.4 lakh crore in terms of royalty, cess, direct and indirect taxes.[8] For allocations to be made in the near future the industry had to import coal at high prices, which in turn impacted consumer pricing.

Long-term Repercussions

While the Court is entitled to render a decision on the illegality of allocations, it must also be cognizant of its repercussions. Courts should not be unaware that investments in sectors of the economy are made on the basis of extant policies. Investors are unaware of the legality of such policies. Indeed, no investor could possibly have contemplated that a policy that was in practice from 1993 to 2012, in the context of allocation of coal blocks, would be set to nought in 2014. The unwary investor cannot be charged with culpability in the event of the State discontinuing a policy that has stood the test of time. This is not the appropriate place to critically examine whether or not the decision was based on sound legal reasoning.

There is much to be said for the government in making the allocations through the screening committee in which the private sector, the Union government, and the state where the coal block was located were active

---

[7] https://indianexpress.com/article/india/india-others/sc-scraps-214-coal-blocks-leaves-1-lakh-crore-30000-mw-question/
[8] https://timesofindia.indiatimes.com/business/india-business/SC-rejects-Rs-9-lakh-crore-impact-of-coal-block-cancellation/articleshow/43383419.cms

participants. Assuming that the Court is completely justified in coming to the conclusion that it did, the question that must be answered is whether the Court could have cancelled all allocations, including those in which there was no element of culpability or wrongdoing. Can the Court, through its decision, foist individual investors with serious economic consequences without them being charged or found guilty of any wrongdoing? Should the Court not have recognized that the unwary investor should not be penalized because of alleged government lapses in policy-making and its implementation?

The deallocation of coal blocks resulted in the government putting up coal blocks for auction which led to litigation. This can be explained with the help of an example. If an entity set up a power plant, next to a coal block which was allocated to it, at a cost ranging from ₹5,000 to ₹20,000 crore, after the cancellation of the said block such an entity is deprived of two advantages. First, the loss of the coal block captive to its power plant and, second, if the plant is in the hinterland, it would have to seek an allocation from another coal block which may be some distance away increasing transportation costs, provided that it is successful in the auction. The transportation of coal would also have an adverse impact on the environment. In the event the entity is not successful in getting an allocation, it would have to import coal at a much higher price. All these factors ultimately would have a serious economic impact on the enterprise.

The reality is that the deallocation of coal blocks set back the process of extraction and effective utilization of coal by seven to eight years. The Court responded to this reality by stating, 'whether they are 95 per cent ready or 92 per cent ready or 90 per cent ready for production is wholly irrelevant, the allocation was illegal and arbitrary as already held, and therefore we quash all these allotments. Learned Attorney General identified 46 coal blocks which could be "saved" from the guillotine, since all of them have commenced production or are on the verge of commencing production. As these allocations are also illegal and arbitrary, they are also liable to be cancelled...'[9]

The above extract of the judgement clearly suggests that the Court

---

[9]http://www.prsindia.org/uploads/media/Coal%20Mines/SC%20order.pdf

was aware of the massive economic dislocation that would destabilize the entire coal sector, which, in turn, would impact sectors like power, steel and cement. The consequence, apart from loss of investments, was that from 2011 to 2015 there has been a substantial increase in the share of coal imports to fulfil industry demand. Imports have increased at the rate of 25 per cent annually, with the total value of coal imports in 2015 at ₹955 billion.[10] The import of coking coal has increased by about 75 per cent over this period, whereas import of non-coking coal has increased by a whopping 250 per cent over the same period. Despite the fact that our country is endowed with a large quantum of coal (315 billion tonnes[11]), of which 90 per cent comprises non-coking coal, this resource is unavailable for exploitation. Clearly, industries which could have used the enormous resources of non-coking coal were deprived of the same. They had to pay a higher cost for the import of non-coking coal, which, in turn, impacted prices. Considering that huge investments are required in infrastructure, it has resulted in an increase in the cost of setting up infrastructure projects, apart from the fact that projects which relied on domestic coal were delayed on account of the sudden requirement to import non-coking coal.

Nowhere is this detrimental impact more visible than in the power sector, in which 57.3 per cent of installed capacity is coal-based.[12] While installed capacity of power utilities increased at a Cumulative Aggregate Growth Rate (CAGR) of 13 per cent between 2009 and 2015, coal-based generation increased by a CAGR of only 8.5 per cent. The lack of supply of raw material meant that several power plants remained idle. The result is that the average plant load factor (PLF) for coal-based power plants has decreased to 62.01 per cent in 2016–17 from 63.86 per cent a year ago.[13] The challenges being faced by the power sector are commercial and financial—apart from regulatory factors—that have resulted in lowering the PLF.

---

[10]https://www.pwc.in/assets/pdfs/publications/2016/icc-pwc-coal-report-june.pdf
[11]http://pib.nic.in/newsite/PrintRelease.aspx?relid=177058
[12]https://powermin.nic.in/en/content/power-sector-glance-all-india
[13]https://www.pwc.in/assets/pdfs/publications/2016/icc-pwc-coal-report-june.pdf

In 2015, coal consumed by the steel sector in India was 66 million tonnes, of which two-thirds was imported. It is estimated that the requirement of coking coal for the steel sector would increase to 96 million tonnes by 2020. Likewise, nearly two-thirds of the coal consumed in the cement sector in 2015 was imported. Rapid urbanization, increase in infrastructure investment by government, infrastructure projects like smart cities and dedicated freight corridors, development of Metro Rail projects, modernization and expansion of airports will drive demand for cement. Coal requirement in this context would be in the range of 72 to 82 million tonnes by 2025.[14] Clearly, the importance of coal as a raw material to fuel the economy cannot be underestimated. The omnibus cancellation of 2G licences and deallocation of coal mines without regard to the economic consequence in the absence of individual culpability has had a catastrophic impact on the economy.

Further, India is a signatory to Bilateral Investment Promotion and Protection Agreements (BIPA), according to which foreign investments are required to be protected.[15] On account of the decision of the Court, several foreign investors have filed claims against the Government of India seeking compensation for the loss caused on account of these cancellations.

The Supreme Court judgement, therefore, created consequences that have jeopardized the future of investments in India. It has also resulted in defaults in bank loans, increasing the number of NPAs, apart from the fact that several investors have been involved in litigation.

Recently, Attorney General K.K. Venugopal told a Supreme Court Bench that the apex court's orders cancelling the 2G licences and deallocation of coal blocks have adversely affected these vital sectors of the economy. 'FDI was hit by the cancellation of licences. Coal prices have shot up and there is a shortage of coal,' the government's seniormost law officer said.[16]

---

[14] https://www.pwc.in/assets/pdfs/publications/2016/icc-pwc-coal-report-june.pdf
[15] http://dea.gov.in/bipa
[16] https://economictimes.indiatimes.com/news/politics-and-nation/ag-venugopal-blames-sc-for-hitting-mining-telecom-and-coal-sectors/articleshow/65330853.cms

Coal Block Auction—Not a Bonanza

Auctioning of coal blocks has not provided the bonanza the government was looking for. Since 2014, 89 coal blocks have been allocated so far, 31 through e-auctions and 58 allotted to PSUs.[17] However, there is no visible increase in the production levels of coal.[18] Our coal sector continues to remain under stress.

Different auction procedures are adopted for the power and non-power sectors. For the non-power sector, the government adopts an ascending system in which it sets a floor price and the participants bid. The first two auctions fetched high bids, but then the price of imported coal fell, making exploitation of the mines uneconomic. Transferring these mines to new bidders too ran into problems.

For the power sector, the government adopted the method of reverse (negative) bidding. Here, the successful allottee bears the cost of mining and also pays a premium to the government. Thus, the power sold to discoms does not allow recovery of cost of mining. Reverse bidding has also resulted in unremunerative outcomes.

In the absence of an adequate number of power purchase agreements, the government's target of producing one billion tonnes of coal per annum by 2020 is a distant dream.[19] In 2017–18, Coal India's production increased by a mere 1.4 per cent, compared to 4 per cent in 2016–17 and 9 per cent in 2015–16.[20,21] Simultaneously, PLF at thermal power plants plunged to 59.68 per cent in 2017–18, down from 77.5 per cent in 2009–10.[22] With the slow pace of the economy, demand has gone down but other factors

---

[17] http://pib.nic.in/newsite/PrintRelease.aspx?relid=177212

[18] https://www.financialexpress.com/industry/scrapped-captive-coal-mines-production-around-half-the-financial-year-2015-peak/1118007/

[19] https://timesofindia.indiatimes.com/business/india-business/govt-may-revise-coal-production-target-of-1-bn-tonnes-set-for-2020/articleshow/63632760.cms

[20] https://coal.nic.in/sites/upload_files/coal/files/coalupload/chap6AnnualReport1718en.pdf

[21] https://www.bloombergquint.com/business/2018/04/02/coal-indias-output-grows-at-slowest-pace-in-four-years

[22] https://www.business-standard.com/article/companies/cerc-mulls-three-part-tariff-structure-as-plant-load-factor-falls-to-60-118052700144_1.html

too have contributed to decrease in demand, including falling tariffs and demand for renewables. However, increase in PLF will require Coal India to increase supplies which, at present levels of production, does not seem possible. In fact, in 2017–18 import of coal has increased by 8.1 per cent.[23]

Increased demand can only be met through commercial and captive mining. Clearly, we need a comprehensive reform agenda to set right the malaise that afflicts this sector. Given the track record of this government at the end of four years in office, no well-thought-out roadmap is likely to be unveiled. Auctions, in the manner conducted so far, have not helped the sector. We must design auctions in such a way that government shares in the prosperity of the sector.

The experience in auctioning coal blocks after the Supreme Court's regressive judgement will lead to monopolies. Not just coal but all minerals being auctioned only to enrich the coffers of the government is a highly flawed policy. We need to take care of regional needs, since coal is available for mining only in a few states. Additionally, the need for coal and its beneficial use also depends on the location of industrial consumers of coal. The quality of coal and its optimum use for particular industries is also a relevant factor. Courts of law, which order auctions as the only fair way of dealing with natural resources, are ill-equipped to deal with highly complex issues of optimum use of national wealth. The caveat, of course, is to ensure that national interest alone must determine allocation of these resources, without the odour of crony capitalism at work. In the context of the concern for the environment, such resources must be utilized with the least environmental impact.

The sector will further suffer since mines allotted to government agencies on nomination basis have been non-starters with mining plans yet to be finalized. This, along with a spate of litigation challenging auctions on several grounds, lack of compensation to prior allottees and changing the rules of the game after auctions are held, have hardly served the cause of a resource most vital for nation-building.

The wisdom of the concept of revenue-sharing seems to be gaining

---

[23] https://www.business-standard.com/article/economy-policy/after-two-years-of-fall-india-s-coal-imports-grow-8-1-in-fy18-118051700016_1.html

favour once again. The bluster and noise of auctioning natural resources served a political purpose, unrelated to economic optimization of the resource with concomitant social benefits. The government has taken a decision to form a panel to review coal block allocations. The panel, according to the Coal Minister, will explore the revenue-sharing model of coal block allocations.[24] The sector with ₹1.74 lakh crore of stressed assets, needs urgent attention.[25]

The alleged coal scam was just one of the many factors that soured the UPA's story. The people of India were inclined to accept the charges made by the massive media campaign against the UPA. In fact, Modi's rise is attributable to circumstances that were created owing to the unholy alliance between the media and the Opposition that emerged after the findings of the CAG report.

In 2014, people forgot all the good work done by the UPA since 2004. The Opposition rejoiced at its successful demolition. More than four years down the road, the campaign against the UPA continues despite the fact that the economy is on a downturn and people are still waiting for the change that Modi had promised.

---

[24]https://economictimes.indiatimes.com/industry/indl-goods/svs/metals-mining/panel-looking-into-coal-blocks-auctions-process-to-submit-report-in-6-8-months-piyush-goyal/articleshow/62571951.cms
[25]https://www.business-standard.com/article/news-ians/stressed-power-projects-have-rs-1-74-lakh-cr-debt-parliament-panel-118030900018_1.html

EPILOGUE

By the time this book is published, we will be about six months away from the Lok Sabha elections in 2019. Politics will be heating up. In the next few months, we will witness the nature and quality of public discourse until the election. Apart from that, the Opposition will attempt to build bridges in order to bring about opposition unity to challenge the BJP in the next election. The NDA has more or less been dismantled. The Shiv Sena may not have an alliance with the BJP. Chandrababu Naidu's Telugu Desam Party (TDP) will certainly not be part of the NDA. In Punjab, the BJP may not be in a position to bargain with the Akalis. The only major alliance partner presently with the BJP is the JD(U). However, the party is faced with a dilemma given the success of the BJP in Bihar in the last elections, riding on the popularity of Prime Minister Modi. The JD(U) will wish to be given a sufficient number of seats, which will be a cause of tension in forging a stable alliance. Nitish Kumar has already indicated that with 17 per cent of the vote share in Bihar, he does not wish to cede to the pressures of the BJP, which would wish to garner a larger number of the Lok Sabha seats in the state. How that dynamics will work is yet to play out. The All India Anna Dravida Munnetra Kazhagam (AIADMK) government in Tamil Nadu, headed by E.K. Palaniswami, is unpopular. Dinakaran is drawing crowds but the Dravida Munnetra Kazhagam (DMK) seems to be in a strong position to win most of the seats in Tamil Nadu in 2019. Even if Palaniswami allies with the BJP, it will not help the party in any significant way, the government being fairly unpopular. The BJP is all set to challenge Naveen Patnaik's Biju Janata Dal (BJD) in Odisha. Given this scenario, the BJP will be fighting the next election on its own. On the other hand, the key players of the Opposition seem to have decided to enter into a strategic alliance at the state level to defeat the BJP.

The attempt to form a Mahagathbandhan at the national level is not going to be easy. With less than 50 seats, the Congress on its own cannot dictate terms, especially since in several states, it has no significant presence. The Congress needs to form strategic alliances in those states so that in the aftermath of the Lok Sabha elections, the alliance partners stand with it to ensure a non-BJP government at the Centre. The results in Uttar Pradesh and Bihar will decide who will be in government at the Centre. If the Congress and the RLD become part of the alliance comprising the SP and BSP, it will be a formidable force. The BJP will find it difficult to get any significant success in the 80 Lok Sabha seats in UP. The RJD along with the Congress in Bihar can also be a formidable force to reckon with. If, in these two states, the BJP is not able to get a substantial number of seats, it will be difficult for Narendra Modi to be the prime minister in 2019.

In the meantime, the Congress will have to decide who it wishes to ally with in West Bengal. Our partnership in Tamil Nadu with the DMK should prove beneficial for us in the long run. Wherever the BJP and the Congress are pitted against each other, it is very likely that the BJP will be cut to size. In Maharashtra, Sharad Pawar has already declared that his party, the Nationalist Congress Party (NCP), would be in alliance with the Congress to fight the next election. That augurs well. It seems that the politics of liberal, secular parties is on track and that of Modi, in decline.

However, election results can never be predicted. The mood of the nation cannot be gauged in advance. Demonetization has destroyed lives, while a flawed GST has negatively impacted businesses, especially in the informal sector. Rising NPAs, lack of credit facilities and rampant unemployment with GDP at 6.75 per cent in 2017–18 will certainly not help Modi in the coming election. The agricultural sector has been badly hit by demonetization. Modi has betrayed the agricultural sector by not fulfilling his promises. His belated attempt to increase MSP of crops for the current kharif season is not going to change the lives of farmers for the better, especially since the ills of the sector are not entirely related to an increase in MSP. There are fundamental issues in agriculture that need to be addressed. Modi has failed to do that for four years. No significant reforms in the education and health sectors have taken place and the recent decision to set up a Higher Education Commission has not gone down well with the academic world.

For Modi, it is politics all the way, as has been the case in the last four years. He moves from one event to another, coins an acronym every other day. Despite event management, control of the media and the trolling army that tirelessly supports him, the Modi magic has soured. His exhortation, 'If you have given the Congress 60 years, give me 60 months and I will change India' shall sound hollow at the end of his 60 months.

But you never know what the voter will do. We will have to wait until 2019.

ACKNOWLEDGEMENTS

To write about contemporary politics is no easy task for the simple reason that the impact of decisions taken by a government has long-term implications, the effect of which can only be assessed later. One must also understand the present in the context of the past. Making value judgements can become a very hazardous exercise. Therefore, one should be humble enough to accept that one's conclusions may not necessarily turn out to be as analysed.

In the course of this exercise, given the fact that I am also practising law and active in politics, it was difficult to take out time for research, collate my thoughts and pen them down. This could not have been done by me alone. Such an enterprise is essentially a collaborative effort.

I must, at the outset, thank my publisher, Rupa Publications, for providing me with the services of Esther Ruolngul, who would take down my somewhat random thoughts which ultimately resulted in this book. I was then confronted with the task of finding time to understand what I dictated. It required elaborate corrections. I sometimes completely restructured the narrative. I cannot possibly miss out the contribution of Rajesh who was patient enough to make the corrections by working till late at night.

Many a times, I did not have easy access to the data that was necessary to support my conclusions. There is hardly any contemporary work which gives easy access to the data that I was looking for. Here, I must acknowledge the unstinted dedication of Arun Nawani without whose efforts this book would never have been written. Apart from collecting data, he occasionally guided me on some issues that needed to be addressed. Without his critical inputs, it would not have been possible for me to give shape to the book in its present form. I also need to acknowledge Mohammad Nizam Pasha's cautious approach and valuable advice after meticulously going through the manuscript.

Twelve hours in a day are not enough to do justice to those I represent in court, to the politics that I actively pursue and to the writing of this book. I had to, therefore, take time out that otherwise belonged to my family. I am, therefore, extremely grateful to Promilaa, my wife, who never complained. She was resigned to my working even during vacations to make it possible for me to complete what I had set out to do.

This, of course, resulted in me not spending time with my two sons, Amit and Akhil, and my grandchildren. They did not complain and I am thankful to them for that.

Last of all, I thank my publishers, Rupa Publications, for making sure that the book could be published before the next Lok Sabha elections.

*My India where
I love to live
taught not to take
only to give*

INDEX

AADHAAR, 92–99
   functioning of Act, 95
   challenges in implementation, 93–95
   principle of proportionality, 96–97
Aakash tablet, 184–85
Abhinav Bharat, 43
Accelerated Irrigation Benefits Programme (AIBP), 25
Acharya, P.B., 52, 62 Governor, Assam (additional charge), 52
Achhe Din, wait for, 8–10
Adityanath, Yogi, 46, 61, 64
Administrative Reforms Commission (ARC), 215
Advani, L.K., 37
Afghan Taliban, 123, 127
Agriculture, growth rate in, 18
Ahuja, Gyan Dev, 63
Ajmer Sharif blast, 41–42, 44
Akalis, 235
Akhil Bharatiya Itihas Sankalan Yojana (ABISY), 50
Akhil Bharatiya Vidyarthi Parishad (ABVP), 43, 48–50
Akhlaq, Mohammad, 63, 214
All India Anna Dravida Munnetra Kazhagam (AIADMK), 235
All India Council for Technical Education (AICTE), 172, 184
All India Manufacturers Organisation (AIMO), 29
Ambedkar Periyar Study Circle, 49
Ambedkar, B.R., 81
Ansari, Mazloom, 214
Anti-graft bill, 217
Anti-Terrorism Squad (ATS), 41, 43
ARAB Spring, 215
Arctic, first Indian expedition, 153–54

Aseemanand, Swami, 43–44
Asif, Khwaja, 103, 105
Atal Mission for Rejuvenation and Urban Transformation (AMRUT), 25–26
Aurangzeb Raj, 68
Automatic Exchange of Information (AEOI), 10
Aziz, Sartaj, 103–5

Babar Bhakt, 68
Babri Masjid, demolition of, 37
Baldeo Sharma, 51
Baliyan, Sanjeev, 46, 63
Balramji Dass Tandon, Governor, Chattisgarh, 52
Banerjee, Mamata, 113
Bangladesh, Bhutan, India, Nepal Initiative (BBIN), 113
bank recapitalization bonds, 15
Barack, Obama, 127
Battle of Perception, 189–91
Beef bans, 36
Benami transactions, 15
Bengal Initiative for Multi-Sectoral Technical and Economic Cooperation (BIMSTEC), 113
Best Bakery killings, 40, 85, *See also* Godhra train burning
Beti Bachao, 35
Bhagwat, Mohan, 60–61
Bharati, Vijnana, 49–50
Bhat, P. Krishna, 83
Bhushan, Prashant, 217, 225
Bhushan, Prashant, 220
Biju Janata Dal (BJD), 235
Bilateral Investment Promotion and Protection Agreements (BIPA), 231
Biotechnology revolution, 138

Biotechnology solutions, 139–40
Birla-Sahara bribery papers, 33
Black money, 7, 9, 15, 27–28, 217, 222
Blasts/lynching/massacres/terror activities
    Ajmer Sharif blast, 41–42, 44
    Best Bakery killings, 40, 85
    Dadri mob lynching (2015), 46
    Godhra train burning, 38–40, 45
    Junaid Khan, 214
    Malegaon blast case, 41, 44
    Mecca Masjid blast, 41–42
    Mohammad Akhlaq, 63, 214
    Mumbai bomb blasts (1993) 37
    Mumbai train blast (2006), 42
    Muzaffarnagar communal riots (2013), 63
    Naroda Patiya massacre, 39–40
    Pehlu Khan, 64, 214
    Samjhauta Express blast, 41–42, 44
Borrowing at high rates of interest, 4

Cambridge Analytica, 94
Cashless economy, faded dream, 31
Central Bureau of Investigation (CBI), 41, 44, 55, 70, 84–85, 209, 218
Central Statistical Organisation (CSO), 26, 29
Central Universities Act, 2009, 174
Chai pe Charcha, 5, 7
Chandra, Lokesh, 50
Chelameswar, Justice, 53, 82–83, 86
China–Pakistan Economic Corridor (CPEC), 121, 131
Choice-based credit system, 174
Choubey, Ashwani Kumar, 68
Chouhan, Shivraj Singh, 33, See also Vyapam
Civilizational levels, 4
Coal Mines Nationalisation Act, 1973, 227
Coal Scam, 226–34
    coal block auction, 232–34
    deallocation of coal blocks, 229
    long-term repercussions, 228–31
Common Reporting Standard (CRS), 10
Commonwealth Games Organizing Committee, 218
Comprehensive Economic Partnership Agreement (CEPA), 11
Constitution Amendment Bill, 80
Constitutional Positions, Saffronization of, 51–56
Corporate Social Responsibility (CSR), 163
Council of Scientific and Industrial Research (CSIR), 138–39, 147–50, 159

Cow politics, 63–65
Crime against women, 32
Crude oil price of, 10–12

Death of Civility, 67–69
Deendayal Upadhyaya Gram Jyoti Yojana (DDUGJY), 25
Defence Research and Development Organization (DRDO), 20
Demographic imbalance, 61
Demonetization, 9, 13, 15, 22–24, 27–31, 34, 68–69, 73, 97, 185, 222, 236
    dip in revenue, 29
    impact of, 30
    job losses, 29
    lingering impact of, 28
    rationale for, 30
Desai, Morarji, 12
Desai, Subash, 38
Destruction of Key Institutions, 69–71
Deuba, Sher Bahadur, 109
Developmental agenda, 10
Dhankar, O.P., 16
Digital India, concept of, 192
Direct Benefit Transfer (DBT), 24
Doklam, 114, 118–20
Doppler radar, 143
Double Taxation Avoidance Agreement (DTAA), 9
Double-digit growth, 21–22
Drainage facilities, 3
Dravida Munnetra Kazhagam (DMK), 235–36
Dress codes, 36
Drip and sprinkler irrigation technologies, 18
Dwivedi, Sudhakara, 43

E-commerce, 96
Economic revival, 6
Economic Surveys, 28–29
Education
    investment in, 15
    politicization of, 186
    saffronization of, 49–51
Electronic Voting Machines (EVMs), 59–60
Employment, 4, 14, 20, 22, 29, 109, 130, 148, 181–82
Export performance, 11

Fair-trade regime, 131
Fake degree racket, 187
Fake encounters, 40

Fake news, 71, 154–55, 214
Farmer suicides, 5, 16
Fertilizer subsidies, 92
Fibre optic network, 157, 163, 165, 184, 192, 197, 212
Financial Action Task Force (FATF), 127
Foreign Policy
   Afghanistan, 116–17
   Bangladesh, 112–14
   Bhutan, 114
   China, 117–22
   Chinese Foreign Direct Investment (FDI), 121
   Chinese proximity with Pakistan, 121
   Doklam, 118
   Europe, 123
   Israel, 124–26
   Japan, 124
   Maldives, 114–16
   Neighbourhood First Policy, 100–1
   Nepal, 108–10
   Nepal–China military exercise, 110
   One Belt One Road (OBOR), 110
   Pakistan, 101–3
   Pakistan's Joint Intelligence Team (JIT) visit, 106–7
   political Immaturity, 106–8
   resumption of dialogue with Pakistan, 105
   Russia, 123
   Sino–Indian bilateral trade, 121
   Sri Lanka, 110–12
   surgical strikes, 107
   transgressions by Chinese soldiers, 118
   United States, 126–28
   Xi Jinping's visit to India, 117

Gandhi, Indira, 124
Gandhi, Rahul, 67–68
Gandhi, Rajiv, 24, 68
Gandhi, Sonia, 68
Gaur, Vivek, 23
General Agreement on Tariffs and Trade (GATT), 130
Generic drugs, 149
Geospatial Information Systems (GIS), 154–57
Geospatial technologies, 157
Ghar wapsi, 36, 46
Global climate change, 152
Global warming, 122
Godhra train burning, 38–40, 45
Goel, Sunil, 23

Governors as Partisan Players, 66–67
Green Revolution, 149
Gross Domestic Product (GDP), 11, 13–15, 19–20, 26–29, 57, 69, 141, 159, 207, 236
GST, 21, 23, 185, 207
   flawed, 73, 236
   poorly implemented, 97
Gujarat State Petroleum Corporation Ltd (GSPC) scam, 33

Haqqani militant, 127
Harkat-ul-Jihad-al Islami (HuJI), 42
Hasina, Sheikh, 112–13
Hazare, Anna, 67, 190, 192, 215–16, 218–22, 224, 227
Hegde, Anantkumar, 61, 69
Higher education
   autonomy to some institutions of, 172
   curriculum framework of, 183
   radical changes in, 165–67
Higher Education Commission, 170, 237
Higher Education Empowerment Regulation Agency (HEERA), 184
Hindu Ekta Manch, 32
Hindu Mahasabha, 47
Hindu Rashtra, 60–62
Hinduism, 47
Hizbul Mujahideen, 36

Ibrahim, Dawood, 37, *See also* Mumbai bomb blasts
ICT-enabled education, 176
Import duties, 11
Income Declaration Scheme (IDS), 15
India Against Corruption (IAC), 215, 217, 222
India Aspiration Fund, 22
India Start-up Outlook Report 2017, 22
Indian Council for Cultural Relations (ICCR), 50
Indian Council of Historical Research (ICHR), 50
Indian Penal Code (IPC), 72–73
Indira Awas Yojana, 24
Industrial growth, 13
Inflation, 10, 12–13, 26
Informational privacy, 96, 98
InnoVen Capital, 22
Inspector Raj, 15
Institutional reform, 88
Inter-caste marriages, Khaps intolerance, 73
International Seabed Authority (ISA), 152

Irani, Smriti, 48
Islamic State (IS), 116, 123
IT sector, 21, 127

Jafri, Ehsan, 39
Jahan, Ishrat, fake encounter case, 41, 84
Jaishankar, S., 33, 102
Jaitley, Arun, 10
Jamdar, Vishram Ramchandra, 51
Jan Lokpal Bill, 217
Janata Dal (United) JD(U), 235
Jawaharlal Nehru National Urban Renewal Mission (JNNURM), 25–26
Jinping, Xi, 113, 117–20, 128, 131
Joseph, KM, 66, 85
Joshi, Maharashtra, 38
Judicial appointments, 77–79
Jumlas, 10, 14, 20, 27–32
    developmental agenda, 10
    make in India, 20
    demonetization, 27–32

Kalmadi, Suresh, 218
Kalota, Mohammad Hussain, 38
Kapse, Nikhil, 37
Karkare, Hemant, 43
Katheria, Ramshankar, 51
Kathua rape case, 32
Katiyar, Vinay, 61
Kausar Bi and Sohrabuddin Sheikh's fake encounter, 85
Kejriwal, Arvind, 192, 220, 225, *See also* Hazare, Anna
Khadi Village Industries Commission (KVIC), 58
Khan, Junaid, 214
Khan, Pehlu, 64, 214
Kohli, O.P., Governor, of Gujarat, 51
Kumar, Kanhaiya, 49
Kumar, M. Jagadesh, 50

Land Boundary Agreement (LBA), 112
Lashkar-e-Taiba (LeT), 40, 42, 116
Legal and Technical Commission (LTA), 152
Liberalization, 19, 21, 130
Lokpal, 8–9, 192, 215, 217–24
Love jihad, 36, 46, 63–65
Loya, Justice, 54–55

Mahagathbandhan, 236
Maharaj, Sakshi, 61, 63–64

Maharana Pratap, 65–66
Mahatma Gandhi, 18, 47, 65, 220
Maheshwari, Dinesh, Justice, 83
Majoritarian sentiment, 37–46
Make in India, 19–22, 35, 158
Malegaon blast case, 41, 44
Mallya, Vijay, 33–34, *See also* Modi, Nirav
Mann Ki Baat, 36
Maritime Silk Road (MSR) initiative, 115
Marrakesh Agreement, 130
McMahon Line, 117
MCOCA (Maharashtra Control of Organised Crime Act) court, 41
Mecca Masjid blast, 41–42
Media planners, 9
Medical Council of India (MCI), 156, 166, 178–81
Memon, Yakub, 48
MGNREGA, 188–89, 192
Migration, 3
Minimum Support Price (MSP), 4, 17–18, 236–37
Misra, Dipak, Chief Justice, 54
Modi, Lalit, 33, 36
Modi, Narendra
    agrarian distress, 16–19
    betrayal of agricultural sector, 236
    careless statements, 56–58
    Chinese relations, mismanagement with, 120
    critical comments about Manmohan Singh, 101–2
    decline of popularity, 47
    demonetization (jumla), 27–31
    destruction of key institutions, 69–71
    diplomatic moves, 100
    doublespeak, 32–34
    employment promise (jumla), 14
    Indo-Pak relations, poor track, 105
    informal dialogue with Putin at Sochi, 132
    informality level, 127
    make in India, 19–22
    Mann Ki Baat, 36
    media campaign, 9
    meeting with Sharif, 105
    NaMo's objectives, mismatch, 31
    political immaturity, 106–8
    political strategy, 35
    portray as Lord Rama, 107
    promise of change, 5–8
    start-ups, 22–24

wait for Ache Din, 8–10
Modi, Nirav, 34, *See also* Mallya, Vijay
Moral policing, 36
More crop per drop, 18, 140
Mukherjee, Pranab, 220
Mumbai bomb blasts (March 1993), 37
Muslim community, ghettoization of, 41

Naidu, Chandrababu, 235
Naidu, Venkaiah, 55, 63
Naik, Ram, Governor of Uttar Pradesh, 52, 62
Nanavati Commission of Inquiry, 40
Naroda Patiya massacre, 39–40
National Academic Depository (NAD), 186
National Assessment and Accreditation Council (NAAC), 166, 169
National Book Trust (NBT), 51
National Commission for Higher Education, 166
National Commission for Scheduled Castes (NCSC), 51
National Company Law Tribunal, 206
National Crime Records Bureau (NCRB), 16, 32
National Curriculum Framework (NCF), 165
National e-Governance Plan (NeGP), 24
National Eligibility cum Entrance Test (NEET), 166, 168
National Green Tribunal (NGT), 35
National Institute of Ocean Technology (NIOT), 152
National Investigation Agency (NIA), 42–44, 70, 106
National Judicial Appointments Commission (NJAC), 80, 82
National Knowledge Commission, 165, 170–71, 174, 181–87
National Manufacturing Policy (NMP), 19
National Population Register, 99
National Register of Citizens (NRC), 62
National Security Advisor (NSA), 103–7
National Skill Development Agency (NSDA), 24
National Skill Development Corporation (NSDC), 24, 182
National Skill Development Fund (NSDF), 24
National Telecom Policy, 197–99
Nationalist Congress Party (NCP), 236
Nehru, Jawaharlal, 25, 50, 57, 65
Neighbourhood First policy, 113
New Frontiers of Knowledge, 152

Nirbhaya, 6, 32, 191
No-frills accounts, 24
North American Free Trade Agreement (NAFTA), 129
NPAs (Non-Performing Assets), 15, 173, 228, 231, 236
NSDL Database Management Limited (NDML), 186
Nuclear Suppliers Group (NSG), 121

Obama, Barack, 127
OBOR Summit, 111
Oli, K.P. Sharma, 108–9

Pal, Justice Ruma, 83
Palaniswami, E.K., 235
Panchajanya, 51
Pandya, Arvind, 39
Paramparagat Krishi Vikas Yojana (PKVY), 25
Parrikar, Manohar, 33, 102–3
Patel, Jayant, Justice, 84
Patnaik, Naveen, 235
Pawar, Sharad, 220, 236
Pay Commission, 172
PDS scam, 33
Plastic-based commodities, 10
Polarization, 46
Post-Godhra riots, 6, 39
Prachi, Sadhvi, 46
Pradhan Mantri Awas Yojana-Gramin (PMAY-G), 24
Pradhan Mantri Jan-Dhan Yojana (PMJDY), 24
Pradhan Mantri Kaushal Vikas Yojana (PMKVY), 24
Pradhan Mantri Krishi Sinchayee Yojana (PMKSY), 25
Pragya, Sadhvi, 43
Pratyaksh Hastantarit Labh (PAHAL), 24
Prevention of Corruption Act (PCA), 9
Private sector investment, 14, 162
Procurement prices, 6, 17
Promise of Change, 5–8
Public Cause Research Foundation, 225
Public Distribution System (PDS), 92
Public-Private Partnerships (PPPs), 165
Purohit, Lt Colonel Prasad Shrikant, 43

R&D investment, 151–52
Rafale fighter jet deal, 33–34
Rai, Vinod, 208

Raja, A., 209, 213, 215
Rajapaksa, Mahinda, 111
Raje, Vasundhara, 33
Rajiv Gandhi Grameen Vidyutikaran Yojana (RGGVY), 25
Ram Janmabhoomi issue, 68
Ramdev, 190–91, 193, 222
  silence about black money, 193
Rao, G.V.L Narasimha, 68
Rao, Muralidhar, 48
Rao, P.V. Narasimha, 19, 137
Rao, Y. Sudershan, 50
Rashtriya Madhyamik Shiksha Abhiyan (RMSA), 176
Rath Yatra, 37, See also Advani, L.K.
Rathore, Rajyavardhan Singh, 103
Real estate, 75–77
Real Estate (Regulation and Development) Act 2016 (RERA), 76
Right to Education Act, 162–65
Right to privacy, 92–93, 96, 98–99, 156, See also AADHAAR
Roy, Tathagata, Governor of Tripura, , 62
RSS, 36, 42, 47, 49–53, 60–62, 66, 175, 185, 219, 222, 227

Saakshar Bharat programme, 165
SAARC Yatra, 102
Saffronization of
  constitutional positions, , 51–56
  educational institutions, , 49–51
  textbooks, , 65–66
Sagar Nidhi, Technology Demonstration Vessel, 152
Sahasrabuddhe, Vinay, 51
Saini, O.P., 209
Salian, Rohini, 44
Samjhauta Express blast, 41–42, 44
Sangh Parivar, 47, 51–52, 61–62
Sarpotdar, Madhukar, 37
Scam(s)
  Coal scam, 226–34
  Gujarat State Petroleum Corporation Ltd (GSPC) scam, 33
  land grabbing case in Danapur, 33
  Nirav Modi banking scam, 34
  PDS scam, 33
  Rafale fighter jet deal, 33–34
  Vyapam scam, 33, 70, 175, 178
  demonetization, 9, 13, 15, 22–24, 27–31, 34, 68–69, 73, 97, 185, 222, 236

School-based assessment, 160
Sengar, Kuldeep, 32, See also Crime against women
Service industry, 21
Shah, Amit, 67
Shah-Nanavati Commission, 39
Shakdher, Justice Rajiv, transfer of, 85
Shanmuganathan, V., former Governor, Meghalaya, allegations of sexual harassment, 52
Sharif, Nawaz, 102, 105–6
Sharma, Baldeo, 51
Sharma, Mahesh, 63
Sharma, Rajat, 102
Sheikh, Sohrabuddin, 44
Shiv Sena, 37–38, 43, 235
Singh, Atul, 32
Singh, Dayashankar, 69
Singh, Giriraj, 33, 68
Singh, Kalyan, Governor of Rajasthan, 51
Singh, Manmohan, 19, 57, 68, 102, 209
Singh, Radha Mohan, 16
Singh, Rajnath, 43, 106
Singh, Raman, 33, 64, See also PDS scam
Singh, Satyapal, 158
Singh, Siddharth Nath, 12
Singh, Surendra, 61
Social media campaign, 7
Soil health cards, 25
Soleckshaw, solar-powered electric rickshaw, 148–49
Special Economic Zone, 112
Srikrishna Report, 37–38
Srikrishna, B.N., Justice, 97
Startup India, 22–23, 35, 173
State of Secondary Education, 175–78
Statue of Unity of Sardar Patel, 14
Structural dispensation in MHRD, 169
Surgical strike on black money, 27, See also Demonetization
Surgical strike on Pakistan, 107
Swachh Bharat, 24, 35, 185
Swaminathan Commission, 17
Swaraj, Sushma, 10, 13, 104–5, 109, 124, 137

Tax breaks, 90, 141, 163
Technological solutions for sustainable development, 149
Tehelka magazine, 39
Telecom sector, 21, 198, 202, 204–5, 207–8, 211

Telecom tariffs, 198
Teleconferencing, legal proceedings, 90
Teledensity, 198
Telugu Desam Party (TDP), 235
Terrorist and Disruptive Activities Act (TADA), 37
Text-based assessment, 160
Textbooks, Saffronization of, 65–66
Thackeray, Uddhav, 38
Thakur, Sadhvi Pragya Singh, 43
Thakur, T.S., 8, 53
Thipsay, Justice Abhay, arbitrary transfer of, 85
Tipu Sultan, 65
Transparency International, 34
Tripathi, Kesri Nath, Governor of West Bengal, 52
Trump, Donald, 110, 122, 127–31
Tsunami warning system, 145–46
Tuberculosis (TB), research on, 138
2G Scam, 195
  benefits beyond territorial boundaries, 196–97
  CAG report, 199–203
  connectivity in a digital economy, 212–13
  data expansion, 208
  first-come-first-served (FCFS), 202
  national telecom policy (NTP) of 1994, 197–99
  performance audit, 201
  policy prescriptions, 211–12
  presumptive loss, 202, 208
  public policy dilemma, 210–11
  referee institutions, 210–11
  return on investment (RoI), 207
  telecom and social media, 213–14
  tumult in the telecom sector, 203–8

Umerji, Maulvi, 38
Unemployment, 4, 10, 18, 181, 236
Unified Access Services Licence (UASL), 198
Uniform Civil Code, 61
Unique Identification Number (UIN), 93
Universal health coverage, 5
University Grants Commission, 159, 169–73, 184, 186
Upadhyay, Major Ramesh, 43
Uttar Pradesh elections (2017), 13

Vajpayee, Atal Bihari, 12
Vala, Vajubhai, Governor of Karnataka, 51
Vemula, Rohith, 36, 48
Venkatachaliah, M.N., 215
Venugopal, K.K., 231
Vibrant Gujarat, 7
Vote-bank politics, 18
Vyapam scam, 33, 70, 175, 178

Wani, Burhan, 36
White Paper on Black Money, 28
Wickremesinghe, Minister Ranil, 111
World Economic Forum, 58
World Trade Organisation (WTO), 130

Xeler8, research platform, 23

Yashpal Committee, 165, 170–71
Yeddyurappa, 67
Yeddyurappa, B.S., 67, 219

Zero balance accounts, 24
Zero Liquid Discharge programme, 139